799

Explore Britain's
BIRDS

Edited by Paul Sterry

EXPLORE BRITAIN'S

BIRDS

Produced by AA Publishing

Bird text adapted and illustrations taken from *The Complete Book of British Birds*, first published by The Automobile Association and the Royal Society for the Protection of Birds in 1988.

For *The Complete Book of British Birds*:
Authors: Irene Allen, John Andrews, Ian Armstrong, Colin Bibby, Sarah Brennan, James Cadbury, Lennox Campbell, Stan Davies, Ian Dawson, Mike Everett, Chris Harbard, Rob Hume, Mike Langman, Keith Noble, John O'Sullivan, Fay Pascoe, Richard Porter, Tony Prater, Bob Scott, Ken Smith, Carolyn Stowe, Tim Stowe, Stephanie Tyler, Graham Williams, Gwyn Williams, Nigel Wood.
Artists: Norman Arlott, Trevor Boyer, Hilary Burn, Robert Gillmor, Peter Hayman, Ian Jackson, David Quinn, Chris Rose, Ian Wallace, Anne Winterbotham.

For *Explore Britain's Birds*:
Editor: Paul Sterry
Copy Editor: Rebecca Snelling

Published by AA Publishing, a trading name of Automobile Association Developments Limited, whose registered office is Norfolk House, Priestley Road, Basingstoke, Hampshire RG24 9NY. Registered Number 1878835.

A catalogue record for this book is available from the British Library.

ISBN   h/b 0 7495 1047 1
         p/b 0 7495 1093 5

Colour origination by L.C. Repro and Sons Ltd, Aldermaston.
Printed and bound by Graficromo SA, Spain.

The contents of this book are believed correct at the time of printing. Nevertheless, the Publishers cannot accept responsibility for errors or omissions, or for changes in details given.

CONTENTS

Introduction   6

The Birds   15

Comparing Ducks   32–33

Exotic and Domestic Ducks   41

Comparing Birds of Prey   50–51

Comparing Waders   62–63

Comparing Finches   138

Comparing Warblers   139

Index   159

Smew

*The kingfisher is one of
Britain's most colourful birds.*

INTRODUCTION

Birdwatching for pleasure

As the sun sinks slowly towards the horizon on the island of Unst, in the Shetland Isles, thousands upon thousands of puffins return from a day's fishing far out to sea to feed their young on the seabird cliffs of Hermaness. A visit to this, or any of Britain's outstanding birdwatching sites, is enough to inspire an interest in ornithology in even the toughest sceptic – and the excitement of such a spectacular natural event will live with you for ever.

While special expeditions or days out can provide wonderful opportunities to view Britain's birds, the delight of a hobby like birdwatching is that you can pursue it almost anywhere. Rambles through the countryside may have much to offer, but careful observation from the comfort of your own home can yield a wealth of observations.

USING THIS BOOK

Many people are first attracted to bird-watching by the visual variety of birds in this country, from colourful species such as the kingfisher to the subtly camouflaged, such as the stone curlew. The marvellous, detailed paintings of birds in this book may be browsed through simply for pleasure, of course, but also serve as a practical and accurate guide to bird identification, with many species shown in flight, or engaging in some characteristic behaviour, such as courtship or feeding. Special spreads help to identify groups of birds such as ducks or warblers, with the birds portrayed side by side for comparison.

The notes which accompany each bird portrait are a quick guide to key points for identification, and are designed to enable the observer to distinguish a particular species from a similar one, and to tell the sexes and ages apart. Accurate identification, of course, enables the enthusiast to learn more, and the main text provides practical and interesting background information about each species. Curious aspects of behaviour may be discussed – why, for example, is the nuthatch known as the plasterer? – along with details such as breeding habits, numbers and status in the British Isles, the size of the breeding population and overwintering numbers. A coloured panel for each species is packed with essential information relating to the bird' size, weight, preferred habitat, and breeding and feeding patterns.

Left, sometimes an illustration to show characteristic behaviour is included, like these blue tits at a nest box.

Great tit

Blue tit

Long-tailed tit

Birds in the garden

Birdwatching need take you no further than your own window, especially if you look out onto a garden. Even without extra encouragement, there are sure to be common species such as blackbirds, thrushes, robins and blue tits around in fair numbers.

If you are able to put out nesting boxes and food in the winter, you will attract larger numbers of birds and amost certainly increase the variety of species seen. Different foods attract different birds, and sometimes presentation can be important – for example, siskin are known to favour the red plastic bags of peanuts. A small pond or bird bath is another popular attraction for garden birds, both during the summer months and in winter if you keep it ice-free. Remember to locate bird baths and feeders in open places, where prowling cats cannot hide.

Flocks of fieldfares may be attracted to fruit and berries in a winter garden.

Below, special features allow you to compare birds easily.

Coal tit

Willow tit

Crested tit

Marsh tit

Going birdwatching

Certain fieldcraft skills can be learned, and these will improve with time and experience. For example, your ability to identify species at a glance will develop with repeated observations of common species – as will your ability to find the best spot for watching. You can soon learn to move quietly through woodlands, using your ears as much as your eyes to detect the presence of birds around you. Wherever you are, remember to use natural cover whenever possible to break up your outline. Be patient, and try remaining motionless in one spot: once the birds are used to your presence, you have a better chance of observing their general activity at close range.

If you are going birdwatching in search of a particular species, then it is well worth undertaking some research before you set off. By focusing on the correct habitat, you will greatly improve your chances of successful observation.

Visual clues may be the most obvious way to distinguish species, but do not forget that the calls and songs of birds are also invaluable aids to their identification. With practice, most birdwatchers can learn to recognise the songs of common garden and woodland birds. Flight and alarm calls may take longer to master – not least because you cannot always track down or see the bird in question, to relate the sound to the species. Having a more experienced birdwatcher as a companion and mentor can greatly speed up the learning process, so why not tag along with an expert? Many nature reserves have wardens who can give you general advice, and a guided walk with an expert ornithologist can be a real revelation. Membership of an organisation such as the Royal Society for the Protection of Birds (RSPB) will also offer more opportunities to broaden your knowledge.

The song of familiar garden birds such as the robin may be easily learned.

While seeing rare birds is exciting, beware – unusual species such as this red-crested pochard may have escaped from captivity.

Some basic equipment

Although good eyesight and keen hearing are the best tools to help you enjoy bird-watching, a good pair of binoculars enables closer observation, and along with a good identification guide they can make all the difference. Their powers of magnification allow you to see distant and often shy species without actually disturbing the birds; and they can also add to the enjoyment of watching common and familiar birds by bringing them into close range, allowing you to pick out the detail of every feather.

When selecting a pair of binoculars, the best advice is to try out as many different makes as possible and to buy the best you can afford. Binoculars are described by a set of numbers – 8x30, for example. The first number denotes the magnification, and the second the light-gathering capacity of the lenses. Do not be misled into thinking that larger magnification binoculars are automatically better than their low magnification counterparts. With greater magnification comes greater bulk, and cumbersome equipment is much more tedious to carry around with you or hold steady. Although some people prefer 10x magnification, 8x will be fine for most birdwatchers.

For the dedicated birdwatcher, and especially one with a serious interest in coastal birds, a telescope is essential equipment. Again, try out as many as possible before you choose – and remember, having bought a telescope, you will also need a tripod to hold it steady!

The green woodpecker is the largest of Britain's woodpeckers, but more often heard than seen.

When watching birds in unfamiliar locations or habitats, many people find it useful to carry a field guide with them, to help identify a species on the spot. Without this aid – and sometimes even with a field guide – there will always be birds which defy ready identification. Making some simple notes on the spot can help you here, where relying on memory alone can be extremely misleading. Try and note down the bird's size in relation to others of known species around it. Look for distinctive marks or patterns, both at rest and in flight; beak shape and head markings may be straightforward, while white rumps or wing bars are examples of less obvious but essential diagnostic aids. Try to describe any call or song heard, and note down any interesting or unusual behaviour. Your notes will make it much easier to recall details when you get back to your reference books, or want to ask for somebody's help.

Warblers are notoriously difficult to distinguish from plumage alone, and taking a note of the bird's song may make all the difference when you try to identify the species later.

Birds for all seasons

Watching birds is a delightful activity at any time of the year – provided, of course, that the weather conditions are not too severe! Particular habitats or regions may have more to offer at certain times of year, however, and a little insight and planning can help decide the potentially interesting areas to visit on a trip at any particular season.

Birdwatching is an amazingly popular pastime in Britain. Individuals of all ages are involved, and the degree of enthusiasm and commitment ranges from casual appreciation to nothing short of fanatical pursuit. While many are happy to enjoy the birds that they encounter on their travels, 'twitching' or the pursuit of rarities is an increasingly popular form of modern birdwatching. This is fuelled by the well-developed twitchers' grapevine, which is centred on various recorded-message bird information telephone lines. While finding or seeing unusual species is exciting, it should not detract from the satisfaction to be found in close, careful observation of common species – for birds of all kinds, be they common or rare, are fascinating and more than repay time spent observing and studying them.

Spring is a wonderful season for the bird-watcher. In woodlands everywhere it heralds the start of the breeding season, and the songs of the resident species are augmented by those of newly arrived migrants. Dawn is the best time for hearing the widest range of birdsong. Migrants and the flow of migrating birds are also clearly seen in spring along Britain's sea shores, where headlands and estuaries offer excellent opportunities to see the birds.

Summer is a comparatively quiet time of year for the birdwatcher, although not without its highlights. Family parties of songbirds may be found in woods and hedgerows – those migrant species feeding eagerly on ripening berries are storing energy for their forthcoming travels. Lakes and reservoirs often attract large numbers of swallows, martins and swifts which feed on the abundance of insect life, while estuaries around the coast witness the first gatherings of migrating waders and wildfowl. This is probably the liveliest time to visit seabird colonies on the cliffs: ravenous, fully grown young are being fed continually at this time of the year, so there is plenty of activity.

For the birdwatcher with access to the coast, autumn is perhaps the most exciting season: everywhere there are signs of migration, and the estuaries begin to fill up with ducks, geese and waders. As the weather deteriorates towards winter, inland birds of many kinds tend to move out to the coast, where the proximity of the sea moderates extremes in the weather.

Winter can be a surprisingly good season for the woodland birdwatcher. The lack of leaves makes observation among trees and bushes comparatively easy, and many of the smaller birds band together in roaming flocks, often being joined by winter visitors. Grassy downs, heaths and marshes can harbour birds of prey at this time of year, and estuaries and wetlands are often outstanding.

Seeking expert advice will help you plan your birdwatching trips, especially if you hope to see something specific, such as this family group of shelducks.

Birds may appear quite different at varying times of the year and life-cycle. While a puffin is most familiar in its bright adult, summer colours (left and bottom), these illustrations show the changes from four weeks old, at around six weeks, during a first winter, an adult in winter, and an adult in summer time.

Whatever the season, it is always worth keeping a careful eye on the weather, for sudden changes or extremes can have a dramatic influence on the numbers and species of birds to be seen. For example, westerly gales in the autumn will drive migrating seabirds, normally only seen well out to sea, close to the shore, making them easy to observe. Longer periods of southerly or south-easterly winds in spring can result in excellent conditions for migration, with large numbers of birds arriving in this country overnight; in the autumn these same winds can result in all sorts of interesting and unusual sightings, as birds are blown off their regular migration routes. Sudden and prolonged periods of severe cold in winter can cause large numbers of birds to move towards the warmer south and west of the country, with even more individuals arriving here from Europe.

The Birds

Above, sedge warbler

Red-throated Diver

❊

GAVIA STELLATA

Red-throats take off more easily than other divers and can take advantage of smaller pools, but are restricted to areas with very little human disturbance. The range has expanded recently to south-west Scotland. The nest is a mere cushion of aquatic vegetation, often so close to water that on larger lochs, where strong winds can whip up high waves, eggs are often swamped. Adults are very ungainly on land, but young have been recorded moving in short leaps over dry ground between pools encouraged by a calling parent.

Young birds and adults from the far north start moving south in late August, usually appearing in the south in September. They stay until April, even May, often in large, loose groups but more usually in ones and twos. By May many birds will have acquired their smart summer plumage, a sight not often seen outside Scotland. They are then distinguished from other divers by their unpatterned backs, but a close view shows delicate striping on the nape and sides of the neck; the white breast is more obvious. In summer they are seen in flight more often than the black-throated, as they move from their breeding loch to and from their feeding places on the coast, usually calling loudly as they go.

In winter, adults have paler face and neck than juveniles, with the dark eye obvious against white background. Upper parts have fine white speckling, not seen on other divers. Longer body and thicker neck distinguish it from grebes.

Length: 53-69cm; **Weight:** 1,200-1,600g
Where to look: breeding birds are confined to lochs and small fresh water pools on moors. In winter widespread around UK coasts, off both rocky and sandy shores. **Nest:** a flat pad close to water. **Eggs:** 1 or 2, dark, speckled brown. **Food:** nearly always fish, but some crabs, shrimps. **Voice:** only in breeding season, wailing and rhythmic goose-like calls; loud, deep quacking in flight, rapidly repeated *kwuk-uk-uk.*

On water the general appearance is of a slim, long-necked bird, low in the water, with head and bill uptilted. Swims long distances under water.

A flying red-throat in winter is best identified by its slim build and pale head and neck, with the white face often obvious. Feet look smaller than other divers'.

Black-throated Diver

❊

GAVIA ARCTICA

On water, black-throats look relatively bulky. The summer plumage is distinctive and, in winter, the dark upper parts, greyer nape and white flank patch are useful identification features.

Length: 58-73cm; **Weight:** 2,000-3,000g
Where to look: breeding birds on large Scottish lochs; in winter moves south, to both sandy and rocky coasts. **Nest:** beside water, often on island. **Eggs:** 1 or 2, olive-brown with black spots. **Food:** almost entirely fish. **Voice:** raven-like croaking, often repeated, and wailing calls building up to loud, far-carrying climax.

Like all divers, the black-throated faces many potential dangers all year round. Because it feeds in the larger lochs where it breeds, instead of flying to the sea it has been persecuted by man in the past. Now the problem is disturbance by boats or noisy groups of people which cause the sensitive divers to desert their nests. Even on ideal lochs, breeding density is low because each pair needs a territory of up to 350 acres. And whereas red-throated divers can breed on acidic, peaty pools and feed out at sea, there is some evidence that black-throats have been affected by acid rain reducing fish stocks in the large lochs they use. In autumn and winter all divers can fall victim to fishing nets in inshore waters, or to oil. Despite these problems, the British population, though small, seems stable after a decline prior to the 1940s.

Divers dive smoothly without forward leap of shag. Young cormorants have pale undersides but longer tails. In flight, divers look hump-backed, legs trailing. Black-throats form small groups, have pale, horizontal, dagger-like bills and white flank flash; red-throats have uptilted bills.

Breeding birds may be helped by the provision of artificial, floating islands to remove the problem of flooded nests, but this idea, which seems a very good one, has yet to be proved successful.

Great Crested Grebe

❊

PODICEPS CRISTATUS

Large young remain striped until they moult into winter plumage. The stripes help the young conceal themselves in vegetation around the edge of the water. They make long whistling calls.

The head ruffs are lost during the winter. The pink bill is specific to the great crested grebe.

Winter plumage

Grebes move long distances under water and can be frustrating: after a long dive they come up far from where you expected.

Length: 46-51cm; **Weight:** 800-1,400g
Where to look: inland lakes, especially gravel pits, occasionally on slow-flowing rivers and often off sandy stretches of coast in the winter. **Nest:** often a floating heap of aquatic plants anchored by surrounding vegetation. **Eggs:** 3-4, white but frequently stained by water plants on nest. **Food:** small fish, insects, molluscs and sometimes vegetable matter. **Voice:** barking *rah-rah-rah* and a clicking *kek;* loud whistles from chicks.

The display of the great crested grebe is as incredible as its history. In the mid 19th century these beautiful grebes were the height of fashion, when skinned and converted into ladies' hats – so much so that by 1860 the UK population had been reduced to just 42 pairs. Today, after a steady increase, the population is standing at around 5,000 pairs. This remarkable recovery has been aided by the flooding of many old gravel pits which, after a few years, provide an ideal habitat with overhanging bank vegetation in which grebes can nest.

The extraordinary springtime display was first recognised and documented in the early 20th century. 'Cat display', 'penguin dance', 'habit preening' and 'head shaking' are all parts of the ritual in early spring. The fluffy, striped young are regularly carried aboard the parents' backs from soon after hatching. It is thought the young do not recognise their parents by sight during the first six weeks as they have been known to follow anything that moves – including boats! The first two weeks of a great crested grebe's life are especially hazardous as they often fall prey to large fish like the pike.

Grebes are not particularly worried by people on the shore but their eggs might be taken by predators if disturbed. Escaped mink present a new menace to these elegant birds and the wash from powered boats is also a threat, sometimes swamping nests.

Red-necked Grebe

PODICEPS GRISEGENA

Red-necks are similar to great crested grebes, but can be told by their smaller size, stocky build and, in summer, by their red neck and white cheeks. They are seen mainly as winter visitors to reservoirs and sheltered coastal waters.

Little Grebe

❋

TACHYBAPTUS RUFICOLLIS

Length: 25-29cm; **Weight:** 140-230g
Where to look: shallow-edged lakes, small ponds and slow-moving rivers. **Nest:** floating tangle of aquatic vegetation attached to larger plants. **Eggs:** 4-6, white, but often stained. **Food:** small fish, shrimps and many types of aquatic insects. **Voice:** distinctive, high-pitched, tittering giggle.

From a dumpy little puffball on the surface the little grebe transforms to a sleek, highly developed hunter beneath water. All of its features are geared to fast movement when submerged. Its legs are set well back on the body to allow as much movement as possible. Its tail is reduced to mere bristles so as not to collide with its thrusting feet. The toes, with wide lobes, can be folded over each other on the forward stroke, and even the bones in the leg are flattened to give extra propulsion on the backward stroke but less resistance on the forward stroke.

Beneath water the little grebe appears silver because air bubbles are trapped under its feathers. This helps to keep the grebe warm and also enables it to float to the surface while concentrating on holding on to its prey – often diving beetles and sticklebacks.

Little grebes, or dabchicks, are found on tiny ponds and narrow rivers, but also on the bigger, more open waters that larger species inhabit, especially in winter. Then they appear smaller than ever.

In flight its very small size and upper wing with no white make the little grebe easy to distinguish from other grebes.

Young birds have unusually striped heads. They dive to find their own food at a very early stage.

The rich burgundy sides to the face and neck show up well.

Slavonian Grebe

❋

PODICEPS AURITUS

Length: 31-38cm; **Weight:** 350-450g
Where to look: rare breeder in the highlands of Scotland. In winter almost exclusively found around the coast, particularly in sheltered bays and estuaries. **Nest:** made of floating weed anchored by surrounding vegetation. **Eggs:** white, but soon stained by vegetation used to cover the nest as the adult bird leaves. **Food:** fish.

Winter birds have well-defined black and white plumage.

Summer plumage unmistakable.

The spectacular golden-yellow eye stripe and tufts are only present during the summer when they are used in great crested grebe-like displays. It is during these displays that the North American name, horned grebe, seems more appropriate. A penguin-like dance varies from the great crested grebe's in several ways. Aquatic plants are gathered from the bottom of the pond and the birds surface to face each other as though to start the dance. When raised out of the water the two grebes immediately turn parallel to each other and race across the surface together. This ceremony is termed the 'weed rush'. The first records of Slavonian grebes nesting in Britain were in the early 1900s. Today they are still increasing and spreading slowly, with about 60 breeding pairs. During the winter they move from the coast or estuaries only when the weather is too bad for them to fish easily. The stocking of lakes with trout causes some concern for the well-being of these rare grebes. Lake ecology is altered by the great numbers of voracious trout, to the detriment of the birds.

Black-necked grebe

PODICEPS NIGRICOLLIS

The summer plumaged bird is easy to identify; in winter, the appearance is similar to the Slavonian grebe, but note the peaked forehead and uptilted bill.

Manx Shearwater

❋

PUFFINUS PUFFINUS

The Manx shearwater has remarkable navigational abilities: a bird released in Boston, USA, took just over 12 days to return the 3,200 miles to its nesting burrow on a Welsh island. Even to feed they may travel more than 200 miles. Perhaps the most remarkable colony in Britain is to be found 2,000ft up on a mountain on the Hebridean island of Rhum. The birds are vulnerable to predators on land, and so gather at dusk in rafts offshore before coming into their burrows in darkness.

Like other members of the shearwater family, the adult abandons its young in the nest burrow, where it lives off its fat reserves for two weeks, and then finds its own way to the sea, and winter quarters, 5,000 miles away off the South American coast.

Manx shearwaters are perhaps easiest to see after dark on some of the Welsh seabird islands, including Skomer. During on-shore gales, however, they often pass close to shore and can then be seen during the daytime from headlands off the west coast of Britain.

A few rapid stiff-winged flaps interspersed with glides, close to the surface, the lower wingtip almost cutting the water. They revel in strong winds, flying in higher arcs, gliding even more.

Stiff-winged cruciform silhouette of birds flying past, flashing alternately black and white as they tilt from side to side.

Length: 30-38cm
Wingspan: 76-89cm
Where to look: mainly off west coast, spring to autumn. Ashore only at colonies at night. **Nest:** in burrows on islands. **Egg:** 1, white. **Food:** small fish, squid. **Voice:** excited cackles.

Length: 14-18cm
Wingspan: 36-39cm
Where to look: at sea, off west coast during gales. Following boats. **Nest:** in holes, burrows on islands. **Egg:** 1, white. **Food:** plankton. **Voice:** churring from burrow.

Storm Petrel

❋

HYDROBATES PELAGICUS

It is a memorable sight to see Britain's smallest seabirds, only sparrow-sized, battling against a fierce autumn gale, apparently at the mercy of the elements. However, the weak-looking, bat-like flight with rapid wingbeats and very short glides is deceptive, for much of their life is spent far out of sight of land, and birds 20 years old have been recorded. They only come to land, after dark, to breed in colonies. Inland records are quite exceptional.

Their habit of following ships, fluttering back and forth across the wake, has made them familiar to sailors. Large numbers can be attracted by 'chum' – a mixture of fish oil and offal; within minutes, an apparently empty sea is dotted with tiny black fluttering birds heading purposefully low over the surface towards the slick, attracted by the smell.

Petrels are named after St Peter, from their habit of apparently walking on water. In fact they simply flutter and patter with their feet or merely lower their legs to stabilise themselves above the waves.

The pale underwing bar can show well. At a distance recalls a sea-hugging house martin. Feeds by dipping to surface with bill, wings raised, legs dangling.

Boat trips in late summer, or sea watching in autumn gales, can be very exciting. Huge numbers of kittiwakes and gannets may pass; petrels and the rarer shearwaters are keenly sought. Identification of distant 'tubenoses' rests largely on their flight action – a few stiff-winged flaps and long glides of shearwaters and weak fluttering of storm petrels.

Fulmar

※

FULMARUS GLACIALIS

Fulmars are perhaps Britain's longest-living birds, many probably reaching 40 years of age; and at least one has celebrated its 50th birthday. Immature birds remain at sea for several years, not breeding until nine or ten. Young birds looking for future nest sites are sometimes trapped in old roofless buildings: in three years 274 were found in this way on North Ronaldsay, Orkney.

In the last 200 years there has been a spectacular spread from Icelandic stock, with birds first recorded breeding in Britain, away from the ancient colony of St Kilda, on Foula in 1878. In 1969/70 the British and Irish breeding population was 305,000 pairs, with 40,000 on St Kilda. Today more than 550,000 pairs nest around the British and Irish coasts. This increase is thought to have resulted from the availability of whaling and trawling offal as food. The St Kilda population has remained stable and still has a plankton-based diet; it also behaves differently, avoiding ruined buildings, so it is possible that a new adaptable type of fulmar arose on Iceland, capable of exploiting man's fishing waste – just as the collared dove has extended its range more recently by filling a vacant niche.

Fulmar-oil is a foul smelling liquid, ejected by both adults and young as a form of defence, although also used, mixed with regurgitated food, for feeding the young. It is rich in vitamins A and D. The smell of fulmars is said to stay on oil-stained clothing for many years. Predators including peregrines have been found dead, completely coated in the oil.

A heavy body, straight wings and lack of neck distinguish the fulmar from superficially similar gulls such as the herring gull.

The stout, hooked bill is made up of several plates, topped with a prominent pair of nostril tubes. The dark patch of modified bristly feathers in front of the eye may help to reduce glare.

Fulmars swim buoyantly, and may spend much of the day resting on the water. They feed from the surface, and also occasionally by shallow plunge-diving.

The downy white chick is attended constantly for the first two weeks. Later, the parents only visit briefly to feed the chick.

Length: 45-50cm
Wingspan: 102-112cm
Where to look: present round entire coastline where cliffs suitable, all year except late autumn. Non-breeders at sea. Very rarely inland. **Nest:** in colonies on cliff ledges, less often unused buildings, sand-dunes; grass or soil preferred to bare rock. **Egg:** 1, white. **Food:** offal, crustaceans, carrion, refuse, small fish, usually taken from surface. Attends trawlers in large numbers. **Voice:** loud, excited cackling and crooning at nest, grunts and cackles in feeding flocks, otherwise silent.

Fulmars are faithful to their mate and nest site. They wave their heads and bow and cackle at their mates and rivals. The inside of the bill, shown in display, is a striking mauve or purple.

At fledging, the young bird resembles its parents. Despite the long period of immaturity, there are no plumage differences with age, sex or season.

The nest site is vigorously defended, though once incubation has started the adults are rarely together.

Gannet

❊

SULA BASSANA

Britain and Ireland now hold 186,000 pairs of this largest and most spectacular seabird of the North Atlantic, a large proportion of the world population. It was formerly taken for food by sea-fowling communities; the fat, unfledged young or 'guga' providing considerable quantities of protein and fat. The inflated, dried stomachs were used on St Kilda as containers. Cessation of most persecution has enabled numbers to increase to a new peak, doubling between 1949 and 1969, and still rising, with several new colonies.

Gannets have no brood patch, so the egg is incubated under the large webbed feet, and the newly hatched chick brooded on top of the webs. Another special adaptation is the lack of external nostrils, enabling the birds to dive head-first into the sea from up to 30 metres (100ft), reaching 100kph (60mph) as they hit the water.

Each young gannet eats about 30 kilos (65 pounds) of fish before leaving the colony. After 13 weeks, they jump off the cliffs and flop-glide to the sea below, unable to take off again for a week or more, until their excess fat reserves have been used up. They move south to waters off the West African coast and may remain there for two years, before returning north.

The central long, thin, angled wings, long, pointed bill and tail give characteristic silhouette.

Gannets take about four years to attain full adult plumage, each stage being recognisable. First-years have white underparts, head and neck, but otherwise are all dark above; second-years have largely white forewings but still have dark flight feathers. Third-years resemble adults, but retain some black feathers on the inner wing and tail. They hang around the colony edge in 'clubs'.

The magnificent adult is gleaming white with black outer wing, and rich buff head and nape.

In flight the body is often angled above the horizontal, and the bird has steady, powerful wing-beats.

Distant birds of all ages are identifiable by their shape.

Fishermen may use the spectacular sight of fishing gannets to locate fish shoals. Many hundreds of birds may gather if the fishing is good, feasting, for example, on mackerel or other shoal fish. To watch a diving mass of gannets it is a wonder that they do not impale one another.

One or other parent is always in attendance at the nest to defend it and to tend the downy, white chick. As it grows older, dark juvenile feathers replace the down. When fledged, juveniles are black ,to avoid being taken for trespassing adults.

Length: 87-100cm
Wingspan: 165-180cm
Where to look: breeds mainly on rocky islands in north and west, but seen off all coasts, less numerous in winter. Vagrant inland. **Nest:** pile of seaweed, vegetation, earth. In large, dense, noisy colonies. **Egg:** 1, pale blue, chalky, turning white, then staining. **Food:** fish, especially mackerel and herring, caught in spectacular plunge-dive; also offal. **Voice:** arr, urrah.

Cormorant

❋

PHALACROCORAX CARBO

Length: 80-100cm
Wingspan: 130-160cm
Where to look: breeds round all coasts, but large gaps in the east; otherwise widespread on estuarine and inland waters, especially winter. **Nest:** pile of twigs, seaweed, lined with finer material, in loose colonies on cliff ledges. Abroad, also in trees, reed beds inland. **Eggs:** 3-4, chalky white. **Food:** fish, especially bottom-dwelling species, eels. **Voice:** guttural croaking at nest and roost.

Cormorants are widely distributed over five continents. They eat a variety of fish, many of no commercial value, but fishermen, who see them as competitors, have long persecuted them. When not feeding, cormorants sit like bottles, upright in rows on a sand bank, buoy or other man-made structure; shags prefer rocks.

The cormorant uses its large webbed feet to incubate its eggs, carefully placing them under the eggs, so they are warmed between the feet and body. The young are born blind and naked, and look distinctly reptilian at this stage. They were formerly eaten in the Netherlands, where some tree colonies are very large – the famous Nardermeer colony has 3,800 nests.

Cormorant feathers have modified barbs which allow air to escape and water to penetrate the plumage. This makes for more efficient underwater swimming. However, it also means that the bird becomes waterlogged and must dry out its plumage, standing in the familiar heraldic posture. Vultures have been observed in similar pose, and it is thought this may also aid digestion in some way.

In full breeding dress they are very handsome; black, glossed blue and bronze, with a white throat and thigh patch, flashed in courtship display. A few white plumes adorn the loosely crested nape formed of elongated feathers. Outside the nesting season adults are much duller, and lose most of their white.

Immatures are brown with varying amounts of white underneath.

Shag

❋

PHALACROCORAX ARISTOTELIS

The shag, or green cormorant, like most British seabirds, has been steadily increasing this century, despite periodic disasters. it is highly susceptible to paralytic shellfish poisoning, contracted from a natural toxin produced by a small marine organism, and concentrated in the fish upon which the shags feed. In 1968, 82 per cent of Farne Island breeding birds died within a few days. However, in the following year, numbers were rapidly replaced by incoming young birds, which had dispersed from the colony. Shags take four years to mature, and, once adult, have a high life expectancy. Young birds are prone to disorientation in adverse weather and may end up inland in considerable numbers. Such influxes are called 'wrecks'.

It is an early breeder, nesting usually timed so that the young are in the nest when most sand eels are available in May and June, but occasional nests have been found in winter. The long fledgling period of 53 days is followed by a further four weeks during which the adults still feed and tend the young. The female chick loses her voice after five weeks, able only to hiss and click!

The shag is confined to European Atlantic coasts as far south as Morocco, and the Mediterranean and Black Seas. It is largely resident, with little more than local dispersal from most colonies, so they must be sought near rocky coasts all year round.

In flight shows proportionately shorter and less pointed wings than cormorant, and more rapid wing-beats, with the neck usually fully extended. They hug the sea more closely.

The dapper spring adult with its dark, oily green plumage, yellow gape, and comic, upturned crest is easily distinguished from the larger cormorant.

Length: 65-80 cm
Wingspan: 90-105
Where to look: rocky coasts, absent from much of east and south England. Immature birds disperse more widely in winter. Not inland except after gales. **Nest:** heap of weed, vegetation, on sheltered ledge, sea cave, among boulders. **Eggs:** 3, pale blue, with chalky deposit. **Food:** fish, mainly sand eels and herrings. **Voice:** grunts and clicks.

Grey Heron

❊

ARDEA CINEREA

A heron standing motionless beside a river or pond is a very familiar sight, and the actions of a hunting bird that has succeeded in catching an eel are truly spectacular as this most accomplished of fishermen tries to swallow the most agile of fish. Frequently the eel actually knots itself around the heron's bill. So successful is the heron at fishing that for many years it was thought that the legs of the bird produced some magical substance which attracted fish as it stood in the water. Anglers were not slow to capitalise on this belief by scattering pieces of herons' legs around a fishing ground. There is, of course, no foundation to the idea.

The grey heron population of England and Wales is probably better known than that of any other bird. First counted in 1928, there has been an annual monitoring ever since, and the population now numbers some 4,000 breeding pairs (plus a further 1,000 or so in Scotland). The largest colony is at the RSPB Northward Hill reserve, Kent, where in most years the colony totals some 200 pairs.

Herons have special powdery down on the sides of their chests. They rub any feathers (usually head and neck) that have become sticky or scaly against the down after feeding, and the powder soaks up the fish slime, making the feathers much easier to clean.

The large, dagger-shaped bill is a highly efficient tool for fishing. Normally yellow, but turns bright pink when breeding.

In both flapping flight and when gliding and soaring, the heron is immediately identified by the broad, rounded wings, 'kinked' neck and long, trailing legs.

The claw on the third toe has a serrated edge which enables the plumage to be preened clean.

Length: 90-98cm; **Weight:** 1,100-1,700g
Where to look: ponds, lakes, rivers, marshes and other fresh water sites, sometimes seen at coastal localities, particularly in winter. **Nest:** large stick construction in tree-top colonies, although occasionally singly or on ground. **Eggs:** 4-5, pale blue. **Food:** varied, fish, small mammals and birds. **Voice:** a loud, harsh and distinctive *frank*; young birds chatter or give a pig-like squeal, especially before being fed.

If you visit the south coast of England and see what looks like a pure white heron, the chances are it is a little egret. Once rare in Britain, these elegant birds are now present year-round, with several hundred in the country at any one time. Many people believe that it will not be long before the little egret is firmly established as a breeding species.

Bittern

BOTAURUS
STELLARIS

A combination of drainage of wetlands, and human persecution in the 19th century has resulted in a very restricted bittern population, now probably numbering just 15 nesting pairs each year. The majority are confined to only two or three sites, and East Anglia is still the strghold of the species.

The skulking and secretive nature of the bittern, the camouflage of the mottled and barred golden-brown plumage, together with the motionless stance, can make it extremely difficult to observe. Consequently, bitterns are most easily seen by birdwatchers in flight; hides at the RSPB's Leighton Moss reserve offer perhaps the best opportunities for observation.

The presence of bitterns in spring is best established by listening for the distinctive territorial 'booming' call of the male. This strange noise, although not loud, is far-carrying and may be heard up to three miles away, most frequently at dusk in April or May.

Although a member of the heron family, when seen in flight the brown plumage with rounded wings can give the impression of a giant woodcock or owl.

Juveniles are uneven, dirty grey-brown at first, growing more white feathers during their first winter, when the bill brightens.

Downy chicks call noisily, with head upstretched, if they are lost, cold or hungry. They clamber on to the hen's back with no active help from her.

In flight the wings of a mute swan make a unique humming, throbbing sound that replaces the contact calls of other species.

Mute Swan

❊

CYGNUS OLOR

Big, white swans are symbols of grace, elegance and serenity, but also strength and power. Adult humans enjoy their beauty and shapeliness; children prefer to ask if it is really true that a swan can break a leg with one swipe of its wing! Probably not, but they are certainly big and impressive, and a very characteristic part of the British scene. Numbers have declined in central England where they seem most obviously at home.

Associated with an increase and spread in western Europe, mute swans in Britain became much more numerous early in the 20th century and by 1955/56 there were 3,500-4,000 breeding pairs and another 11,000 non-breeding birds. Hard winters, increased disturb-ance from boats and the effects of lead poisoning from lost fishing weights combined to cause a decline, though it has been most marked in central England and balanced by increases in the north. By 1983 there were 3,150 pairs and 12,600 non-breeders, but some of the most famous herds, on the Thames and at Stratford-upon-Avon, have declined almost to the point of disappearance. Swans used to be kept for food, but their need for water and the problems of feeding and catching, such big birds eventually caused a change-over to domestic geese.

Male mute swans can be very aggressive and will chase off intruders, flying and then swimming quickly towards them. They also perform a spectacular display known as 'busking', with arched wings, breast thrust forwards, head aimed back and neck feathers fluffed out; serious fights sometimes develop.

Adult pulls up food and passes it to chick on one side, using same action as in nest-building; foot movements attract chicks and stir up food particles for them.

Length: 145-160cm; **Weight:** 8-13kg
Where to look: shallow lakes, slow rivers, marshes, wet meadows, sheltered coasts.
Nest: beside water, huge heap of vegetation with shallow depression. **Eggs:** 5-8, huge, chalky, greenish, April-June.
Food: aquatic vegetation obtained by dipping head and neck or up-ending; grasses taken when grazing on meadows or salt marsh; some snails, worms. **Voice:** hoarse, strangled trumpeting, snorting and hissing calls; wings noisy in flight.

Bewick's Swan

❄

CYGNUS COLUMBIANUS

Length: 115-125cm; **Weight:** 4-8kg
Where to look: flooded meadows. salt marshes, shallow lakes and reservoirs.
Food: roots, shoots, aquatic plants, grain and waste potatoes. **Voice:** varied soft or loud and far-carrying, musical, bugling calls.

Bewick's swans used to be common in west Scotland and rare in England, but since the 1930s the opposite has been the case. They breed in remote tundra at the far northern edge of Siberia, from which only a few thousand come to Europe each winter. In England the main flocks are found on the Ouse Washes and at Slimbridge, where artificial feeding brings them close to observation hides; normally they are very shy. Their appearance on these Wildfowl Trust reserves is predictable, but the big flocks remain spectacular. Elsewhere it is an exciting event to discover a newly arrived party of these wild and wonderful swans on a frosty November day.

They are noticeably smaller than other swans when seen side by side, but the shorter, straighter neck, black and yellow bill and shorter, less pointed and, when swimming, less elevated tail are the best distinctions from the familiar mute swan. Whooper swans are much more like them, but with a longer, flatter head profile and more yellow on the bill.

In flight Bewick's call loudly, but their wings simply 'swish', without the hum of the mute's.

Adults have rounded yellow side patches on otherwise black bill; young birds are dingy grey with pink and black on the bill.

The typically thick, goose-like neck can be raised erect, and then appears long and thin.

Length: 145-160cm; **Weight:** 8-14kg
Where to look: wet meadows and stubble fields by rivers and estuaries, upland pools, large lochs. **Food:** leaves, stems and roots of aquatic plants, waste grain and potatoes. More often on dry land in recent years.
Voice: loud, trumpet-like or bugling call, stronger than Bewick's.

Whooper Swan

❄

CYGNUS CYGNUS

Small, quiet lochs in the Scottish hills, grassy fields beside the mouth of a river, or wild, remote farmland with meadows and stubble not far from a lake make the ideal winter home for whooper swans. In some places, especially at the Wildfowl Trust reserve on the Ouse Washes, all three swans mix together in winter, but it is generally true to say that whoopers prefer the north

Plumage is like Bewick's, but longer bill and flatter forehead are obvious; notice that the yellow extends forward in a point on the side of the bill.

All swans are prone to reddish staining from oxides in water, but whoopers perhaps show it most often. They, and Bewick's, walk more freely than the waddling mute and are quicker to take to the air

and west of Britain to the softer south. Most of Britain's winter whoopers are from Iceland, where there are 5,000-7,000 birds, though only a small proportion nest in any one year. Like other swans and geese, the numbers here in any winter depend very largely on the breeding success of the previous season. As young birds are obvious and family parties stay together all winter, the productivity of the whooper swan is easily studied.

The weather in Iceland also plays a part in how many come to Britain and Ireland, as more will stay there in a mild winter, but a spell of bad weather even in mid-winter can trigger off a new movement south and flocks can cross to and from Iceland at almost any time from September to April. They can migrate at enormous heights, presumably in very cold air indeed. Very occaionally a pair or two of whooper swans will remain in Britain to breed. The north and north-west of Scotland are classic locations for this.

Length: 60-70cm; **Weight:** 1.5-2kg
Where to look: meadows and stubble beside salt marshes and on islands. **Food:** leaves, stems, seeds and roots of grass and other vegetation. **Voice:** short, sharp bark, often repeated in yapping chorus from flocks.

In flight the black chest and white belly make an obvious contrast; from above, the rump is eyecatching.

With its beautiful barring, glossy black chest and immaculate appearance, the barnacle is perhaps the most lovely of all geese. The neat little beak and, for a goose, rather long legs, add a distinctive touch at close range. Barnacles that breed in Greenland spend the winter in western Scotland, especially on the island of Islay, and in Ireland. There will usually be over 20,000 of them. Another group from Spitsbergen winters only on the Solway Firth; these have increased to over 10,000 birds. A third group breeds in the northern USSR and spends the winter in the Netherlands, but some reach England each winter. On Islay they have been the cause of great controversy, because they prefer to eat the rich, green grass of meadows improved for sheep rearing, to the detriment of the sheep. An RSPB reserve is managed in order to attract the geese away from other farms on the island, in an attempt to reduce the conflict. The success of the scheme remains to be evaluated.

Grazing flocks look greyest of all geese in dull light, sharp contrasts in sunshine.

Barnacle Goose
❈
BRANTA LEUCOPSIS

On a dark, misty winter's day in south-east England, only the comfortable sounds of the brents' deep, nasal, rronk-rronk calls, echoing around the marsh, may give them away. The flock may be hidden in the gloom, or tucked away in a muddy creek or out of sight behind the sea-wall, but these little geese are as much a part of the wilderness of Britain's low-lying coasts as the life-giving mud and marsh on which they live. They feed and roost in tight-packed groups, even when they fly to the fields, an increasing habit of recent years, so that counting them is a hard job. Dark-bellied birds come here each winter from the northern tundra of the USSR, to feed in the southern estuaries; pale-bellied birds from Greenland visit Ireland, and others from Spitsbergen come to Lindisfarne. Both races are rare in world terms. The pale-bellied birds number some 20,000 in Ireland and 3,000 in Northumberland.

Length: 55-60cm; **Weight:** 1.2-1.5kg
Where to look: muddy estuaries and adjacent salt marshes and pastures; sandy bays. **Food:** grazes and up-ends to feed on eel-grass, green algae, growing cereals and marsh plants. **Voice:** deep, rolling bark.

Brent Goose
❈
BRANTA BERNICLA

When eel-grass was reduced by disease in the 1930s, numbers of dark-bellied brents fell by at least 75 per cent. The population of this race is enormously variable depending on breeding success, but with careful protection has recently reached over 80,000, in turn renewing calls for their control.

Black neck, chest, face, marked only on sides of neck, unique; juvenile has no neck patches at first, and barred wing coverts.

Dark birds browner beneath, black chest less contrasted than on pale race; sometimes hard to tell.

Though only as long as mallard, brents look larger, heavier in flight, with white rump obvious. Flocks usually shapeless masses or lines, low and fast-flying.

Canada Goose

❋

BRANTA CANADENSIS

As on other geese, the 'stern' is strikingly white — clearly an obvious mark for other birds to follow, especially in flight

Both parents tend the young, which are able to feed themselves.

Chicks use frequent contact calls and perform greeting displays after accidental separation.

Chicks leave nest on hatching and are vulnerable to predators; they fly after seven weeks.

Pairs — formed at about two years old — remain together for life; young are tended by both parents but driven away next spring.

Length: 90-100cm; **Weight:** 4-5kg
Where to look: ornamental lakes, flooded gravel pits, reservoirs, and nearby meadows. **Nest:** on ground near water, often below tree or bush; a pile of leaves, grass, reeds. **Eggs:** 5-6, cream or white, March-April. **Food:** roots, stems, leaves and fruits of water and waterside plants; mostly grazes, also up-ends in water. **Voice:** loud, resonant honking calls, usually obviously two notes - *gor-rronk*, etc. Also various loud, quicker and shorter honking and trumpeting notes in display or alarm.

In North America, the Canada goose is a highly-migratory species with many distinct races and traditional migration routes and wintering grounds. It is odd that such a bird should be so successfully introduced into Europe (to Britain in the 17th century) and remain content to live all year round on the lakes where its ornamental qualities were required. Nevertheless, the lakes and pools of Britain's stately homes, surrounded by ample flat, grassy expanses for easy grazing, proved ideal and the adaptable birds soon became established and familiar.

So long as food is readily available, Canada geese seem content to settle anywhere, even on a city-centre lake; if food is insufficient to support them, they simply fly elsewhere. By the late 1960s there were over 10,000 birds in Britain and their increase continues. In favoured sites in central England it is possible to find flocks of several hundred birds in late summer and autumn, which undoubtedly look spectacular and allow everyone to enjoy the sight and sound of 'wild geese', but they somehow lack the romantic associations and appeal of their truly wild relatives, which would not be seen dead in a town! Consequently, they are rather neglected – even despised – by many birdwatchers.

The Canada goose is easily recognised by the brown-barred back, creamy chest and black neck and head, with white 'chinstrap'. Winter flocks are well organised and often large, with considerable aggression being common between members of the group and towards threats from outside. Within the flock a hierarchy exists with large families dominating small ones; these in turn dominate pairs, with unfortunate single birds at the bottom of the 'pecking order' in every respect.

White-fronted Goose

❄

ANSER ALBIFRONS

Length: 65-78cm; **Weight:** 1.5-2.5kg
Where to look: meadows in broad river valleys, beside estuaries. Very restricted, in reduced numbers, mostly in Gloucestershire, Kent, Hampshire. Greenland race in wilder places, very rare in Wales, more widespread Ireland, Scotland. **Food:** grass, roots. **Voice:** most musical of geese, with ringing, laughing, yodelling quality to flock calls; usually high-pitched *lyo-lyock, klick-klek,* etc. Hissing and yapping calls on ground and 'creaking' wings taking flight.

To many people in the south of England this was once the most familiar of the wild 'grey geese', as greylags and pink-feet are more northerly in their distribution. Nowadays, however, flocks of introduced graylags are much commoner, while, coincidentally, wild white-fronts have declined dramatically. Only in the North Kent Marshes, the Avon Valley of Hampshire, the Tywi Valley of South Wales and on the Severn Estuary around Slimbridge, are there now regular flocks of birds from the Siberian tundra, and all have declined in numbers. In the north and in Ireland, darker birds from Greenland appear, around 20,000 all told in an average year. White-fronts are fascinating to watch, like all geese, and the hides at Slimbridge in mid-winter offer the best views. They are noisy, busy and quarrelsome, quick to take alarm and difficult to approach except behind the Slimbridge screens. In flight, white-fronts *en masse* are unparalleled, as they cross the sky in huge 'Vs', lines and chevrons; in full voice they create a yapping, squeaky, babbling chorus that can be quite deafening from a really big flock – in the Netherlands it is often possible to see 10,000–15,000 together. In flight the white-front shows a white rump and some grey on forewing above. They are more agile in flight than greylags, especially when landing and taking off. The calls of geese are difficult for a beginner to identify, though each species has its characteristic tone and pattern. The calls of white-fronts have a distinctive 'catch' to them.

Usually wary and difficult to approach, but gets used to hides, as at Slimbridge.

Immature birds best recognised by plain, brownish colour, orange legs, dull, pinkish bill, and parents!

Adult of Soviet race has pink bill, variable barring; can look strongly contrasted or plainer.

Bean Goose

❄

ANSER FABALIS

Only in south-west Scotland, where a very few birds appear each winter, and in Norfolk, where a reduced but recently recovering flock can be found, are bean geese regularly seen in Britain. Most winters one or two will be found mixed with Russian white-fronts, but otherwise only irregular parties appear from time to time. At the traditional wintering places they are creatures of habit, seeking out the same preferred fields year after year. Britain's wintering birds breed in the birch scrub and coniferous forest south of the north European tundra.

Beans are big geese, though not so heavy as greylags, and their long proportions – especially the neck – give them a special elegance. Adults are particularly cleanly barred above, but have none of the blue-grey cast so often evident on pink-feet, nor do they show the same fawn-buff colour on the breast. Choosing open spaces in winter, with a wide view, bean geese are shy and unapproachable birds.

Dark upperwing, long, rather slender neck and deep calls are helpful features in flight.

Bean has longish, orange and black bill; pink-foot has short bill with pink band; greylag has paler head, massive orange bill with paler tip, no black.

Length: 65-80cm; **Weight:** 2-4kg
Where to look: pastures and arable land. **Food:** in Britain grazes mainly on grassy fields, but on the Continent also in stubble. **Voice:** generally quieter than other grey geese, resembles deep pink-footed, without the higher-pitched notes.

Greylag Goose

※

ANSER ANSER

Chicks quickly follow their parents and soon learn the rank of the family within the flock.

Length: 75-90cm; **Weight:** 3-4kg
Where to look: open arable land, marshes and lakes. Feral birds in more enclosed space. **Nest:** on ground in sheltered hollow or in reeds. **Eggs:** 4-6, creamy-white, April-May. **Food:** grass, spilt potatoes and grain; moving to growing cereals in late spring. **Voice:** clattering clamour in flight, less bugling or trumpeting than other geese, more rattling in effect.

Wild breeding pairs frequent remote lochs; 'feral' birds, introduced but now living wild, may be much tamer and breed on quite small, even well-wooded, pits in unlikely places

The large, bright orange bill, generally pale appearance and loud, rather rattling calls (without the musical quality of many other geese) help to identify the greylag. Visiting birds in winter have pink legs; but some of the wild breeding stock, and some feral birds, have orange legs, although either colour may be hard to distinguish at a distance! Old birds have a few spots of black on the belly and chest, but never so much as a white-front.

All geese vary greatly in appearance according to the light. Greylags are essentially pale birds, but strong sun can create sharply contrasting highlights and shadows, and swimming birds can often appear misleadingly dark-headed as their barred backs catch the light.

Britain's winter-visiting greylags –

in record years there may be up to about 100,000 of them – come from Iceland in October, mainly to Scotland, where they need a safe, quiet roost on water and undisturbed feeding places. The greylag is not generally long-lived, studies showing that average adult life expectancy is under four years. Pairs form for life and will be together all year round, and families remain together during the winter within the spectacular flocks.

Greylags are heavier and slower than pink-foots, with larger heads.

Length: 60-75cm; **Weight:** 1.8-33kg
Where to look: estuaries, salt marshes, lakes, nearby arable and pasture land. **Food:** grass, spilt barley and other grain, waste potatoes. **Voice:** musical, deep di- or tri-syllabic honking; also high-pitched, sharp *wink-wink*.

Pink-footed Goose

※

ANSER BRACHYRHYNCHUS

Barred, greyish back, pale buff forebody and very dark head and neck; rounded head, short, dark bill, legs pale to deep pink.

This is perhaps the prettiest, most attractive grey goose. It may have white around the bill.

White-front (inset, left) and pink-foot.

In central and southern Scotland, where it mixes with greylags, and in northern England, especially on the Lancashire mosses, this is the most abundant winter goose. In late 1985 the number wintering in Britain reached a new record of 128,000. They come from Iceland and east Greenland and, like other northern geese, are very dependent on good weather during the short summer at such high latitudes. In a bad season they may rear virtually no young at all and fewer are seen in Britain as a result.

At places such as the north shore of the Solway Firth it is one of the great birdwatching experiences to stand between the inland feeding grounds and the estuarine roost at dusk, when stream after stream of noisy geese fly overhead. After many years with reduced numbers, the traditional Norfolk flocks have recently recovered, and it is now often possible to see several thousand

there, too – much to the delight of more southern birdwatchers. The reason for the increase – in 1950 there were only 30,000 – seems to be largely to do with improved food supplies and better refuges in Britain rather than changes in the breeding grounds, which are threatened with development.

In flight, pink-footed geese have forewings that show blue-grey, more extensively than white-fronts but darker than greylags. The flight action is fast and aerobatic, while the head and neck look relatively small.

Flying birds show such a striking pattern that they are hard to miss.

The broad sharp bill is ideally suited to sieving through wet ooze and dealing with molluscs.

Downy chicks start to cheep as they hatch; later they have high-pitched piping noises, with the same rhythm as the female's quack.

For 15-20 days the family stays in the feeding territory, then the chicks join with others in a crêche up to 100 strong. The crêche is often looked after by adults that have failed to breed

Shelduck

TADORNA TADORNA

Shelducks have startlingly white plumage, even on the dullest day, exaggerating their size and making them stand out from all the duller birds around. On a sunny day in summer the brightness of the bill is almost unreal, and the sharp, clean lines of the plumage are equally breathtaking.

Numbers have increased this century and today there are thought to be 12,000 birds nesting in Britain and Ireland. Because most of the shelducks of north-west Europe go to the same place to moult, this figure is small compared with the great gatherings in the Waddenzee. At least 100,000 gather there, safe for the dangerous period when they shed all their flight feathers at once – a characteristic of all ducks and geese – and are unable to fly. Their distribution abroad is quite wide,

though largely limited in Europe to the coasts of France and those countries bordering the North Sea and the Baltic; but shelducks nest in scattered places in the Mediterranean and then eastwards beyond the Caspian into central Asia. This sporadic distribution shows a liking for rather warm climates and a need for productive shallow-water habitats. In the past the range was probably more complete, and the isolated remnants have survived through their adaptability to changing conditions. It seems odd to find the same species on a cold Scottish mud flat and on a hot, reed-fringed Mediterranean marsh.

Although shelducks are primarily birds of the coast, they are quite frequent in land on migration or during harsh winter weather. They have even begun to breed inland, especially by flooded gravel pits.

Length: 60-70cm; **Weight:** 1-1.8kg
Where to look: sandy and muddy shores, dunes, flooded gravel pits, reservoirs, marshes. **Nest:** in burrow, hole in tree, haystack. **Eggs:** 8-10, white, April to June. **Food:** molluscs, insects, crustaceans dug or sieved from wet mud or from water. **Voice:** male whistles; deep, quick quacks from female.

Males in spring are glorious, with brilliantly red bill topped by a large knob; females have no basal knob and show white facial marks, less black below.

An attacking bird chases others from its territory with head held low; the intruder runs off with its head raised and plumage sleek.

Most pairs persist from year to year, and move to territorial feeding places on the shore by late March. At the same time they look for nest sites, often miles away, visiting them each morning. Nests may be close together, with no territories around them. When the young hatch, the family goes to a new, nursery area, with a 'mobile territory' centred around the chicks.

Wigeon

❊

ANAS PENELOPE

Note small size and steep
forehead; white and black
undertail of male; grey legs
and small bill.

The British breeding population of wigeon rarely exceeds 500 pairs, but in the winter months birds from Iceland, northern Europe and Russia move south, and as many as 200,000 are present during the January peak. The main wintering sites are coastal, apart from the Ouse Washes, where the creation of reserves to prevent disturbance, and the establishment of a water management regime on grazing meadows, has resulted in a dramatic increase to over 25,000 birds at a peak. The most evocative sound of a salt marsh is the whistle of a male wigeon. Feeding flocks move forward in dense groups; good sunlight reveals their beautiful colours.

Length: 45-51cm; **Weight:** 600-900g
Where to look: shallow, fresh water when nesting, salt marsh or pasture in winter.
Nest: on ground in cover. **Eggs:** 6-12, pale buff. **Food:** vegetable, mainly algae and eel-grass. **Voice:** whistling *whee-oo*; grating purr.

Eclipse males resemble females, but retain white forewing.

The wigeon is a highly gregarious duck, between mallard and teal in size, with a short neck and tiny bill used for cropping vegetation. In flight, often with complex aerial manoeuvres, the distinctive whistle and prominent white patch on the upperwing of the male, plus the short pointed tail, are all distinguishing features. The overall impression is of a small, light duck with a dark head.

Teal

❊

ANAS CRECCA

In a group or 'spring', teal leap vertically from the water and then dash about the sky over a pool, so active that, although in shape they resemble small wigeon, they will often give the impression of a party of dark waders. By contrast, when walking they are, if anything, rather clumsy and less agile than the larger mallard. The smallest of the wintering ducks, and only a third the weight of a mallard, the 100,000 or so that are present in December are to be found at both inland and coastal sites, with over 20,000 on the Mersey Estuary alone. The favoured areas are where shallow water only a few centimetres deep covers soft mud into which the birds can easily thrust their bills, for they rarely feed by up-ending as do the larger species.

In areas where they are not disturbed, they become extremely tame and are often found feeding close to observation hides. Normally, however, because they are persecuted by hunters, they tend to be rather wary and difficult to see, looking very dark and dull except for the horizontal white bar across the males.

Very active when feeding, but resting birds can remain motionless for long periods. Preening birds show the striking green and black speculum with white edging, a useful pointer.

Creamy and black undertail very obvious during take off, which is vertical. White underwings.

Small size with rapid wing-beats and twisting flight. Whitish underparts hard to see.

Length: 34-38cm; **Weight:** 240-360g
Where to look: shallow waters. **Nest:** on ground in cover. **Eggs:** 8-11, off-white. **Food:** seeds, invertebrates. **Voice:** distinctive high-pitched, chirping *krick*.

Mallard

ANAS PLATYRHYNCHOS

The commonest, most wide-spread of all ducks, the mallard needs no introduction, being encountered everywhere from the town park to the village pond, from the reservoir or gravel pit to the wildest sea loch or estuary salt marsh. Except for her yellowish bill and orange legs, the female is a rather undistinguished brown colour. This contrasts sharply with the male, with his striking bottle-green head and curled feathers above the tail. There are few sounds more familiar than the quack of a female mallard; the male has only a weak rasping raehb.

The brown plumage of the female provides camouflage so that she remains hidden among vegetation while incubating eggs.

Males have a dark green head, white neck ring, purple-brown breast and grey back.

During the summer months the male's plumage assumes an appearance similar to that of the female; this is called 'eclipse' plumage.

Highly adaptable, mallards often nest well away from water, high in a tree or on a building, and newly hatched young face a perilous journey. The British breeding population is difficult to estimate, but it could exceed 150,000 pairs, which together with an arrival of European birds, provides a winter count in excess of 700,000.

Mallard drakes tend to defend territories around a small headland or other feature.

Out of water the birds walk easily, their bodies parallel with the ground. Both sexes have orange legs.

Length: 50-65cm; **Weight:** 950-1,300g
Where to look: almost anywhere with water. **Nest:** usually on the ground, can be high in tree. **Eggs:** 9-13, bluish-green. **Food:** variable; opportunistic feeder. **Voice:** female gives familiar quack, male a weak nasal note.

Goldeneye

BUCEPHALA CLANGULA

Despite the recent welcome rise of the Scottish breeding population, the goldeneye is still best known as a winter visitor to Britain and Ireland. The peak winter population is 10,000-15,000 birds, widely distributed over inland waters (mainly large reservoirs) and also along the coast. The drakes are among the most handsome and distinctive of winter wildfowl, strikingly black and white, but females and first winter birds are both less obvious and less distinctive, looking hunched and dark. Through the provision of large numbers of nest-boxes, goldeneyes have colonised Scotland in the last 20 years; in 1986 there were 44 successful nests, with 381 ducklings seen. Planned and supervised by the RSPB, this highly successful conservation operation also owes much to co-operative landowners. Look for a small, mainly grey duck, with or without a white collar below the brown head, showing a white flash on the side. Goldeneyes dive continually and are usually nervous and easily put up: watch for the white wing patches and listen for the distinctive wing noise.

Comparing ducks

❊

With over 120 species in the world, ducks come in a range of shapes, sizes and colours. In general, males are more colourful than the brown females, which are dull so that they can remain hidden while incubating eggs. There are two basic types of duck, the surface feeding, or dabblers, and the diving species.

Wigeon: *short-necked, rather dumpy species with tiny bill. Flocks 'graze' when feeding.*

Mallard: *The largest, commonest and most familiar of the surface feeding species. The 'basic' duck.*

Pintail: *a long-necked, slender duck, the pointed tail of both sexes most obvious in flight.*

Goosander: *the largest of the 'sawbills'. A long, low body with largish head and long, thin bill present very distinctive shape. Female resembles merganser.*

Pochard: *fresh water diving duck, often in flocks with tufted duck. Has hump-backed, tail-less shape.*

Goldeneye: *rather small but large-headed duck, found on both fresh and salt water. Both sexes have white panels in wings.*

Teal: *the smallest duck, only garganey similar in size. Leaps straight from water to fly.*

Gadwall: *often an overlooked species, commonest in eastern England. Female mallard-like but greyer with white in wing.*

Shoveler: *the squat, low-in-water appearance, with short neck and huge bill, makes this the most distinctively shaped duck.*

Tufted duck: *the commonest of the diving ducks. Striking male, dull-all brown female.*

Gadwall

※

ANAS STREPERA

The very first gadwalls to nest in Britain were a pair trapped in Norfolk in the mid-1800s which were released after wing-clipping. From this pair the population increased and spread northwards, although the large numbers at Loch Leven, Scotland and Tresco, Isles of Scilly, are of less certain origin. The numbers are continuing to increase and the present breeding population probably exceeds 500 pair. There is a wintering peak of some 5,000 birds, mainly from mainland Europe, which is still very much concentrated in East Anglia. Further introductions in the 1960s and 1970s have established groups in Gloucestershire and Lancashire.

Rather drab-looking birds, gadwalls can be overlooked among other ducks, where they may be dismissed as females, for the male lacks the bright plumage of other dabbling species. The best distinguishing features are overall greyness, black

The female gadwall is easily distinguished from the female mallard when speculum visible.

The male appears very grey with a contrasting black tail, steep forehead and fine black bill.

In flight, gadwalls show white underwings and belly, plus clearly visible white speculum; they have yellow legs and feet.

undertail of male and the white speculum of both sexes. Female gadwalls have obvious orange sides to the bill and plainer heads than mallards.

Length: 46-56cm; **Weight:** 600-900g
Where to look: inland lakes and marshes, usually well vegetated. **Nest:** on ground beside water. **Eggs:** 8-12, pale pink. **Food:** seeds, plants and insects. **Voice:** a quiet quack from female, a nasal *mair* from male.

Garganey

※

ANAS QUERQUEDULA

Unique among British ducks, the garganey is a summer visitor and hence its alternative name of 'summer teal', for in size it is closest to the more numerous teal. Although a very common duck in world terms, the garganey is scarce and decreasing as a British species, with less than 50 pairs present in most years and all confined to the south and east. The continual loss of shallow floods and water meadows suggests the population is likely to decrease further.

One of the earliest of the summer migrants to arrive in spring, appearing on the south coast in late March, the male is immediately identifiable by the prominent curved white stripe from above the eye to the back of the lower neck. The overall impression is of a pinkish-brown and pale grey duck with fine mottling. The female

Distinctive flight characteristics are the blue-grey upper forewing, the dark leading edge to the pale underwing and the dull speculum edged with white.

resembles a rather pale teal, but shows very strong facial markings with a pale spot at the base of the bill and very pale throat. In flight, the white bar across the mid-wing is less obvious than a teal's, but the rear edge is more so, giving two parallel lines as on a mallard.

Garganey winter in large flocks in Africa, both on the coast and on large lakes inland.

Usually seen in pairs in spring, with the male's distinctive head pattern and pinkish plumage aiding identity. Female shows face-markings with pale spot near bill; no bright green on wing (see teal).

Length: 37-41cm; **Weight:** 320-500g
Where to look: shallow flood water. **Nest:** on ground in thick tussock. **Eggs:** 8-9, light brown. **Food:** insects and aquatic vegetation. **Voice:** main call is a mechanical-sounding rattle by male; females quack quietly.

Pintail

❉

ANAS ACUTA

Female looks pale, greyish-brown with blue bill and pointed tail.

Length: 51-66cm; **Weight:** 750-1,000g
Where to look: open areas with shallow water. **Nest:** rare, usually in open. **Eggs:** 7-9, yellowish. **Food:** variety of plant and animal matter. **Voice:** quiet whistle from male, short quacks from female; silent in flight.

The white stripe and breast of the male is distinctive.

Subtlety of colour and an elegant form make the pintail one of the most attractive ducks. The gleaming, distinctively coloured, slightly off-white breast of the male is visible from a considerable distance when no other details may be obvious. In flight the shape is unmistakable; even the female shows a long pointed tail and long slender neck.

Less than 50 pairs breed in Britain, almost all confined to Kent and the fenlands of East Anglia, but, in winter, birds from Iceland, Scandinavia and Russia concentrate on some of the west coast estuaries, with counts of over 15,000 birds on the Mersey. Only here and on the Dee Estuary do counts regularly exceed 5,000. On these coastal sites they feed on the tiny snail called Hydrobia, but increasingly the species has developed night flighting away from the more traditional coastal sites to exploit the stubble and potato fields of inland farms. They are much quieter birds than mallards and most people see them far less often, and usually in very small groups. In flight, pintails look long and thin with pointed tails; the underside is pale and the upperwing dark with a pale line on the trailing edge.

Shoveler

❉

ANAS CLYPEATA

Swimming slowly forward, bodies almost awash, shovelers filter water through their big, broad bills, pushing it out through the sides and trapping food particles with the special serrations that line the edges. Feeding in this manner will often involve small groups which appear to work in unison. To be successful this technique requires a rich food source – seeds and invertebrates – suspended in shallow water.

The male shoveler is distinctive both in shape and colour, while the brown-plumaged female shows the similar distinctive short neck and large bill. Both sexes show striking blue areas on the leading edge of the wing, although these are duller in the female. Especially as they take off, the wings of shovelers make a loud, deep 'woofing' noise, quite unlike mallards.

Something like 1,500 pairs may breed in Britain. They are mainly confined to the south-east, with the largest concentrations on the Ouse Washes. In the winter, populations from eastern Europe move westward and as many as 10,000 reach Britain.

In flight the distinctive front-heavy look, with broad bill and tail-less shape, is apparent. The blue-grey forewing is also very obvious.

In all plumages the body shape and size of bill is distinctive. Eclipse male differs from female in the redness of plumage.

Length: 44-52cm; **Weight:** 400-850g
Where to look: shallow water. **Nest:** on ground. **Eggs:** 9-11, buff. **Voice:** quiet *tuc* by male, female quacks.

Pochard

❋

AYTHYA FERINA

Length: 42-49cm; **Weight:** 800-1,200g
Where to look: well vegetated lakes and pools in summer and open fresh water in winter. **Nest:** on ground near water. **Eggs:** 8-10, greenish. **Food:** water plants, seeds and invertebrates. **Voice:** harsh growling notes.

Although one of the most familiar diving ducks, the pochard is actually a very scarce breeding bird in Britain. There are no more than 200-400 pairs, mainly in south-east England, with important concentrations in the North Kent Marshes and the Norfolk Broads. Most of the birds which come to Britain and Ireland are winter visitors from central Europe and as far away as the USSR. The wintering population may be as high as 80,000. About 85 per cent of their food is plant material, including many seeds, which is obtained by diving in shallow fresh water, hence the birds' preference for shallow and well-vegetated lakes and gravel pits. Reservoirs and other deep-water sites are more often used for roosting and resting. The males are usually unmistakable, but females sometimes cause confusion – especially when asleep. They have quite pale, greyish-brown bodies with pale marks at the eye and the base of the bill. The bill, when visible (pochards sleep for much of the day), has a broad pale band around the middle and a black tip.

In flight, the female looks very plain, but note the pale belly. Neither sex shows prominent wing markings.

Females are a warm mixture of grey and reddish-brown.

Males have a reddish-chestnut head, black breast and vermiculated grey back.

Ruddy Duck

❋

OXYURA JAMAICENSIS

In the late 1950s, about 20 unpinioned young ruddy ducks escaped from the Wildfowl Trust reserve at Slimbridge. From their original strongholds on reservoirs in Somerset and Staffordshire these North American 'stifftails' spread quite rapidly, having nested in the wild for the first time in 1960. There are now probably some 3,000 birds, mainly in the southern half of England, but with records from Wales (including Anglesey) and Northern Ireland. The species has also bred in one area in Scotland. Males in breeding dress are unmistakable, but winter males, females and immature birds need to be compared with various other ducks and also grebes which have dark crowns and white or pale cheeks. Look for the long tail, often held in a stiff cocked position, and the rather long, broad bill. When breeding, ruddy ducks prefer shallow waters with good surrounding vegetation, but in winter they use more open water and may occur in large flocks. Already several sites have become 'traditional' places and attract as many as 400 birds each year.

Female has a brown cap with pale cheeks crossed by a dark stripe.

Summer male is bright chestnut with white cheeks contrasting with black cap. Note blue bill and stiffly cocked dark tail.

In winter, the male closely resembles the female, but still has clear white cheeks and a black cap. The large, broad bill becomes greyish. Note typical shape and posture (tail not always cocked). See smew.

Length: 35-43cm; **Weight:** 500-700g
Where to look: lakes, ponds, reservoirs, gravel pits. **Nest:** well hidden, near water. **Eggs:** 6-10, whitish. **Food:** mainly insect larvae, seeds. Dives. **Voice:** largely silent.

Scaup

❋

Aᴀʏᴛʜʏᴀ ᴍᴀʀɪʟᴀ

Scaup are principally sea-ducks in winter, many of them coming to Britain's shores from Iceland. At present, probably only 5,000-10,000 winter here. Although widely scattered around the coast ,they are most numerous in the Forth, the Dornoch Firth, Islay, the Solway, on the Cheshire Dee and at Carlingford Lough, Northern Ireland. Gone are the days when up to 30,000 could be seen in the vast flock which wintered off Leith in the Forth, attracted by waste grain from breweries and distilleries and by the small worms which lived on the raw sewage. Fewer grain discharges and better sewage treatment led to its abrupt disappearance. Males are easily distinguished from similar ducks. Females are not difficult, but beware of female tufted ducks with white face-

marks; scaup are slightly larger and broader-looking, as well as much less dark in appearance. Their bills are longer and broader and, except on young birds, the white is always more extensive. Tufted ducks have broad black tips to their bills; scaup have only a narrow black mark, useful on dull-faced juveniles.

> **Length:** 42-51cm; **Weight:** 900-1,200g
> **Where to look:** shallow coastal waters, bays and estuaries. Does not breed in UK.
> **Food:** mainly molluscs, also waste grain.
> **Voice:** harsh *karr-karr* while flying.

Female looks larger, broader and paler than female tufted. It has a white patch on the face.

Male looks black fore and aft, and pale in middle with their white flanks and grey back: unlike tufted duck of either sex or any age.

Tufted Duck

❋

Aᴀʏᴛʜʏᴀ ꜰᴜʟɪɢᴜʟᴀ

> **Length:** 40-47cm; **Weight:** 600-1,000g
> **Where to look:** areas of open water, including rivers. **Nest:** well hidden, near water. **Eggs:** 8-11, greenish-grey. **Food:** some aquatic plant material, but mainly molluscs, insects, etc. **Voice:** various harsh growling notes.

After the ubiquitous mallard, the tufted duck is the most widespread and best-known duck, often occurring on park lakes and on rivers in towns and cities, where it soon becomes very tame. It is a remarkably successful species which has been quick to make use of the many new artificial water areas created by man, including gravel pits and reservoirs. In a mere 25 years the breeding population in mainland Britain has trebled to its present level of about 7,000 pairs; there are at least 2,000 more in Ireland. Similarly, the winter population has increased over the same period (by about 50 per cent) with a mid-winter peak of over 60,000 birds. Scottish birds are known to go to Ireland in winter, but those in Ireland and the rest of Britain apparently do not move far. Large numbers reach the British Isles from Iceland, northern Scandinavia and Russia, arriving from late September onwards to stay until early spring. Being so common and often so tame, tufted ducks can be watched and

'learned' thoroughly in all their plumages, which makes it that much easier for the birdwatcher when a scaup appears among them! They are more lively than nearby pochards during the day, as pochards are more nocturnal feeders. Tufted ducks are sociable, often displaying together in groups.

Dives normally last 15-20 seconds, generally to a depth of about 2.5 metres (8ft). Up to 100 dives per hour are common, with pauses of about 10 seconds between dives.

Female tufted duck is a small, dark bird with pale flanks and always a suggestion of a crest. Some females show white on face, but never as much as female scaup. White undertail is not uncommon.

Male is strikingly black and white, with a long, drooping crest.

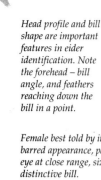
Eider

❋

SOMATERIA MOLLISSIMA

Head profile and bill shape are important features in eider identification. Note the forehead – bill angle, and feathers reaching down the bill in a point.

Adult male is only duck with combination of white breast and back with black underparts and stern. Note also heavy, broad-bodied appearance.

Female best told by its rather plain, barred appearance, pale line over the eye at close range, size and distinctive bill.

Length: 50-71cm; **Weight:** 1,500-2,500g **Where to look:** coastal waters, usually close to shore. **Nest:** on ground, often exposed. **Eggs:** 4-6, greenish-grey. **Food:** dives (or feeds from surface) mainly for molluscs. **Voice:** except when courting, rather silent.

Nests singly or in a loose group; sometimes well hidden, but often out in the open.

Even at very long range, an adult drake eider, uniquely white on top and black beneath, is easy to identify. Young males, passing through a variety of piebald plumages as they grow older, can be more tricky, but at least the bill shape and their size and bulk are distinctive. Eiders are essentially birds of the northern and north-western seaboards. They are usually close inshore, riding the swell in a sandy bay or out beyond the breaking waves on a rocky beach, often strung out in long lines. The creches of youngsters with their attendant 'aunties' may be seen running over mud in some northern estuaries, where they can be in danger of being snatched up by large gulls. A herring gull will make short work of a duckling.

Courtship begins in late winter, as with many wildfowl. The cooing and crooning calls of the beautiful drakes are familiar sounds along favoured coasts well into spring. Female eiders nest singly or in loose colonies, sometimes in quite open spots but often in a crevice between big rocks, occasionally in gull and tern colonies. Eiders are increasing, and perhaps as many as 30,000 pairs breed in Britain and Ireland, while the winter total is estimated at 72,000 birds. This is but a small proportion of the total European wintering population of around two million. Eiders eat slow-moving, bottom-living creatures, mainly molluscs, which they take in dives from the surface. They use their feet to swim underwater, but half-open their wings as they roll forward to dive.

Velvet Scoter

MELANITTA FUSCA

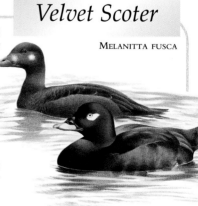

The velvet scoter is both bigger and bulkier than the common scoter, with which it mixes, and is closer to an eider in size. Females and immature birds can be difficult to identify, especially at any distance, but at some stage the characteristic white wing patches will be seen. Eiders have different bill shapes and those which are as dark as velvet scoters will usually show much more white. The female's pale head markings are actually visible even at quite long range in reasonable light.

While individuals turn up quite regularly inland, most velvet scoters are seen on the sea, sometimes very close inshore, and are quite tame. They have been suspected of breeding in Britain in the past, but are essentially winter visitors from Scandinavia and western Siberia. Numbers are very variable from year to year: as many as 10,000 have been recorded, but the more normal total is probably 2,500-5,000. Recent work on winter sea duck populations has shown that the Moray Firth is as important for velvet scoters as it is for common scoters and long-tailed ducks. It is always a pleasure to be able to watch a selection of these attractive marine species close to the shore.

Long-tailed Duck

❈

CLANGULA HYEMALIS

Even where it is common and fairly easy to see, the long-tailed duck remains a blue riband species for the birdwatcher. Fortunately, despite plumage variations, it is not a difficult bird to identify. It occurs off many coasts in small numbers, wherever there are shallow waters offshore, but is commonest from Northumberland northwards to Shetland, and in the Outer Hebrides. It can be seen close inshore in some areas, but often remains well out to sea, flying around a great deal. It is perfectly at home in the roughest conditions. It was only comparatively recently that realistic estimates of wintering numbers became available, following work on sea ducks in the Moray Firth area.

This revealed that the Moray Firth regularly held 10,000-15,000 birds, which must be at least three-quarters of the total for Britain and Ireland. In the sandier inlets of the Firth, displaying groups in spring are at their liveliest and give the most delightful birdwatching.

Length: 40-47cm; **Weight:** 600-800g
Where to look: sea coasts. Does not breed in Britain. **Food:** dives, mainly for animals, especially crustaceans and molluscs. **Voice:** unlike many sea ducks, very vocal – drakes have musical calls.

The winter male is a spectacular white bird with dark cheekmarks, and black on back, wings, breast and, tail, which is very long. Small bill distinctly two-coloured – dark with pinkish band.

Common Scoter

❈

MELANITTA NIGRA

Common scoters breed on a few fresh-water lakes in Scotland and Ireland. In some areas, even in central England, they appear regularly on large reservoirs in late summer. Mainly, though, they are known as sea ducks, winter visitors from Scandinavia and Russia. There are big concentrations in the Moray Firth and Carmarthen Bay. It is often worth looking through flocks in the hope of discovering a few grebes, velvet scoters or long-tailed ducks. Scoters always give the impression of extraordinary buoyancy, and when the males raise their pointed tails and very slender necks, they belie their heavy build. On rare

calm days the sounds of courting birds carry far across the water, a chorus of rippling, piping calls that spread infectiously through the flock.

Common scoters form close-packed, often very large, rafts on the sea, diving under frequently. They fly in long lines or dense packs.

Length: 44-54cm; **Weight:** 700-1,300g
Where to look: coastal waters. **Nest:** well hidden near water. **Eggs:** 6-8, cream to buff. Rare breeder. **Food:** dives for molluscs.

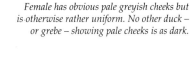

Female has obvious pale greyish cheeks but is otherwise rather uniform. No other duck – or grebe – showing pale cheeks is as dark.

The male is the only totally black duck. Its black and yellow bill can often be seen at very long range.

Red-breasted Merganser

❖

MERGUS SERRATOR

Length: 52-58cm; **Weight:** 900-1,200g
Where to Look: inland lochs, rivers, also coastal waters. **Nest:** on ground, well hidden. **Eggs:** 8-10, buff to olive. **Food:** as other sawbills, fish caught by diving and pursuit under water. **Voice:** mostly silent.

Female is smaller, darker and more obviously crested than goosander. Note lack of clear-cut division between head colour, throat and neck.

Male unmistakable – fine red bill, wispy crest, white neck-band, orange-brown breast.

Although they now breed in north-western England and in parts of Wales, mergansers are most commonly associated with Scotland and Ireland. While many nest well inland on lochs and rivers, the majority breed along the coast, especially in inlets and sea lochs with an abundance of small islands. Some remain on fresh water in winter, but most move to coastal waters, occurring right around the eastern and southern coasts of England as well as their western and northern haunts. Many of these more southerly birds come from Scandinavia, while birds from Iceland join those in Scotland and Ireland. The total winter population is perhaps as high as 11,000 birds.

Seen well, males are unlikely to be confused with other sawbills, but 'redheads' (females and immature birds) can be tricky; they are always thin-billed, darker and generally browner than 'redhead' goosanders, lacking the clear-cut markings of the latter. The facial expression is different, with almost a 'smile' compared with the stern goosander.

Goosander

❖

MERGUS MERGANSER

Large, long and rakish in flight. Drake very white with dark head, 'redhead' more uniform, but head darker and white wing patches.

The goosander is the largest of the three sawbills found in Britain and Ireland; there is little risk of confusion with smew, the smallest species, but 'redhead' (female and immature) goosanders and red-breasted mergansers require care. With practice, they are not actually too difficult to identify and the goosander's clear preference for inland fresh water in winter is a useful extra clue. It haunts fish-rich lochs, lakes and rivers in the breeding season and is very much a bird of large areas of open water, including reservoirs, in winter. Only locally (such as in the Beauly Firth, where there may be as many as 1,500 birds) does it winter regularly on sheltered coasts. Not long ago, the goosander bred only in Scotland, but it is now established in parts of northern England and has also colonised Wales and Ireland in very small numbers. The population appears to be fairly sedentary and, except when hard weather brings influxes from Europe, is not added to by migrants. About 8,000 spend the winter here. They are best sought on traditional sites, albeit often rather modern reservoirs, and are relatively rare away from these regular wintering places.

The female goosander is rather larger than the female merganser and much more uniformly grey, with clearly demarcated red-brown head and neck, well-defined white chain and throat and less wispy crest. Immature similar.

The male – black, white and pink – is unmistakable.

Length: 58-66cm; **Weight:** 1,100-1,700g
Where to look: fresh-water lakes and reservoirs, locally on sheltered coasts.
Nest: usually hole in tree, also in ground or nestbox. **Eggs:** 8-11, whitish. **Food:** fish.
Voice: silent except during display.

Exotic and Domestic Ducks

❋

Ducks have had a close association with man for many centuries. Several species have been domesticated, hybrids are not unusual and exotic species are kept as ornamental waterfowl on many lakes. All cause identification problems for the birdwatcher.

Muscovy: *large species from South America. Common. Black with varying amounts of white.*

White mallard: *an albino variety, common at farms and on town ponds.*

Cayuga mallard: *domesticated form now common in wild populations. Black body with varying amounts of white on breast of male.*

Khaki Campbell: *Commonest form of domesticated mallard. Uniform pale brown with deep body shape.*

Hybrid Mallard x pintail: *one of the mast frequent hybrids. Males show features of both.*

Ruddy shelduck: *Asiatic species, perhaps rare visitor to Britain, but escapes from collections.*

Wood duck: *North American species very similar to mandarin.*

Bahama pintail: *South American species breeding readily in captivity. Escaped birds can include the albino form.*

Red-billed whistling duck: *from South America, the commonest captive 'tree-duck'. Stands very upright on long pink legs.*

Golden Eagle

❊

AQUILA CHRYSAETOS

Golden eagles and buzzards both soar on raised wings, so caution needed at a distance. The eagle is much larger with a more protruding head; longer wings are often 'pinched-in' at the body.

Soaring majestically on outstretched wings over a wild, mountainous landscape, the golden eagle is a genuinely thrilling sight. Like many of Britain's rarer raptors, its home is in Scotland, where it nests on crags and hunts over moorland and bare hillsides. Therein lies one of the main threats to its future, for such areas are becoming the target for forestry plantations. As blanket coniferous forests start to swathe the Scottish glens and moors the eagle's vital feeding grounds are lost.

Around its eyrie, a golden eagle hunts over a 'home-range' which can vary from 8,000 to 18,000 acres. Much of its food is carrion, particularly in winter when dead sheep can form nearly half its diet. Otherwise it feeds on medium-sized mammals and birds, notably mountain hares and red grouse.

The eagle has declined in many countries and Scotland is no exception. During the last century it was intensely persecuted; during World War II numbers rose, only to be reduced again by killing on grouse moors. Then followed reduced breeding success through eating sheep carrion contaminated by dieldrin sheep dip.

Britain's largest bird of prey, with a 2-metre (7ft) wingspan. Adult brown, but young distinctive with white flashes in wings and tail.

When seen close to, the massive bill, accentuated by the flat crown, is impressive. The crown and rather shaggy hind neck are washed golden-yellow.

Today the illegal use of poisonous baits is almost certainly having its effect on the eagle population, and nests are still robbed by egg collectors. Scotland has 420 pairs of golden eagles, one of the highest numbers in Europe. This gives Britain an international responsibility to ensure that poisoning, egg collecting and, particularly, blanket afforestation are kept in check.

Seen in flight, an adult golden eagle appears rather uniform in colour. Juvenile birds, on the other hand, show a lot of white on the wings and base of the tail, leadingto possible confusion with the white-tailed eagle. The latter's broad-winged silhouette, however, is distinctly different.

White-tailed Eagle

HALIAEETUS ALBICILLA

White-tailed eagles have been successfully reintroduced to Scotland after an absence of more than 50 years. They are almost exclusively coastal, their broad wings giving them a characteristic 'barn-door' appearance in flight, unlike that of the golden eagle.

Adult brown with white tail, variable whitish feathers on head and upper breast, yellow bill. Juveniles more difficult to identify, lacking obvious tail of adult.

Length: 75-85cm
Wingspan: 200-220cm
Where to look: wild mountainous country in Scotland; with luck in the Lake District.
Nest: remote crags, occasionally Scots pine. Eyrie with extensive views; pair often has 2-4 alternate nest sites. Bulky nest of branches lined with grasses. **Eggs:** 1-3 (usually 2), whitish or blotched red-brown.
Food: hares, rabbits and grouse, also carrion; hunts over vast area ('home range').
Voice: thin yelp at nest and whistling *twee-oo* alarm.

Buzzard

❋

BUTEO BUTEO

The fate of the buzzard in Britain has been dictated by two main factors: gamekeepers and rabbits. At the turn of the century it was a relatively rare bird, but with a decline in persecution and in the collection of specimens and eggs, and with rabbits still common and widespread, an increase took place up to the 1950s. An interesting aspect of this was the way buzzards spread eastwards during the two world wars – when keepering was reduced or non-existent in many areas. Between 1952 and 1955 myxomatosis struck Britain's rabbits, resulting in their near elimination. This in turn had a drastic effect on buzzards, which depend largely on rabbits during the breeding season. The buzzard population may have been reduced by half from about 25,000 birds. Today there are signs that it is spreading its range once again.

The buzzard continues to be persecuted, though at a much lower level than in former times. It is particularly vulnerable to poisoned baits and more buzzards are killed by them than any other raptor in Britain.

Length: 50-55cm
Wingspan: 115-130cm
Where to look: hilly country and wooded farmland. **Nest:** trees and crags, bulky. **Eggs:** 2-3, white or bluish, with reddish-brown blotches. **Food:** rabbits, earthworms, carrion. **Voice:** mewing *peeioo*.

Adult has dark band on rear of wing and tail, absent in juvenile. Tail may have faint orange hue.

From below buzzards can be highly variable – from largely dark to largely white – though in Britain most are brownish with pale, lightly barred flight feathers.

Circles effortlessly over hillsides, rising in the updraught or in a hot air thermal.

Wings raised when soaring, but flat in glides. Compact, well-proportioned with broad head and thick-set neck. Soars with tail fanned, often to edge of wings.

Commonest large bird of prey to be seen in western Britain, the Lake District and Scotland.

Honey Buzzard

❋

PERNIS APIVORUS

Varies in pattern below from whitish through to chocolate brown. Typically barred with dark patches on fore-wing and characteristic lines on flight feathers. Bars on tail also a clue to identification. Note well-protruding cuckoo-like head, long tail and narrower wings.

The honey buzzard is one of the commonest large raptors breeding in Europe, so why is it so rare in Britain? Part of the answer must lie in its diet of bee, wasp and insect larvae – the numbers of which can be seriously affected by the wet summers of Britain's Atlantic climate. Another factor is its type of migration. Honey buzzards spend the winter in Africa and do not like making the long sea crossing so they migrate where the sea is at its narrowest – places in Europe like the Bosphorus and Gibraltar. The English Channel, therefore, could act as a serious barrier to those that might otherwise reach our shores.

The few that nest in Britain do so from Hampshire to Scotland, but the population is probably less than 30 pairs. They can occasionally be seen on migration in late spring and autumn when care should be taken not to confuse them with the commoner buzzard: note the honey buzzard's small protruding head and neck, long tail, flat wings when soaring and characteristic tail and wing pattern.

Length: 50-60cm; **Wingspan:** 135-150cm
Where to look: uncommon migrant in south and east. Rare breeder in mixed open mature woodland. **Nest:** in large tree, often built on an existing nest. **Eggs:** 2, whitish with red or chocolate markings. **Food:** bee and wasp grubs, other large insects, small mammals.

Rough-legged Buzzard

BUTEO LAGOPUS

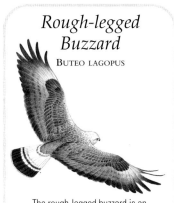

The rough-legged buzzard is an uncommon winter visitor. Its long wings, white tail-base and habit of frequently hovering are good identification clues.

Marsh Harrier

CIRCUS AERUGINOSUS

Like many raptors, the marsh harrier suffered from persecution in the last century and actually became extinct as a breeding bird. Then, just before World War I, a pair nested and heralded the recolonisation of Britain. At first this was slow, but with increased protection in the 1950s numbers grew to 15 pairs in 1958. This success was short-lived, however, because they succumbed to pesticides, and the population crashed to just one pair in 1971. Subsequently, with voluntary bans imposed on the use of the more persistent kinds of pesticides the situation greatly improved, and a quite dramatic recovery took place, with over 30 pairs raising nearly 100 young each year in the late 1980s. Many nest in the safety of reserves or under RSPB protection. Furthermore, birds are spreading from their traditional nest sites in East Anglia, though the best chance of seeing this grand bird of the reed beds is still at RSPB reserves such as Minsmere in Suffolk and Titchwell in Norfolk.

The dark brown female usually has a creamy crown, throat and shoulders. The brown tail is unbarred.

Note the tricoloured wings of the male above; below shows russet-streaked body, whitish underwings with black tips. Flight leisurely with glides on raised wings.

Length: 55cm. **Wingspan:** 115-130cm **Where to look:** reed beds, though often hunts over nearby fields. **Nest:** bulky, among reeds and vegetation in water. **Eggs:** 4-5, bluish-white, often stained. **Food:** mainly frogs, birds and small mammals. **Voice:** a plaintive shrill *kweeoo*.

In good light, the rusty-red tail is very obvious. Note the distinctive buff band on upperwing.

Red Kite

MILVUS MILVUS

Soars on slightly bowed wings held forward. Graceful flight, with the forked tail constantly manoeuvred.

Strict security surrounds Britain's red-kite breeding area in central Wales. Once a common scavenger (even in towns), its population gradually dwindled as hygiene improved and fewer animals died to provide it with carrion. Persecution also took its toll. The Welsh population now numbers nearly 90 pairs, and under careful protection has slowly increased from just 12 birds at the turn of the century.

What problems does it face now? Several succumb each year to the illegal activities of egg collectors, and for this reason nests are guarded. Poison continues to produce victims: poison baits set for crows and foxes (an illegal act in itself) are indiscriminate and can easily kill kites. On one occasion two were found dead on a poisoned carcass. Sadly, about two-thirds of all known kite deaths investigated have been directly attributable to human action. A natural hazard is bad weather in May, which can seriously affect chick survival. The hanging oak woods in which it nests will remain vital.

Length: 60-65cm **Wingspan:** 175-195cm **Where to look:** mature oak woods in steep valleys and nearby hill country in central Wales. **Nest:** of sticks and mud in tall trees. **Eggs:** 3-4, whitish, variably marked. **Food:** small mammals, birds, worms, carrion. **Voice:** shrill, quavering *weeo-weoo-weoo*.

Distinctive colouration below with rusty body and underwing coverts: whitish head, reddish tail, noticeable white wing-patches and black wing-tips.

Hen harrier

❉

CIRCUS CYANEUS

Male is pale grey, white and black below. Note grey hood and dark trailing edge to wing. Dramatic switch-back display over breeding area.

in Montagu's) and the head pattern is a little different with a less bold cheek patch on the hen harrier. Juveniles look like females except that young Montagu's have unmarked

Female very similar to female Montagu's, but larger with different head pattern: compare the two. Juveniles are similar to females.

rufous underparts – a useful point.

Many hen harriers breed on heather moorland and come into conflict with shooting interests because grouse can form an important part of their diet. Whether they cause any reduction in the numbers of grouse available for shooting is a matter of debate, though certainly where grouse numbers are healthy, scientists have shown hen harriers have little or no effect on the population.

Most birdwatchers see hen harriers as winter visitors. They particularly favour the coastal areas of south and east England.

Harriers fly low and more quickly than often imagined over open ground, wings often held up in a slight 'V'. Female and young hen and Montagu's harriers are very similar and, in spring and autumn when they are most likely to overlap, many are simply noted as unidentified 'ring-tails'. The hen harrier is the larger of the two, broader in the wing (especially near the tip which is particularly long and slender

Length: 45-50cm
Wingspan: 100-120cm
Where to look: moorland and bracken-covered hills, newly afforested areas, but marshes and farmland in winter. **Nest:** on ground in heather, lined with rushes and grasses. **Eggs:** 4-5, bluish-white, occasionally with reddish marks. **Food:** small birds and mammals. **Voice:** rapid, chattering *ke-ke-ke-ke* in nesting area.

Montagu's Harrier

❉

CIRCUS PYGARGUS

The female Montagu's and hen harrier are similar, with a white band at the base of the tail. A 'ring-tail' from November to late March is seen only on the hen; in summer both species display this feature – take care!

Wintering in Africa, Montagu's harriers arrive on their breeding grounds in April and May. They are not uncommon on the continent, with perhaps 1,000 pairs in France and 6,000 in Spain, but in Britain they are rare birds. The highest numbers this century were in the 1950s, when some 40 pairs bred, mainly in Devon and Cornwall. A period of decline followed with a 'low' in 1975 when none bred. There has been an improvement since and now several pairs regularly nest in southern England. But there has been a change

of habitat. Traditionally they nested on heaths, reed bed fringes and new conifer plantations, but now all the nests are in corn or rape fields. Therein lies a problem. When the fields are to be cut, the young are still in the nest and earlier spraying operations can flatten them. Thus, nests have to be located and protected from certain farming activities and, if necessary, an area around them left uncut until the young fly. This is a case where farmers and conservationists have worked closely together.

The main features to look for on the male are dirty-grey plumage, black wing tips and bars on the underwing.

Length: 40-45cm
Wingspan: 105-120cm
Where to look: cereal and rape fields in southern England, previously in reed beds, moorland and young forestry. A very rare summer visitor. **Nest:** in crops, lined with grasses etc. **Eggs:** 4-5, pale bluish-white with obscure rusty markings. **Food:** small mammals and birds. **Voice:** high-pitched *yik-yik-yik* over breeding area.

Osprey

❋

PANDION HALIAETUS

Long-winged with shortish tail. In most positions the wings are decidedly angled which, with colouration, gives the appearance of a large gull.

Small head and relatively small bill with a long hook for dealing with bony fish. White head, with brown eye stripe, contrasts with all-brown upperparts.

Unmistakable from below; white body and wing linings contrast with greyish flight feathers; black wrist patches. Note breastband.

Fish are held head-first in torpedo-like manner. It is possible that prey up to 3kg (6.5lbs) in weight might be carried by adult. Occasionally two fish are caught in one dive.

Adaptations for capturing fish include strong legs and feet, long claws, spiny scales on underside of toes and a reversible outer toe.

The osprey was formerly a common, breeding summer visitor to Scotland, but persecution by egg collectors and trophy hunters at the turn of the century brought it to extinction in Britain. No more that spectacular dive into a loch to emerge holding a pike or trout torpedo fashion to carry off to its eyrie high in a pine. No more, that is, until 1955 when a pair returned to nest at Loch Garten. Immediately protected by the RSPB, a success story followed, with these birds or their future offspring showing off their families to over a million visitors, while at the same time increasing to over 40 pairs.

Since their return nearly 600 young have been raised.

Ospreys migrate to West Africa, where they spend the winter in tropical climes: summer in the pines among lochs, winter in the palms along rivers with hippos, or by golden Atlantic beaches.

What of the future? They continue to increase in Scotland, and with the help of artificial nesting platforms might well be encouraged to start breeding in England. However, they will always face danger on migration.

Circles or hovers over water then dives feet first when fish is sighted.

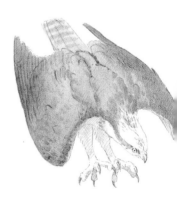

Length: 55-60cm
Wingspan: 145-170cm
Where to look: by open water stocked with fish. Summer visitor to Scotland and uncommon passage migrant in spring and autumn. Winters in Africa. **Nest:** near water, usually in conifer-top, but also island ruins. Same eyrie of sticks (lined with grasses and finer material) used annually and added to until large size; but remains inconspicuous in tree top. **Eggs:** 2-3, white, boldly blotched deep chocolate or reddish-brown. **Voice:** repeated, short, shrill whistle *tchip tchip tchip.*

Sparrowhawk

❋

ACCIPITER NISUS

The long legs and long central toe – for catching and holding prey – indicate the sparrowhawk is a bird eater. Prey is caught by surprise attack either from a concealed perch or flight close to a hedgerow or woodland edge. Very rarely will it 'stoop' on its prey. Sparrowhawks can carry prey as heavy as themselves.

The female is much larger than the male and double its weight. She is duller and browner than the male with grey brown barring below and grey brown above, not so bluish as adult male. Her eye is yellow, whereas that of the male is orange.

Length: 30-40cm
Wingspan: 60-80cm
Where to look: widespread resident, but less common in south-east England; coniferous and mixed woodland, farmland with hedgerows; look for displaying birds in spring, or soaring birds at any time. **Nest:** built of sticks, sometimes uses foundation of old nest of another species, high in conifer near trunk. **Eggs:** normally 4-5, whitish, many without markings. **Food:** small birds caught on the wing in swift dashes. **Voice:** harsh *kek-kek-kek-kek.*

Birds form almost the entire diet of the sparrowhawk, Britain's second commonest bird of prey. It does not take its prey in proportion to the numbers that occur in the wild: those species which are conspicuous or feed away from cover are taken far more commonly. Detailed research has shown that for certain birds, sparrowhawks may account for more than half their total mortality.

Like most raptors, sparrowhawks were seriously affected by the introduction of DDT and other chemicals, such as dieldrin and aldrin, to control insects and other invertebrates that are harmful to agriculture. During the late 1950s and early 1960s a population decline started and sparrowhawk numbers were reduced by 50 per cent in western Britain. In the east, where agriculture was more intensive, the bird was practically wiped out. With the voluntary and legal bans on the use of pesticides the situation is now improving. Once again sparrowhawks can be seen over the woods and fields of East Anglia, Kent and Sussex; indeed in some areas they may be as common as kestrels, though few would realise this because of the sparrowhawk's secretive behaviour. Woodland dweller, spends most time perched in thick cover. Wing and tail shape adapted for flying between trunks and branches. Fairly widespread in Britain, but commoner in the north and west. The secretive nature, however, means it is not commonly seen.

Goshawk

❋

ACCIPITER GENTILIS

The female is much larger than male, approaching the size of a buzzard. Upperparts dark brown, underparts whitish and barred.

For the birdwatcher, the goshawk presents a problem: it is easy to confuse the smaller male with a female sparrowhawk. Note carefully the goshawk's shorter tail with a rounded (not square) end, longer, broader wings with a more 'S'-shaped rear edge, bulkier size and slower wing-beats.

Male distinguishable from female sparrowhawk by bulkier size, relatively longer, more 'S'-shaped wings and shorter, rounded tails.

Note protruding head, conspicuous stripe above eye and noticeably banded tail. Soars and glides on flat wings.

Goshawks probably became extinct in Britain in the early part of the century, but in the early 1960s they started to breed again. There was initially some debate as to their origin, but it is now generally accepted that the recolonisation was the result of falconers' birds escaping or being deliberately released. Now the population of this shy forest dweller could number over 200 pairs, yet such a figure will never appear in national reports, for most birdwatchers or recorders are reluctant to submit their observations. Understandably they are concerned that publication – however vague – may result in sites becoming known, which could lead to an increase in egg collecting or robbery of the young (for falconry), two activities that seriously affect the goshawk population in the best-known localities.

Length: 50-60cm. **Wingspan:** 95-125cm
Where to look: extensive pine or beech woodland. Shy and quite rare. **Nest:** substantial, of sticks in tree. **Eggs:** 3-4, bluish-white. **Food:** squirrels, pigeons, jays etc. **Voice:** only at nest, rapid hoarse *gek-gek-gek-gek.*

Kestrel

❀

FALCO TINNUNCULUS

Few people can fail to notice kestrels hovering over roadsides and, particularly, motorway verges. This, Britain's commonest and most familiar bird of prey, can be seen on most days by anyone with the opportunity to look for it. Kestrels require open areas to hunt over, particularly grassy meadows and banks; and safe nest sites, such as holes in trees and quarry ledges. They readily take to nestboxes and are also venturing into towns where they nest on ledges on buildings. The RSPB knows that a number of kestrels are taken illegally each year as chicks which are then reared in captivity. The would-be falconers may attempt to fly the birds, but more often the birds are abandoned and this inevitably means that they will die.

Kestrels have been less affected by pesticides than other raptors, but nonetheless they became scarce in the intensively farmed arable land of eastern England during the late 1960s and early 1970s. Numbers are back to their former levels, and the population is estimated at about 70,000 pairs. Now that the pesticide problem seems to be under control, the future conservation of the kestrel lies with the maintenance of its food supply, notably voles and mice. Conversion of rough grazing land to cereals and stubble burning can seriously affect the abundance of these small mammals.

The handsome male has a chestnut back and wings spotted black, blue-grey head and faint black 'moustache'. The blue-grey tail has a conspicuous black band.

Pointed wings and hovering flight when hunting instantly distinguish it from the sparrowhawk, the second commonest raptor in Britain. The female is much duller than the male, being muted chestnut brown above, with a heavily barred, blackish tail. Colour relieved sometimes by tinge of grey on head and tail.

Black flight-feathers contrasting with chestnut upperparts are a good feature at a distance.

Conspicuous woodland birds such as chaffinches and tits form a large part of the kestrel's diet.

Length: 33-36cm **Wingspan:** 70-80cm
Where to look: many places, even in city centres; can be most easily observed over roadside verges. Most widespread bird of prey in Britain. **Nest:** hole in tree, crevice in wall or cliff face, ledges (even on buildings) and other structures; may use old crow's nest.
Eggs: 4-5, white with red-brown markings, laid in mid-April in scrape with no lining.
Food: usually field voles, mice, insects, worms; urban kestrels, especially, take small birds. Hunts by hovering or perching in readiness to pounce on prey. **Voice:** *kee-kee-kee-kee* generally at nesting area.

Merlin

❊

FALCO COLUMBARIUS

The tiny merlin has a certain dash and energy about it which gives it a special appeal. It is Britain's smallest falcon and a bird of the upland heather-covered moors, and therein lies one of the main problems it faces. These areas are under threat from forestry planting or conversion to grass through sheep grazing or re-seeding. True heather moors are disappearing at an alarming rate and their future protection as a habitat for the merlin is closely connected with the continuation of grouse shooting. But grouse numbers are falling and this, coupled with the high cost of running moors, is encouraging some owners to move towards an income from trees and sheep – two factors definitely detrimental to merlins.

Merlins are not persecuted, and keepers enjoy having them on their moors as much as birdwatchers do. Problems through the use of pesticides are probably largely over and so habitat destruction is almost certainly the major cause of their decline.

Length: 27-32cm **Wingspan:** 50-70cm
Where to look: uplands, especially moors and fells in Scotland, northern England and Wales. Quite rare. In winter, coastal marshes and farmland. **Nest:** scrape in cover of heather on lower slope of moor. Will use old nest of crow. **Eggs:** 3-6, usually 4, cream stippled with red-brown spots. **Food:** small birds, especially meadow pipits, chaffinches and tits, which are caught in flight. **Voice:** a rapid, grating chatter, *quik-ik-ik-ik*, when nest site intruded upon.

Male is pale rusty below with dark streaks, the underwing coverts are whitish-buff streaked reddish brown and the flight feathers whitish with dark bars. Female is brown above, creamy-white below and heavily streaked reddish brown.

Hobby

❊

FALCO SUBBUTEO

A summer visitor mostly confined to southern England, and thus only likely to be confused with the kestrel as there is no other similarly shaped raptor present. Look for hobbies over heathland, gravel pits and farmland with conifer clumps.

The graceful hobby is a trans-Saharan migrant which spends the winter in Africa and is present in Britain for about five months in the summer. It arrives in May, and the breeding season is late, with young in the nest from mid-July onwards, coinciding with the appearance on the wing of young swifts, swallows and martins, which are easily caught by the parent hobbies. Look out for hobbies at swallow and martin roosts in early autumn. In addition, dragonflies and other insects are taken in flight – dextrously grasped in an outflung talon, they are quickly transferred to the bill for plucking and devouring.

Hobbies are secretives and a nesting pair can easily go undetected, especially on farmland. As a consequence, informed opinion now believes the population may be as high as 500 pairs, well above the often quoted figure of 100-150 pairs. Unlike many of Britain's birds of prey, the hobby does not seem to be under threat from habitat destruction, pesticides or human persecution, though a few clutches are lost to egg collectors each year.

Swift and agile. Fast, stiff wing-beats, interspersed with short glides when hunting: at other times, wing-beats relaxed.

Whitish underparts broadly streaked black, fairly uniformly chequered underwings and, especially, rusty-red undertail coverts are important field marks. Dark slate-grey above with a prominent black 'moustache' on whitish cheeks. Lightly barred under tail.

Length: 30-35cm
Wingspan: 70-85cm
Where to look: heaths and downs in southern England, also farmland. **Nest:** old crow's nest, does not build. **Eggs:** 2-3, yellowish with red-brown blotches. **Food:** birds, especially martins; insects. **Voice:** rapid *kew-kew-kew*, musical for falcon.

Comparing Birds of Prey

❊

Birds of prey (raptors) are among the most difficult groups to identify. Views may only be brief or distant. This makes familiarity hard to achieve. Wing shape and position, and tail length, are important to distinguish families, but then one should concentrate on plumage, especially wing patterns.

Golden eagle: *much larger than buzzard, with longer wings and tail and powerful bill on well-protruding head. Soars on wings raised in shallow 'V'*

Buzzard: *large-sized raptor with broad wings raised in shallow 'V' when soaring. Note wing pattern and compare with the rare honey buzzard, which has longer neck and tail and soars on flat wings. Commonest in western and northern Britain.*

Red kite: *the forked, reddish tail and white wing patches are the main characteristics. A rare bird for which a journey to Wales must be made.*

Marsh harrier: *like all harriers, soars and glides on raised wings. Note male's wing pattern and rusty body. Female brown, often with yellow head and wing markings.*

Hen harrier: *like all harriers, males and females differ in plumage. Female difficult to distinguish from female Montagu's, but note head pattern. In male look for white underparts, grey head and upper breast, black tips to wings and dark trailing edge, white rump.*

Male

Male hen harrier.

Female marsh harrier

Female hen harrier.

Falcons are small to medium-sized raptors with rather long tapering wings and medium-length tails, their shape designed for fast flight and rapid acceleration enabling pursuit of their prey – flying birds in open country. The kestrel is the exception, locating its prey on the ground by hovering or watching from a vantage post. Hawks have short, rounded wings and long tails and are woodland dwellers, their wings shaped for manoeuvrability between trees and branches.

Osprey: long wings bowed when gliding and soaring, and white body with large black patches at bend of wing make this easy.

Peregrines

Hobby chasing swift

Peregrine: large falcon with thick-set body, broad-based pointed wings and rather short tail. When chasing prey its speed is impressive. Note the large black 'moustache', white cheeks.

Hobby: small falcon with long, narrow pointed wings and silhouette not unlike large swift. Streaked black underparts, small 'moustache' and reddish undertail-coverts are characteristic.

Female merlin

Merlin: the smallest falcon, with shorter wings than other species, and bold dashing flight. Note blue-grey upperparts and black tail band of male(above).

Sparrowhawk: note short rounded wings, long tail and flight: rapid wing-beats interspersed with glides. Secretive woodland dweller.

Male kestrel

Kestrel: persistent hovering is the most characteristic feature of this common bird of prey. Often seen over roadside verges.

Peregrine

❋

FALCO PEREGRINUS

A peregrine requires about 100g (4oz) of food a day. Its prey includes game birds, waders, pigeons and other medium-sized birds such as thrushes. On an estuary in winter the falcon's presence will cause alarm to wildfowl and waders.

In silhouette note compact shape, broad-based pointed wings (wings often appearing triangular-shaped) and square-cut or slightly tapering medium-short tail.

At Symonds Yat Rock in Gloucestershire there is a public viewpoint each summer.

Powerful, swift and agile in flight with stiff, shallow wing-beats and occasional short glides. Stoops on prey from a height on nearly fully closed wings. The actual speed of the stoop- by which its prey is caught - is the subject of much debate, but can reach between 100 and 200 mph.

The life and times of the peregrine are among the best documented of any bird. Before World War II it was heavily persecuted by keepers and collectors; during the war it was shot to protect pigeons carrying messages; after the war it was hit by pesticides and then subjected to high levels of theft of its eggs and young. It was the use of pesticides that was the most damaging, reducing the population to an all time low in the early 1960s. Quick action by conservationists in studying just why peregrines were starting to lay thin-shelled eggs (which therefore broke) or failing to raise young resulted in the discovery that levels of pesticides were building up in their tissues through eating prey that had fed on contaminated insects. Being persistent, these chemicals accumulated in 'top' predators like the peregrine. Once discovered, action was swift and voluntary bans on the manufacture and use of these dangerous substances were introduced. So, in many ways, the peregrine was a barometer of the health of the environment, and for that we should be grateful.

The peregrine is a large, powerful falcon, with the female noticeably larger than the male. Adults are dark bluish-grey above; underparts are white to warm buff, densely barred black, but the white chin and cheeks have a conspicuous black lobe-like strip from beak to eye. The underwing is lightly barred, with little contrast between coverts and flight feathers.

These days, the best places to look for peregrines include the rocky wests coasts of England and Wales and in Scotland. Resident pairs of adult birds are often present in the same location throughout the year, while juvenile birds tend to wander further afield. To this day peregrine nests are still robbed of eggs and

Juvenile birds are dark brown above, rusty-buff below, streaked (not barred) dark brown, 'moustache' thinner than adult's.

young, and many are guarded by vigilant wardens during the breeding season.

Length: 40-59cm
Wingspan: 80-115cm
Where to look: mountains, moorland and sea cliffs, but not in south-east England in breeding season. Estuaries and coasts in winter. **Nest:** ledge or crevice on cliff or quarry face; may use old raven's nest. **Eggs:** 3-4, lightly dappled tawny to reddish brown, laid in bare scrape.
Food: medium-sized birds such as pigeons, crows, seabirds, grouse; taken on wing in powerful stoop; also mammals. **Voice:** in breeding season a shrill chattering *kek-kek-kek-kek*, harsh *kaark*.

Red Grouse

※

LAGOPUS LAGOPUS SCOTICUS

Whirring wings and short glides, accompanied by abrupt, cackling calls; note dark wings and tail.

The head-to-toe feathering of the red grouse enables it to withstand the frequently appalling weather conditions of Britain's moorlands. Regularly feeding beneath snow, this dark, rusty-coloured bird avoids its predators – peregrines and eagles – but faces months of hardship. The closely related willow grouse, of Scandinavia, actually changes to white plumage in winter like the ptarmigan.

The red grouse was once unique to Britain, but has been introduced to other parts of the world; it has also lost its status as Britain's only unique species, being reclassified as a race of the willow grouse. The 'Glorious Twelfth' is 12 August, the start of the grouse shooting season, and most grouse are on ground maintained by keepers. Management of heather by burning allows fresh new growth with succulent shoots – ideal food – but over-burning and over-grazing destroy the heather which the grouse rely on. When flushed, the grouse utters a rapid staccato call which changes to a distinct 'go-back go-back' – the sound is evocative of the wild habitat and, taken litera lly, probably good advice as the mist and clouds roll in over the high, exposed moor.

Length: 37-42cm; **Weight:** 550-690g
Where to look: moorland with good cover of heather; also on damp cotton-grass or sedge. **Nest:** on ground. **Eggs:** 4-9, cream, blotched brown. **Food:** heather, seeds, berries. **Voice:** explosive, rapid barking notes.

Although mostly on open moors, will take grit from edges of roads to help digest heather.

Males are more rusty-red then buff-speckled females.

Perfectly hidden on mountain screes, only movement and blinking white eyelids give them away. Never so rich brown as red grouse; males often quite grey or patchy in summer, females more buff. In winter all white except for tail; male has red wattle and a black eye patch.

Ptarmigan

※

LAGOPUS MUTUS

The snow lies thick on the high Scottish mountains for three months or more and the ptarmigan in their smart white winter dress crouch unnoticed. As spring begins to melt the snow, and rocks and vegetation show again, they develop mottled plumage to merge with the new background. When all the snow has gone in mid-summer, ptarmigan disappear against the lichen-covered rocks with their grey-brown and black plumage patterns. These mountain grouse really are masters of disguise, but despite their superb camouflage many still fall prey to the golden eagle.

In late autumn and winter large parties of ptarmigan may gather, using the theory that many pairs of eyes are better than one. The largest flock recorded in Scotland was of 470 birds! Normally, flocks number several dozen at most, with males and females in different groups. The males put themselves in the front line against predators and harsh weather by feeding in the more exposed places. If many males die, the remainder become highly polygamous in the following spring, often having three or more mates. Ptarmigan seem oblivious to humans and are often surprisingly approachable.

Length: 34-36cm; **Weight:** 400-600g
Where to look: Scottish mountains, lower in extreme north. **Nest:** on ground. **Eggs:** 5-9, cream with brown spots. **Food:** heather, other plants. **Voice:** quiet, rattling *karrrrakakaka*, belching *AAr-aa-ka-ka*.

Black tail, white wings all year; only the body feathers change colour.

Black Grouse

❊

TETRAO TETRIX

As a silvery dawn breaks, with dew heavy on the ground, male black grouse gather to display at favoured, traditional sites called leks. In Britain, groups may number up to 40 birds, but in the USSR leks may hold 200. The curious ritual is practised throughout the year except for a break in late summer and autumn, when the birds are moulting. Males fluff up their white undertail coverts and raise their lyre-shaped tails, inflate their blue necks and make a bubbling, dove-like cooing in a regular repeated pattern. The males – blackcocks – bustle about in mock fights, while the females – greyhens – watch nearby. The display will continue even without greyhens present – and so vain are the blackcocks that they will even strut about alone! Although the black grouse has disappeared from many of its old haunts, due to over-shooting and loss of habitat, its population is increasing in a few parts where new conifer plantations provide temporary havens.

Male is always unmistakable.

Female greyer than red grouse; has slightly forked, paler tail and faint pale wingbar.

Feeds mostly on buds, often in trees; at dusk, gathers in pines or birches beside the moor.

Length: 40-55cm; **Weight:** male 1,300g female 1,000g **Where to look:** typically edges of moor on heath near trees; bogs, plantations. **Nest:** on ground in long grass. **Eggs:** 6-10, buff with brown spots. **Food:** buds, shoots of birch, pine. **Voice:** far-carrying dove-like bubbling; hissing sneeze.

Capercaillie

❊

TETRAO UROGALLUS

May be flushed from clearings in forest where juniper and bilberry provide good feeding.

These giants of the forest, though the size of turkeys, can be elusive, disappearing into the pines away from a frustrated observer – either clattering through the branches or creeping silently away on the ground. A quiet onlooker may be lucky enough to see one crash out of a tree to fly off on large, rounded wings. In the early spring, dripping water may stimulate the male's song, which starts with a similar *pelip-pelip* sound and continues into a fast *plip-plip-plip-itit-t-t klop*! The last note sounds like a cork popping from a bottle. The turkey-like display attracts females and keeps other males at bay, indeed even other animals. Occasionally an unpaired male will display to anything that moves – even people have been attacked by raving male capercaillies. The species became extinct in Britain in the late 18th century due to over-hunting and loss of habitat. Today's population of several thousand birds has built up from a few birds introduced from Sweden in the 1830s. Most are found north of the River Forth, generally preferring old forest to plantations.

Length: 60-87cm; **Weight:** male 4kg **Where to look:** old conifer forests of north Scotland. **Nest:** on ground near tree. **Eggs:** 5-8, buff speckled brown. **Food:** pine needles, buds, also seeds, berries. **Voice:** male – clicking song; female – pheasant-like crow.

Large size and broad, fanned tail separates hen from other grouse; note orange breast and richly coloured plumage with many black bars. Male is unique.

The cock's black and brown plumage glistens green in good light. The white shoulder patch and pale bill are often obvious.

Pheasant

❋

PHASIANUS COLCHICUS

The vivid plumage of the splendid male serves to attract females – up to 18 have been recorded in one harem. The male scuttles around each hen, trailing the near wing, twisting over his tail and inflating his facial wattles to show off his finery. Once the females have settled down on a nest, the male appears to ignore them. This is for the best – his colours would soon attract the attention of predators such as fox or stoat, whereas the female and young are well-camouflaged. Although introduced to Britain, probably before the Norman Conquest, pheasants are now a familiar and characteristic part of the British landscape – even favourite Christmas card birds! It seems odd to think that they are not 'British' at all.

Smaller, short-tailed females resemble large partridge, but their pointed tail is never rusty; beware half-grown young birds that can already fly, thus causing confusion.

Length: 53-90cm; **Weight:** 1-1.5kg
Where to look: woods, agricultural land with dense cover, marshes. **Nest:** on ground, well hidden. **Eggs:** 8-15, olive. **Food:** grain, seeds, berries, insects; even lizards, mice. **Voice:** loud crow and shorter *hic-up*.

Long-tailed male quite unlike any other British bird; more likely to run than fly from danger.

Quail

❋

COTURNIX COTURNIX

Short, quick flights on rather long wings characteristic.

A rare breeding bird, appearing sporadically, mainly in southern counties, the quail has periodic 'good years' which bring more to nest here. A decline noted during the early years of this century was thought to be due to over-persecution by egg collectors and shooters rather than any agricultural changes. Today it is much more a characteristic bird of rolling cereal fields shimmering in the heat of Spain or southern France, where the dawn and dusk chorus of penetrating, triple calls can be quite dramatic. If flushed – not an easy thing to accomplish – the quail flies on relatively long, narrow wings before dropping back into the vegetation with a lark-like flutter, as much like a big lark or small snipe as a partridge. Usually quails will scurry away through vegetation without ever being detected, and they are nearly always 'heard but not seen'. This is Britain's only migrant gamebird, and most move to central and southern Africa after the breeding season. On migration European quails suffer enormous losses at the hands of trappers and gunmen in North Africa, especially in Egypt and Libya. It is difficult to judge just how damaging this is to the long-term well-being of the quail population.

These days, quails in Britain seem to prefer barley fields, especially where strips of set–aside lie adjacent to the crop.

May stand higher to peer over short vegetation.

Length: 16-18cm; **Weight:** 70-150g
Where to look: arable land on limestone or chalk; open downs. **Nest:** scrape on ground. **Eggs:** 7-12, buff, variably blotched brown. **Food:** shoots and seeds, also insects. **Voice:** loud, liquid *whic whic-ic*; doll-like *mama*.

Female lacks facial markings and chestnut streaks of male.
Small size makes confusion unlikely with other gamebirds except half-grown, but flying, young partridges which have rusty tails. Quail usually crouch.

Red-legged Partridge

✹

ALECTORIS RUFA

There are as many red-legged partridges as there are grey, but the red-legs are less widespread. Red-legs are much easier to see, as flocks up to 20 strong wander over ploughed fields and open pastures. Despite their rather bright colours, however, they can conceal themselves remarkably well even on open ground. Crouched low into a depression, the black and white face and striped flanks help to break up the outlines of the birds and make them less eyecatching. When approached, they will run away rather than fly, but if taken by surprise at close range they burst into the air with whirring wings then glide down to the ground before scampering away on bright-red legs. Watch them walk over rough ground and you will see that the head remains very steady while the legs and body act as a 'suspension', absorbing all the irregularities – better for seeing food and possible danger. Red-legs often perch on high objects – walls, haystacks, even old farm building; a grey partridge is unlikely to do this. The 'French partridge' is often more familiar than the grey these days.

Length: 32-34cm; **Weight:** 500g
Where to look: often drier arable land, heaths, dunes. **Nest:** on ground in dense vegetation. **Eggs:** 10-15, spotted brown. **Food:** shoots, seeds; also slugs, insects. **Voice:** harsh, loud, chuffing *CHUkaarr .. CHUkaarr.*

Flies with long glides between bursts of whirring wing-beats, showing rusty tail and plain sandy-buff upperparts.

Uniform buff-brown back, well-marked face and red bill and legs all distinctive.

Crouching bird looks like a clod of earth; surprisingly large when seen well.

Less secretive than grey partridge, and happy on open ground, heaths and rough places near gravel pits; sturdy legs carry it very fast when threatened.

Introduced into Britain nearly 200 years ago and now common, particularly in southern and eastern England where harsh calls are familiar.

Grey Partridge

✹

PERDIX PERDIX

Length: 29-31cm; **Weight:** 350-400g
Where to look: arable land, lower moorland edges, rough pasture. **Nest:** in thick cover. **Eggs:** 12-19, olive-buff. **Food:** mostly vegetable, but chicks eat insects. **Voice:** loud, like creaky, rusty gate *SKERrr-ik; ik-ik-ik* in flight.

Whirring flight, frequent glides; streaked back, rusty tail.

Smaller than red-legged, with orange face, speckled upperparts and less bold flank stripes. Creaky calls quite different. Male has more obvious horseshoe mark on belly than female.

Takes to flight rather than running if threatened, usually with short, clicking calls.

Although feeding predominantly on plants, insects form a vital part of every partridge's diet during the first few weeks of its life. A mixed diet of animal and vegetable helps chicks to develop more quickly. Unfortunately, many of the insects they eat are crop pests, like aphids, weevils and sawfly larvae. In cereal crops these have been greatly reduced by effective use of pesticides – and so the partridge has declined. Other changes in farming practice have not helped. Loss of hedges reduces nesting places, herbicides kill off food plants like grasses and chickweed, and more efficient harvesting leaves less waste grain in fields. Because the numbers have declined many have been imported from Europe for shooting and in some places so many have been released that it is difficult to class the bird as 'native'. Other species of partridge, especially the chukar, have also been introduced in hundreds – surely not the best way to protect wild birds that are already under pressure. Autumn coveys (or flocks) give an idea of the breeding success – up to 20 birds at times, but after a bad year as few as three or four. Without its partridges, the countryside would be the poorer.

Water Rail

❋

RALLUS AQUATICUS

A winter cold spell of four or five days' duration is usually enough to drive this normally very secretive bird out of a frozen reed bed to areas of unfrozen running water. The true shape of the water rail cannot be appreciated during winter as it fluffs up its striped flanks to retain body heat. The skeleton illustrates how incredibly slim it really is; looking almost as though it had been squashed from both sides, it

Its slim body glides between reed stems without touching them, so that not even a twitching reed head will point a hungry marsh harrier in the right direction.

Long toes prevent feeding birds sinking into deep mud.

The buff undertail is shown when the tail is jerked up. Brown horizontal streaks on upper parts and vertically striped flanks help to hide the bird in vegetation.

More often heard than seen, the strange squeaks, hisses and squeals will give away its presence. These noises inform other water rails of its position; the calls become quieter and die away as birds meet in the cover of a reed bed. A quiet, still, patient observer may be rewarded by a good view.

Length: 23-28cm; **Weight:** 90-150g
Where to look: thick reed beds and marshes; also overgrown ditches, older thickets. **Nest:** in very dense cover of dead reeds and other aquatic vegetation. **Eggs:** 6-11, buff, with a few grey or brown spots and blotches. **Food:** mostly insects and grubs, but also berries and seeds. Larger prey such as fish, small mammals, eggs, birds and carrion also eaten. **Voice:** varied pig-like squeals and grunts; other calls include whistles, squeaks and hisses.

enables the bird to slip between reed stems quickly and quietly.

The long red bill is used to probe into mud or shallow water for grubs, but can be turned on unsuspecting small birds and mammals with deadly accuracy. Water rails have been observed eating larger dead birds like moorhens, which had probably frozen to death.

Flying as a last resort, water rails will normally dart into a clump of vegetation and will only move when virtually stepped on. Sometimes one gives an unexpectedly clear view when it hides its head behind a stem, leaving the rest of its body exposed!

Corncrake

❋

CREX CREX

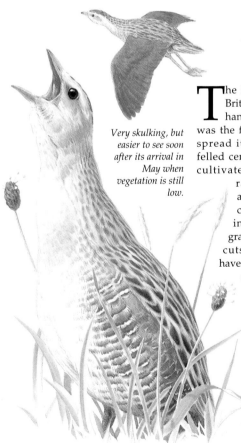

Very skulking, but easier to see soon after its arrival in May when vegetation is still low.

The future of the corncrake in Britain seems now to be in the hands of farmers. Strangely, it was the farmers who first helped it spread its range. As forests were felled centuries ago, giving way to cultivated grassland, corncrakes rapidly moved in, taking advantage of the newly created habitat. The introduction of mechanical grass cutters and the repeated cuts of grass to make silage have forced the corncrake out of many areas in recent decades; changes in Africa's climate may also have been disastrous though the habitat remains good.

Also called the landrail, the corncrake resembles a moorhen in shape, but its striped buffish plumage with greyer head and its habitat (especially hay meadows) are good identification

The rasping call would have been familiar to all country dwellers in the early 1900s. Today it is only a few crofters farming in traditional ways in western Ireland and the Hebrides who hear the corncrake summoning spring after its long-distance migration from wintering grounds in central Africa. The call which gave the corncrake its Latin name is likened to the teeth of a comb being drawn rapidly across the edge of a matchbox twice, but at close range is a much louder, harder sound. In the autumn, corncrakes are occasionally seen along the south coast, especially if unfavourable weather halts their migration southwards

Length: 27-30cm; **Weight:** 150-200g
Where to look: hayfields, iris beds. Formerly common throughout Britain, now rare. **Nest:** hidden in dense tussock. **Eggs:** 8-12, creamy with brown blotches. **Food:** mostly insects, worms; a few seeds. **Voice:** distinctive, repeated *crek-crek*.

Moorhen

❄

GALLINULA CHLOROPUS

At close range the bright bill, brownish back, black head and slatey underside look very different from the 'black and white' of a distant bird.

When swimming, the head and tail move in a jerky, deliberate fashion. The bird's tail is held nearly as high as the head, unlike the more horizontal body of the coot. Notice the flank streaks.

Moorhens are very adaptable birds, being able to climb trees, walk or run on flat ground, swim, wade and clamber through undergrowth. Yet they never appear to be quite at home, often moving awkwardly or cautiously with their big feet getting in the way. The long, spread toes enable them not only to wade on marshy ground without sinking, but also to swim confidently – they are among the few British birds able to swim well without webbed or lobed toes. Their cautious nature is exaggerated by jerky movements and frequent stops to survey the surrounding land. At the first sign of danger the tail is flicked to warn other birds, before an ungainly waddling exit, with head held low, into the nearest area of dense cover. A moorhen caught out by a predator on open water will dive and stay submerged by clasping on to underwater plants until the threat has gone. Two or three broods are reared each year. The black, downy young follow their parents persistently, waving tiny wings as though rowing through the air, trying to attract attention. They may be fed by older brothers and sisters from earlier broods.

Although moorhens regularly use trees to roost and even nest in, unwary observers are often caught out by finding this 'water bird' in a tree or even a hedge. Moorhens feed mainly on plant matter and small invertebrates, but they will sometimes feed on unusual items. In severe cold, for example, they are often seen feeding on carrion.

Length: 32-35cm; **Weight:** 200-400g
Where to look: fresh water from small pools to large lakes or rivers, always requires good plant cover. Feeds on wet meadows. **Nest:** floating heap of vegetation, or up to 5 metres (15ft) high in trees or bushes beside water. **Eggs:** 5-11, glossy buff with brown and black blotches. **Food:** water weeds, seeds, fruit, grasses, insects, worms and larvae. **Voice:** variable, often urgent *kittik*, a loud, abrupt or metallic *kaak* and *kic-kic-kic*.

Dangling legs and rather bowed wings are characteristic in flight, which is usually only over short distances

The long legs and toes (typical of the crake family) allow easy movement on moist ground.

Juveniles have browner backs, buff underparts, and a greenish bill (quite unlike the adult).

Downy black and red chicks pester the adult birds continuously for food; older juveniles are grey with white face and breast.

The silky black plumage helps to show off the white bill and frontal shield; the glowing red eye is a common feature of nearly all European crakes and rails.

Coot

❋

FULICA ATRA

During the breeding season coots do not tolerate each other's company, often fighting viciously with their long, sharp claws. With head almost flat on the water and wings bunched high over its short tail, a coot will drive off birds much larger than itself – even swans and geese. Noisy calls and splashing fights are frequent in summer wherever there are coots.

Large winter flocks, often several hundred strong, will gather on favourable waters to dive for food. Many of these birds will be migrants from mainland Europe who have come to Britain to take advantage of its milder climate. When on the surface the broad body appears unsinkable, but air is pushed out of the feathers by flattening them and a leap well clear of the water before submerging helps the coot dive to depths of 7 metres(20ft). The lobed grey feet are quite unlike the moorhen's and enable it to swim and dive very efficiently.

Coots spending the winter on ponds near humans will become very tame, even taking food from the hand. Their urge to feed will often lead to a squabbling mass of black and white as they clamber over each other. Moorhens are always far more timid, pushed out to the edge of the bustling, self-important coots. The two species are, however, seldom seen without each other's company.

Huge lobed feet.

Length: 36-38cm; **Weight:** 400-800g
Where to look: larger areas of open water with plenty of vegetation. Also town park ponds. **Nest:** aquatic plants, floating, but anchored to safe foundation. **Eggs:** 6-9, buff with small dark spots. **Food:** shoots of reed, roots, algae; also insects, eggs. **Voice:** *kep* or *coot* call, loud and abrupt.

Hastily retreating coots combine a mixture of running and flying across the surface of the water, the long, lobed toes being very obvious. When threatened by predators flocks dive in a shower of spray.

Wings raised to make itself look bigger, an aggressive coot will menace an intruder by showing its white bill and shield. It is turned away in courtship.

Oystercatcher

❋

HAEMATOPUS OSTRALEGUS

Large, with heavy orange bill and red eyes. White patches make dazzling pattern in flight.

This big, boldly coloured bird is a familiar sight on estuaries and rocky shores all around the coast, equally characteristic of cold, bleak mud flats, sunny sandy beaches, beautiful Scottish sea lochs and tangy mussel beds. After a steady rise in numbers, at least 280,000 now spend the winter in Britain, many from the Faroes, Iceland and Norway, although 40,000 pairs breed here. Some winter concentrations are huge – in Morecambe Bay alone there can be 50,000 – and to see them pouring in to their high-tide roost, landing on the run and crashing into those already settled, is a noisy and memorable experience. Numbers in an estuary vary according to the food supply – a good cockle year means more oystercatchers. Unlike most waders, the oystercatcher collects food and takes it to its chicks, because they have yet to learn the specialist feeding techniques that make this bird so successful. Many stalk their prey, waiting for a chance to strike the bill into an open shell; others simply find a shellfish and hammer it open with the powerful, chisel-tipped bill.

The majority of British oystercatchers breed around the coast, favouring sandy or shingle beaches. Not surprisingly, perhaps, pressure from human visitors effectively excludes them from most areas of south and east England, unless specially protected. The west coasts of England and Wales are much more suitable for breeding oystercatchers and in Scotland they are widespread, even at inland sites.

Length: 40-46cm
Weight: 500-600g.
Where to look: on all coasts, some on coastal fields. Also breeds in river valleys. **Nest:** simple scrape. **Eggs:** 2-3, pale buff, spotted brown. **Food:** mussels, cockles, ragworms; worms inland. **Voice:** clear, sharp *KLEEP*.

Robust, orange bill used to chisel open mollusc prey.

Summer bird glossy black above, in winter duller with white collar. Stout, pale pink legs.

Chick is well camouflaged against pebbles and lichen-covered seashore rocks.

The black and white plumage is striking even at a distance.

Avocet

❉

RECURVIROSTRA AVOSETTA

Very white in flight with flickering black wingtips. Legs trail behind and neck protrudes in front. Looks long. Juvenile is like adult, but black areas are dull brown.

The upcurved bill is unmistakable. A tall, elegant eye-catching bird; among gulls looks smaller, pure white; legs often hidden in water.

The typical feeding action is a distinctive sideways sweep of its bill through watery mud.

Breeding birds sit conspicuously on rudimentary nests on muddy islands in a few coastal reserves.

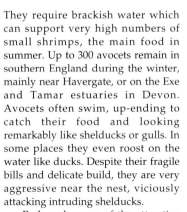

Active protection and habitat management are the main reason why the avocet has managed to gain a strong foothold in Britain. In 1947 two groups totalling 28 pairs were discovered breeding on land flooded as part of war-time defence measures. It is thought that inadvertant protection afforded to Dutch and Danish birds during wartime allowed numbers on mainland Europe to build up. This made colonisation of suitable areas in England more likely. The areas were purchased by the RSPB and sophisticated systems were developed to improve the nesting and feeding conditions, including the salinity of the water. Those areas, Minsmere and Havergate Island, remain the principal breeding places, although birds have spread to many other areas, particularly in north Norfolk. The total number of pairs in Britain is now over 400 and rising.

They require brackish water which can support very high numbers of small shrimps, the main food in summer. Up to 300 avocets remain in southern England during the winter, mainly near Havergate, or on the Exe and Tamar estuaries in Devon. Avocets often swim, up-ending to catch their food and looking remarkably like shelducks or gulls. In some places they even roost on the water like ducks. Despite their fragile bills and delicate build, they are very aggressive near the nest, viciously attacking intruding shelducks.

Perhaps because of the attractive appearance or their rarity value, avocets still suffer from persecution from egg collectors. A careful watch is therefore maintained at nesting sites throughout the breeding season.

Length: 42-45cm;
Weight: 300-400g.
Where to look: muddy coasts in south and east England: breeds mainly on East Anglian coastal lagoons. **Nest:** scrape, little lining.
Eggs: 3-4 buff, spotted. **Food:** small shrimps and worms.
Voice: *klute.*

Comparing waders

Black-tailed godwit: *tall and slim with a long, almost straight bill. Breast with an even, pale wash. Clear stripe over eye.*

All the waders shown on this page are in their first autumn and winter plumages

Bar-tailed godwit: *more stocky than black-tailed godwit; bill stouter, pointed, slightly upcurved. Back streaked.*

Redshank: *clear red legs, reddish bill base. Fairly dark, many fine streaks on underparts, breast darkish. Noisy.*

Greenshank: *very white; long greenish legs. Upcurved stout bill.*

Dunlin: *small, brown-grey with dull greyish breast. Dark bill is distinctly downcurved. Very common. This one is autumn juvenile gaining grey winter feathers.*

Knot: *smallish, but chunky. Grey. Legs greenish.*

Little stint: *tiny, with a small straight bill. Richly brown and chestnut above with distinct white 'V' on back. Usually seen in autumn in juvenile plumage like this one.*

Sanderling: *small. Very white below. Back is mostly grey (all pale grey in adult). Big black eyes, black legs.*

Curlew: *very large with a long, strongly down-curved bill. A dark and pale brown, streaked bird. Very wary.*

Dotterel: *long whitish stripes over eyes meet on nape. Pale breast line. Usually very approachable.*

Golden plover: *rounded shape with many yellow spots on underparts and breast. White belly. Big, dark eyes. Inland.*

Lapwing: *wispy crest very characteristic. Looks black and white at a distance. An inland and gregarious species.*

Grey plover: *a pale greyish, stocky wader of coasts; always looks distinctly spotted above. Big dark eyes, heavy bill.*

Oystercatcher: *large. Sharply black and white. Large orange bill, pale pink legs. Noisy.*

Turnstone: *thickset, smallish wader, mostly blackish and white. Orange legs. Chisel-shaped bill. Often approachable.*

Ringed plover: *small, chubby wader. Brown above, with clear dark breastband and face mask. Legs orange. Bill short.*

Small, chunky wader with stubby yellow and black bill, orange legs. Rather chubby, and a fraction larger than dunlin.

Ringed Plover

❀

CHARADRIUS HIATICULA

Length: 18-20cm; **Weight:** 56-70g
Where to look: sandy parts of estuaries, beaches, gravel pits. **Nest:** scrape, little lining. **Eggs:** 3-4, buffish or bluish, spotted; April-August. **Food:** small shrimps, snails, worms and insects. **Voice:** mellow, rising *too-li.*

Adults have clear black breastband and face mask, in females washed slightly browner. Thin orange rings around the eyes.

Characteristic 'stand-watch-run-pause-bob down' feeding action.

The very distinctive stop-go action when feeding provides an easy way of separating this species from other small coastal waders. Like other plovers, it uses sight to locate prey moving on the surface of the sand. For this reason strong winds, heavy rain or very cold weather make finding food difficult. When feeding in slightly muddier areas it often rapidly trembles a foot; this disturbs invertebrates – which then reveal themselves. About 8,600 pairs breed in Britain; the greatest concentration is on the sandy agricultural land (the machair) of the Western Isles, where over a quarter of the total is found. Elsewhere they are mainly on coastal beaches, but increasingly inland on reservoirs, gravel pits or rivers in northern Britain. Males have a striking display flight in which they hold their wings stiffly and flap slowly, calling loudly with a continuous, piping *leea.* In winter some 23,000 are present in Britain, most of which are native breeders and their young.

Juvenile has brown band through eye and brownish, sometimes incomplete breastband. Streak of white over eye. Looks pale.

Little Ringed Plover

❀

CHARADRIUS DUBIUS

Length: 14-17cm
Weight: 35-45g
Where to look: inland waters; scarce on migration on coastal lagoons. **Nest:** simple scrape. **Eggs:** 3-4, April-July; buff to green-blue with small spots. **Food:** insects, other invertebrates. **Voice:** a clear *peeoo,* sharp *pew.*

In flight looks small, dark; can be told from the rather similar ringed plover by the lack of a white wingbar; calls also characteristic.

The expansion in gravel extraction over the last 40 years has aided this species considerably. Breeding was first recorded in Britain at Tring Reservoirs, Hertfordshire, in 1938; since then the numbers have rapidly increased so that in 1984 over 600 pairs bred. Initially, nearly all birds were in south and east England, but they have now spread into Wales and Scotland. The majority breed on gravel pits and banks of reservoirs, but some do so on their typical continental habitat of shingle river beds. As ringed plovers increase inland, it seems that little ringed plovers find it difficult to compete with the more aggressive , larger species and are being forced away from traditional sites. The two look very similar at first sight, but careful observation will reveal many differences. Sometimes this species can be picked out first by its slightly faster feeding action and relatively small size, then positively identified by its thin, mostly black bill and clear yellow eye-ring. In flight the dark wing without a white wingbar and sharp calls would dispel doubts. It is an early summer migrant, returning in March and April from wintering grounds in tropical Africa and quickly settling into nesting territories.

Similar to ringed plover, but subtly different. Bill thinner, mostly black; legs longer, more yellow or pinkish. Slightly smaller, longer, slimmer.

Very bold yellow eye-ring is characteristic in adults; single black breastband is narrower than on the ringed plover.

In winter, golden spotted breast and white belly. In summer, belly black; face, neck variably black.

Golden Plover

❈

PLUVIALIS APRICARIA

Northern race is very black below with white streak on side. Southern birds are less well marked in summer.

Length: 26-29cm; **Weight:** 150-250g
Where to look: winter – on permanent grassland, cultivated land; summer – on moorland. **Nest:** depression in peat. **Eggs:** 3-4, buff, blotched brown, April-June. **Food:** insects, some seeds. **Voice:** clear, whistled *tooeee.*

A medium-sized bird, standing upright. Always with golden spotted upperparts, prominent dark eye and short dark bill. Fairly wary.

A musical, but sad, rising whistle is often the first clue that a flock of golden plovers is about. Searching the sky should then reveal this fast-flying species, looking almost like small white crosses from below. They wheel around in a tight flock, then, on banking, the dark golden brown upperparts show as they almost funnel down and seem to disappear on landing. When on the ground the flock slowly spreads over the chosen grass field, each bird showing the typical plover run-pause-bob feeding action. Watch one and you will see that it sometimes cocks its head sideways, apparently listening for prey and sometimes clearly watching a spot for movement. It is estimated that about 250,000 spend the winter in Britain. These not only include Britain's breeding birds but also some from Iceland and others from Scandinavia. About 22,500 pairs breed in Britain, mainly on moorland, where their complex aerial display and almost melancholic song seem to suit the open landscapes. The few breeding on Dartmoor are the most southerly birds of their species in the world. Breeding golden plovers often favour bare areas or newly burnt ground with only limited regrowth.

Dotterel

❈

CHARADRIUS MORINELLUS

Superb in summer; clear, very long, white stripe over eye; chestnut and black belly; pale line across the breast. Legs yellowish. Males are duller than females.

As the winter snows melt on the mountain tops of northern Britain, so these spectacular little plovers appear. They will have spent the winter on poor agricultural land around the lower slopes of the Atlas mountains in northern Africa, and in late April and early May they move north, stopping for a day or two at a number of traditional sites, many in eastern England, before reaching the breeding grounds. At least 150 pairs nest in Britain, but they can be extremely elusive. Although brightly coloured, their patterns provide excellent disruptive camouflage against broken backgrounds. Dotterels are among the few waders where the female is more intensely coloured than the male. Her crown is dark brown, not streaked, and the stripes over the eyes (which meet on the back of the head) and breastband are sharply white. Females tend to take the lead in display and very rarely incubate the eggs or look after the young. The sex roles are, therefore, almost entirely reversed. By the time autumn migrants appear in late August the adults have already almost lost their breeding plumage. Dotterels are usually extremely tame, allowing an approach to within a few yards.

Length: 20-22cm; **Weight:** 90-110g
Where to look: mountain tops in northern Britain; migrants mainly in eastern England. **Nest:** usually unlined scrape. **Eggs:** 3, buff, heavily spotted. **Food:** mainly beetles and flies. **Voice:** a trill or *kwip-kwip.*

Pale stripe over eye, and breastline clear in winter and on juveniles. Sandy-buff and brown above. No white on wing or rump in flight. Often tame.

Grey Plover

❋

PLUVIALIS SQUATAROLA

Grey plovers in summer plumage are stunning in the contrast between their black underparts and silvery-white and grey upperparts. There can be few birds as striking as these, which appear during April/May and July/August. Most seek out large, muddy estuaries in southern and eastern England. They are of a similar size to redshanks, but stand out on the mud flats because of their pale grey plumage and hunched, dejected stance, combined with a rather slow feeding action. Sight is the sense which is used when feeding. They watch for tiny movements on the surface, then lunge to catch the worms or molluscs before they retreat into the mud. Because they feed on items at the surface, bad weather (low temperature, high wind, rain) may affect their feeding rate significantly.

Typically, grey plovers spend the winter in warm climates, but during recent years the numbers wintering in Britain have doubled to 21,000. The Wash, Chichester Harbour and the area around Foulness in Essex have over 2,000 birds each. Very few are noted inland, even during migration. All the grey plovers seen in Britain come from breeding grounds on the tundra of northern Siberia.

Long-winged in flight and shows a clear white wingbar and square white rump. Characteristic black mark on the 'armpit' contrasts with white underwing from below.

Winter birds pale below, greyish and pale spotted above. The large dark eye is prominent. Juveniles have pale yellow spots on back.

Length: 27-30cm; **Weight:** 200-250g
Where to look: nearly all are on estuaries, mainly in the southern half of Britain. Does not breed in Britain. **Food:** summer – insects; winter – marine worms, shellfish. **Voice:** a flat *TLEE-oo-EE*. Wistful but far-carrying.

Always a greyish, rather heavy plover with a prominent black bill; tends to have a hunched and neckless stance and is relatively slow moving. When disturbed, normally flies away silently.

When sitting, the buff and brown upperparts are well camouflaged. Note white streaking on the face.

Stone-curlew

❋

BURHINUS OEDICNEMUS

Most peculiar appearance with staring yellow and black eye and striking yellow bill. White and dark on wing.

Secretive and inconspicuous, the stone-curlew is one of Britain's least familiar birds. Ideally, it requires large, open spaces where grass is kept very short by grazing, and where bare ground can be found. Such conditions are now only found in East Anglia's Breckland (where two-thirds of the 120-150 pairs of British stone-curlews breed) and to a lesser extent the upland chalk of southern England. It will also live on agricultural land which has areas of bare earth, but if it does it needs the active help of the farmer in not ploughing up its nest or eggs. It is inactive for much of the day, sitting or standing quietly by patches of taller vegetation. As dusk approaches so it comes to life, searching grass, open soil or dung piles for earthworms, burying beetles and other invertebrates. Even small mice and nesting birds are taken. Activity is intense through the night, and it is then that the extremely varied calls can be heard. These are a mixture of wailing and slurred curlew-like calls interspersed by oystercatcher-like piping. The large eye is adapted to its nocturnal habits.

Length: 40-44cm; **Weight:** 400-500g
Where to look: rare summer migrant to sandy heaths in the Breckland and chalk in south England. **Nest:** simple scrape. **Eggs:** 2, pale, blotched. **Food:** mainly earthworms, beetles. **Voice:** wailing *cur-lee*; whistles.

Lapwing

❊

VANELLUS VANELLUS

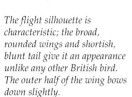

The flight silhouette is characteristic; the broad, rounded wings and shortish, blunt tail give it an appearance unlike any other British bird. The outer half of the wing bows down slightly.

Flies with distinctive, jerky, almost intermittent flaps. This is enhanced by the wings being sharply kinked at the 'wrist'.

In summer, adult males are easy to identify by the all-black chin, throat and breast. The long black crest is longer than in females.

The English names for the lapwing show how well known it is. Lapwing itself describes the flapping, broad-winged flight, green plover the correct plumage colour, while peewit is an excellent description of its call note. In winter it can be found throughout Britain, shunning only the cold mountains and uplands. No accurate figures exist for the numbers present in winter, but there are certainly more than a million. These include not only British breeding birds, but birds from Scandinavia and western Europe east to western USSR. The lapwing is almost always found in flocks, and flocks often number several thousands. In very severe weather, when the food it takes from the surface is almost impossible to find, huge daytime movements take place, with birds seeking milder southern and western feeding grounds. In exceptionally harsh conditions birds can be seen feeding on road verges in towns or even in gardens. Many may die at such times. Territories are taken up during late February and March in southern Britain, but into April further north. It is then that the spectacular display flight can be seen. The birds engage in twisting and tumbling flying, the rounded wings looking almost moth-like.

Britain's breeding population has been estimated at 181,000 pairs. However, numbers have slumped in recent years as agricultural intensification has changed the landscape.

Length: 28-31cm; **Weight:** 150-300g
Where to look: found in many areas in winter; mainly on grassland, some on ploughed fields. On coasts in severe weather. In summer on wet meadows, moorland and spring cultivated land. **Nest:** scrape on dry land, little lining. **Eggs:** 3-5, pale brown, blotched dark; March-June. **Food:** wide range of adult and larval invertebrates, many worms, some plant material. Many food items eaten would harm crops. **Voice:** a rising, two-note, thin, slightly harsh *wee-ip* or *pee-wit.*

The white-naped chicks feed close to the adults, who stand guard.

Adult females in summer have some white speckling on the chin and throat. Crests are shorter than males' and wings glossed blue-green, not dark blue.

Winter adults have a white chin and throat; breastband is black.

A fairly large, rounded wader with a distinct wispy crest. No other British bird has this plumage feature.

Knot

Look for pale grey rump and indistinct wingbars in flight. Flocks usually look very dense.

✳

CALIDRIS CANUTUS

When seen singly, the knot's bulky size and mainly grey colour make it distinctive, but it is a very gregarious wader more often found in flocks of many thousands. Although 250,000 spend the winter in Britain, few occur away from areas with larger, sandier estuaries, such as Morecambe Bay and the Wash, or the rocky coasts of north and east Scotland. They form extremely tight flocks, which carpet the ground, giving rise to the descriptive name of 'a pack' of knots. As the tightly-packed flocks turn in their complex aerial manoeuvres, the colour changes as first the upper, then the lower parts of the birds come into view. Knots are among Britain's most spectacular migrants. Most come from north-east Canada and

Greenland; others, which breed in Siberia, are only seen in May and autumn en route from and to Africa. A very restricted range of food is taken, consisting almost entirely of small cockles and, especially, Baltic tellins, which are obtained by probing. Tiny mussels help the birds put on weight before migration, for which fat is the essential fuel.

A bulky, smallish wader with short greenish legs and straight bill. Looks low-slung. In winter very grey with paler underparts; pale face. Legs more greyish.

Length: 23-25cm; **Weight:** 110-170g
Where to look: large, mostly sandy estuaries; rocky coasts. Does not breed in UK. **Food:** summer – insects; winter – mainly small molluscs. **Voice:** a quiet *knutt* or double *knuup-knuup.*

Transformed in summer to brick-red below and blacker above.

Sanderling

Large white wingbar prominent, dark line down centre of rump. Flicks low along shoreline. In summer reddish back and breast.

✳

CALIDRIS ALBA

Frenzied activity is the sanderling's hallmark as it dashes up and down the beach picking up small shrimps exposed by each wave. So fast do the legs move that the birds look almost as though they are mechanically driven. The

Usually very active in front of waves in small groups.

Strikingly pale in winter; pearly grey above, white below with dark shoulder patch; black legs.

14,000 that spend the winter in Britain are highly localised, many beaches being apparently unsuitable. The Western Isles are favoured. The pale winter dress is very obvious, even where the bird mixes with other waders at roost. Sanderlings breed on tundra near the Arctic Ocean and can be found wintering on beaches all around the world as far as the extreme southern tips of Africa and South America. Those coming to Britain breed mainly in north-east Canada, Greenland and Siberia. Summer plumaged birds are often mistaken for other waders, but the large white wingbar is always distinctive and the belly is always spotlessly white.

Length: 20-21cm
Weight: 50-60g
Where to look: sandy beaches and outer part of estuaries. **Nest:** only on the tundra of the high Arctic. Does not breed in UK. **Food:** summer – mainly insects, winter – tiny shrimps. **Voice:** a quiet, positive *twick.*

Dunlin

❋

CALIDRIS ALPINA

Variability in size and plumage makes this the most likely species to be confused with other small waders. As it is the most numerous wader on the coast, (approximately 430,000 spend the winter in Britain) it is usually best to assume a small wader is a dunlin unless you can prove to the contrary. Muddier estuaries are favoured, although groups can be found on sandy shores and rocky coasts. Small ragworms and the snails called Hydrobia are perhaps its favoured food. When worms are extracted they are often taken to the nearest water and washed before being eaten. Severe weather places much stress on small waders, and at these times dunlins crowd along the tideline where food is most easily found.

Those wintering in Britain breed in Siberia and northern Scandinavia, but others from Iceland and Greenland pass through to spend the winter in south Europe and north-west Africa. There they are joined by the 9,000 pairs which breed in northern Britain. Males have a beautiful song, a descending reedy trill which seems to blend into the wild moorland and marshes. Dunlin are often associated on their breeding grounds with golden plovers, the two species sometimes nesting within a short distance of one another. This relationship has led to the dunlin's nickname of 'plover's page'.

In flight looks quite brown but with distinct, fairly narrow white wingbar. Black line running through pale rump and grey tail.

Dunlins come in many sizes; those from the east are long-billed, but birds from Greenland have much shorter, straighter bills.

In spring the back of the neck of male is grey, but in female it has a strong reddish tinge.

No other small wader has a black belly in summer plumage. Has chestnut markings above which wear to become darker.

The dunlin's delightful song is evocative of its moorland breeding habiat.

Length: 16-22cm
Weight: 40-60g
Where to look: widespread on muddy estuaries, lake shores. **Nest:** in deep vegetation near northern wetlands. **Eggs:** 4, buff, variably marked. **Food:** invertebrates.
Voice: a slurred, slightly harsh *treeep*.

When feeding, they keep their heads down and probe into the mud very rapidly. They run quickly between feeding sites; often quarrelsome.

Juvenile has dark spots and streaks on belly; neat lines of pale fringed feathers on back. Breast and head suffused buff.

Dull in winter, with grey-brown upperparts, white underparts and breast suffused grey, forming a breastband at a distance. Then more easily confused with other small, much scarcer, waders.

Little Stint

❋

CALIDRIS MINUTA

Muddy lagoons, especially those just behind sea-walls, attract most little stints, although any inland wetland might be used. They are less frequently seen on estuaries, but this is due to the difficulty of spotting them. Once seen, their tiny size, thin straight bills, crouching stance and tendency to remain in a small area for some time are distinctive. Often, small dunlins cause confusion, but a genuine little stint should leave no doubt. Most occur between September and November and are the strongly marked juveniles, blown west by easterly winds over the Continent. Normally these Scandinavian and Siberian birds migrate through central Europe to overwinter from Africa to India. Very few (under 20) spend the winter in Britain, and only scattered, chestnut-faced adults in breeding plumage are seen in May or late July/August while on passage. In order to ensure as many young as possible are raised females often lay two clutches, the male incubating one and the female the other, so that two adults rather than four can in effect rear two complete families.

Most often seen in autumn are the juveniles. Prominent white 'V' on back, reddish fringes to brown upperparts and cap; white flanks.

A tiny wader, much smaller than the dunlin and with a diminutive straight bill and black legs. Feeds with very rapid pecks from the mud surface. Often tame.

In flight looks small; narrow white wingbar and dark line over white rump and grey tail.

Length: 12-14cm
Weight: 20-30g
Where to look: exposed mud inland, some on estuaries. Mostly seen in autumn. Does not breed in UK. **Food:** small invertebrates, mainly insects. **Voice:** a quiet but clear *tip-tip* or *stit-stit.*

Curlew Sandpiper

❋

CALIDRIS FERRUGINEA

When feeding, curlew sandpipers often wade out into quite deep water and probe vertically, submerging their heads. Others probe for worms on mud flats. Females have longer bills than males, enabling them to probe more deeply. The neatly-patterned juveniles are seen from late August to October and greatly out-number the adults. In exceptional years, with strong persistent easterly winds after a good breeding season, up to 3,500 have been seen in Britain, but 500-1,000 is more usual. These breed in central north Siberia and over-winter throughout Africa; others fly to New Zealand for the winter, often in large numbers.

The curlew sandpiper is not very vocal, but sometimes can be picked out in a flying flock of small waders by its soft call. Often feeds with dunlins, but wades further out into deeper water, up to its belly. In flight white rump obvious during banking or landing. As its name suggests, the bill is relatively long and downcurved, recalling that of a curlew.

Flying birds show a prominent square white rump and a short-tailed, long-winged shape. A clear white wingbar.

Like tall, long-legged dunlin with longer, downturned bill. On juveniles, note pale stripe over eye, scaly back and pink-buff breast.

Length: 18-23cm; **Weight:** 55-70g
Where to look: mainly coastal lagoons and muddy estuaries: some inland. Most in autumn. Does not breed in UK. **Food:** wide range of invertebrates, especially worms. **Voice:** a gentle rippling *chirrup.*

Purple Sandpiper

❊

CALIDRIS MARITIMA

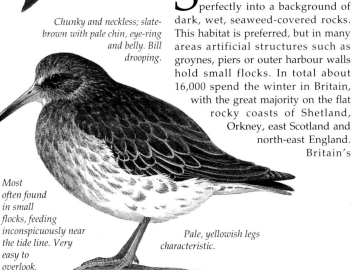

Dark in flight; neat white wing-bar and sides of rump stand out. Tends to fly low over the water.

Chunky and neckless; slate-brown with pale chin, eye-ring and belly. Bill drooping.

Most often found in small flocks, feeding inconspicuously near the tide line. Very easy to overlook.

Pale, yellowish legs characteristic.

Superb camouflage helps the purple sandpiper to merge perfectly into a background of dark, wet, seaweed-covered rocks. This habitat is preferred, but in many areas artificial structures such as groynes, piers or outer harbour walls hold small flocks. In total about 16,000 spend the winter in Britain, with the great majority on the flat rocky coasts of Shetland, Orkney, east Scotland and north-east England. Britain's birds come from breeding areas in Norway and, probably, Greenland. Most arrive in October and November. There have been up to three pairs breeding in Scotland since 1979, making a welcome addition to the list of breeding birds. Relying on their camouflage, they allow a very close approach. They are so tame that their behaviour can be studied in detail as they peck among the seaweed, taking many small periwinkles and a range of other invertebrates. Early in the winter juveniles can be identified by buff edges to the upperwing feathers. Females have noticeably longer bills than males, and there may be tiny differences in the way they feed.

Length: 20-22cm; **Weight:** 55-80g
Where to look: rocky coasts especially in the north-east, often on piers and harbours. **Nest:** on ground in moorland. **Eggs:** 3-4 buff, blotched brown. **Food:** small marine invertebrates. **Voice:** low, single or double *whit*.

Turnstone

❊

ARENARIA INTERPRES

Short chisel-shaped bill and orange legs. In summer, strikingly white-headed and chestnut-backed.

Although most abundant on the rocky coasts favoured by purple sandpipers, turnstones are also frequently seen on mussel beds, rocky outcrops or even shingle beaches where drifts of seaweed occur. They are very scarce inland, even when migrating. The birds seen in Britain are from two distinct areas – Scandinavia and Greenland/Canada. Those fromScandinavia pass through in autumn and spring on their way to and from wintering grounds in central and southern Africa, while the Canada/Greenland birds mostly spend the winter in Europe. About 45,000 of those remain in Britain. Turnstones are aptly named, for with their strong bills and necks they move over feeding grounds turning small stones, lifting up patches of seaweed or digging furiously in sand; the invertebrates there dash for cover, but are rapidly caught. In addition, many small periwinkles are eaten and limpets prised off rocks. Turnstone camouflage is excellent and thus feeding birds are confident and can be very approachable. In breeding plumage, males have much more white on the head than females. Occasionally pairs may breed in Scotland, but turnstones have not colonised Britain.

Length: 21-25cm; **Weight:** 80-150g
Where to look: rocky coasts, outer parts of estuaries: rarely inland. **Nest:** mostly on Arctic tundra, moorland. **Eggs:** 4, green, streaked brown. **Food:** wide range of coastal invertebrates. **Voice:** clear rattled *trik-tuk-tuk-tuk*.

Sturdy and thick-set; in winter, head dark, back brown and black.

Snipe

❋

GALLINAGO GALLINAGO

Feeding birds remain in the same spot, probing a small area rapidly. The bill is held vertically and inserted to its base. When disturbed they remain quite motionless, but alert.

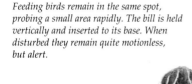

Note the pale belly; the brown bill is darker at its tip and the legs yellow or greyish-green.

On warm summer evenings the males dive in aerial display; the outer tail feathers are spread and they vibrate to give a characteristic tremulous or drumming sound.

Appears to feed in small groups or singly, but camouflage is so effective they are difficult to see.

Displaying birds often choose to stand on posts or lumps of soil and utter the distinctive chipa-chipa call note. Agitated adults with young will stand on posts, calling in alarm if danger is near. When flying up, parallel buff lines on the back are often noticeable. Thin white line along rear of wing; some white on the tail.

The long bill, almost twice the length of the strongly striped and mottled back, is very distinctive.

When flying high overhead looks rather jerky, with fast flickering wing-beats. Wings sharply pointed triangles; short tail; long bill held slightly angled down.

As the drainage of lowland grassland and its conversion to intensive agriculture has taken place, so the lowland population of snipe have decreased substantially in Britain and elsewhere in western Europe. Even so, taking into account the upland breeders, there are probably about 30,000 pairs remaining in Britain. In winter many more flood into the country, especially from Scandinavia and Iceland. Winter totals are not known, but must be much highter. Snipe love flooded grassland where worms have been forced to the surface, and where the ground is soft and there is plenty of vegetation to provide camouflage. In general they rely for protection on being hidden, but fly up if approached too closely. Sometimes they feed out on open mud beside reservoirs. In very cold winters most of their feeding grounds become unsuitable and then they can turn up in gardens, on roadsides and other unlikely places. Many die or become so weak they can be caught by cats or hit by cars. A flock of snipe is given the collective name of a 'wisp', perhaps due to its rapid twisting and turning before the birds drop down again.

When feeding out in the open, snipe often look rather dark. Seen in good light, however, the plumage is an amazing mixture of brown, buff, black and white. Even among low vegetation, this affords the snipe exceptional camouflage.

Length: 25-27cm; **Weight:** 90-150g
Where to look: around edges of fresh-water areas where mud meets vegetation; marshes, wet fields. **Nest:** in tussock of grass or rush in wet meadows, lined with grass. **Eggs:** 4, olive, blotched brown. **Food:** mostly worms; insect larvae, other invertebrates. **Voice:** harsh *scaap* when startled.

Woodcock

❊

SCOLOPAX RUSTICOLA

Large, dark brown; long bill.

at dusk at the edge of a wood on a fine spring evening. Then you may see its distinctive roding flights, and hear its strange calls. If put up, the large size, broad wings, rusty colour and noisy wing-beats make identification easy as the bird flies fast through the trees; the long bill and dark crown bars are distinctive if seen.

Up to 40,000 pairs breed, in both coniferous and broadleaved woods, and many more come to Britain from Western Europe in November and December.

If you are lucky enough to watch a bird feeding in a boggy glade or in damp leaf litter, it has a peculiar to-and-fro rocking action with the head kept remarkably still. The woodcock has a most extraordinary and endearing habit — the adult flies with small young held between its legs when danger threatens. Several trips are needed to move a whole family to safety.

Length: 33–35cm; **Weight:** 290–32g **Where to look:** put up from ground in woods, but easiest in spring display flight over trees. **Nest:** on ground. **Eggs:** 3–5, blotched brown. **Food:** worms, insects, grubs. **Voice:** sharp *pitz* or *tswik* alternating with deep croak.

Relying on camouflage, remaining still until almost trodden on, this bird is rarely seen unless driven into the open by severe weather, but it is worth a look

Jack Snipe

❊

LYMNOCRYPTES MINIMUS

Although widely distributed, this small snipe is scarce and very difficult to see. It may be picked out when feeding among snipe or in vegetation by its remarkable up-and-down rhythmical bouncing action, which is quite unlike any other species. Why it does this is not known. Otherwise it is only flushed from wet marshland when almost trodden on. Occasionally one

may be seen flattened against the ground just in front of the advancing boot! If a good view is obtained look for the dark centre to the crown and the dark, purple tinged back. Birds arrive in Britain in late autumn from their Scandinavian breeding grounds

and return during early spring. Considering how weak its flight appears to be when flushed, it is remarkable that it undertakes quite substantial migrations each year. Perhaps one summer a pair will remain to breed in Britain.

Length: 17-19cm; **Weight:** 40-70g **Where to look:** in marshy areas when small wet, open patches are found among vegetation. Does not breed in Britain. **Food:** mostly invertebrates, many worms. **Voice:** normally silent in Britain, but sometimes a weak *gah* when flushed..

Bill is short, just longer than the striped head. No white in tail.

A small snipe: when flushed it shows prominent pale buff lines on the very dark, glossy back.

Flushes from underfoot and drops back into cover very quickly.

Relies on keeping very still and its almost perfect camouflage.

Black-tailed Godwit

✻

LIMOSA LIMOSA

The outer third of the bill of the black-tailed godwit is packed with sensory cells, enabling it to follow underground movements of its prey. In any flock some birds will be resting their bills on the surface while others will probe deeply. Another characteristic feeding action is seen in shallow lagoons, where the head is thrown back quickly to swallow items caught under the surface. Only 30-40 pairs breed in Britain, nearly all on wet meadow nature reserves such as the Ouse Washes in Cambridgeshire. When breeding, they have a complex aerial display and are very vocal with loud, nasal, slightly harsh *grutto-grutto* and *wicka-wicka* calls. Recolonisation of Britain took place in 1952, but despite optimism its hold is still precarious. Winter numbers have increased greatly over the last 50 years, but have remained at about 4,800 since 1970. The wintering birds breed in Iceland and form a distinct race. Birds breeding in Scotland also belong to this race, but those in eastern England are from the continental race; these migrate to Africa for the winter.

Neck and breast red in summer; flanks barred, belly white.

In flight, a solid black band at the end of the white tail is distinctive.

Winter birds have an even brown-grey wash to back and breast; stripe over eye distinct.

Length: 36-44cm
Weight: 250-350g
Where to look: winter — muddy estuaries in southern England; summer — wet meadows. **Nest:** hollow in grass. **Eggs:** 3-5, olive, blotched brown. **Food:** range of invertebrates. **Voice:** quiet *tuk*, noisy when breeding.

Bar-tailed Godwit

✻

LIMOSA LAPPONICA

There tends to be a clear separation in habitats used by the two godwit species. The bar-tailed is found in sandier areas, while the black-tailed will be inland or on muddier sections. The largest bar-tailed flocks are on major estuaries such as The Wash or Morecambe Bay, where they gather on sand flats rich in lugworms. They scan the surface looking for worms coming up to make their distinctive coiled casts, and then they probe deeply to catch them before they withdraw out of reach. Flocks are often at the tide edge where lugworm activity is greatest. One of the spectacular sights of migration is of bar-tailed godwits sweeping east along the coast of south-east England during late April. The dark brick-red males with their relatively short bills can be picked out from the long-billed females, which have only a tinge of red on their underparts. These birds have come from wintering grounds in West Africa and are on their way to breeding areas in arctic Scandinavia and Siberia. British wintering birds breed there as well and arrive here in October and November. When coming in to roost they often plummet down, twisting and turning as they drop to the sand in an action called 'whiffling'.

Flying birds show white 'V' up back and pale tail; no white wingbar.

Slightly upcurved, long pointed bill; legs are fairly long but look stout. Streaked upperparts. Summer plumage is distinctive.

In winter, upperparts are streaked grey and brown; breast is grey or buff and finely streaked. Stripe over the eye indistinct. Looks chunky.

Length: 37-41cm;
Weight: 200-350g
Where to look: large sandy areas, mainly on estuaries. Does not breed in UK. **Food:** many coastal invertebrates, mainly lugworms. **Voice:** a low barking *kirruc-kirruc.*

Curlew

❄

NUMENIUS ARQUATA

The curlew's bubbling song, given mainly during the hanging display flight, seems to express the nature of the lonely, open spaces where it breeds. Most of Britain's 35,000 pairs nest in the north and west, where some are under pressure from modern agricultural methods. Many of the birds which breed in Britain move to Ireland and France for the winter, while British estuaries are filled with 91,000 birds which breed mainly in Scandinavia. These immigrants start arriving very early in the season; it is not unusual for the first birds to beback by August. When feeding they take a wide range of invertebrates: inland; earthworms are favoured, but on mussel beds and rocky coasts it is not unusual to see them eating small crabs. They break off the legs before swallowing them. High-tide roosts are formed on salt marshes or on fields, but as the species is very wary, they are easily disturbed.

Large white 'V' on back. Leisurely flight action.

Length: 50-60cm; **Weight:** 700-1,000g **Where to look:** estuaries and coastal meadows in winter. Summer — moors, farmland edge. **Nest:** grassy, hollow. **Eggs:** 3-5, spotted. **Food:** wide range of invertebrates. **Voice:** melodic *cur-lee*; bubbling song.

Very long, gently down-turned bill is unmistakable. A very large brown and buff streaked wader. Bland face pattern with no eye stripe.

Flying birds usually give distinctive rippling calls.

White 'V' on back clear in flight. Beats wings faster than a curlew.

Whimbrel

❄

NUMENIUS PHAEOPUS

'Heard before seen' could be the motto for the whimbrel. Its characteristic rippling note carries a long way and is given frequently. One of its colloquial names is the 'seven whistler', as the single note is often given about seven times. Just to create some confusion, it also gives a cur-lee reminiscent of a curlew's call. A very small breeding population of about 400 pairs is found in northernmost Scotland; there the bubbling display song, recalling the curlew, can be heard.

However, over most of Britain it is a relatively scarce migrant. Small flocks, rarely more than 50, may be encountered on the edges of estuarine marshes at high tide or seen flying along the coast. The speed of the wing-beats is closer to that of godwits than of the slower curlew. April and early May is when spring migration is at its peak. Some birds stop on coastal grassland at night. One spectacular flock of over 1,000 builds up on Stert Island in Bridgwater Bay, Somerset. These are on the way from sub-Saharan Africa to breed in Iceland; Scandinavian breeders pass through eastern Britain. They are not familiar birds to most birdwatchers, but at the right time on suitable coasts are not particularly rare.

General colour a dark oily brown, lightly spotted above; darker than curlew. Seen in small parties.

Like a dark curlew, but smaller, with a shorter, more sharply down-turned bill. Head pattern distinctive, with prominent pale stripe over eye between two dark stripes. Narrow crown stripe.

Length: 40-46cm; **Weight:** 350-450g **Where to look:** on migration wet meadows, salt marshes. **Nest:** partly lined hollow. **Eggs:** 3-4, olive, blotched. **Food:** mostly invertebrates; berries in summer. **Voice:** mainly a rippling *bibibibibibibi*.

Redshank

❊

TRINGA TOTANUS

Striking white rear edge to dark wings, white 'V' on the back distinctive. Calls loudly in flight.

Brownish-grey wash to upperparts; little sign of pale stripe over eye.

Bright-red legs characteristic. Bold dark spots in summer.

The title 'Sentinel of the Marshes' is most apt for this widespread, wary and noisy wader as it flies off yelling a warning to other birds. On the face of it, this is an adaptable species, being found on all types of coasts and on inland marshes in winter. However, though 75,000 still winter here, numbers have been dropping in the 1980s. Many that have bred in Britain remain for the winter (although often their young move down to southern Europe) and are joined by birds which bred in Iceland.

Most of the time redshanks feed on small shrimps, snails and worms found on the surface, but they will take a very wide variety of food. A rhythmical, even-paced walk with steady pecks is the typical and instinctive feeding action. By April, most of the British birds are back on their breeding territories. About 32,000 pairs breed in Britain, the favoured habitats being estuarine salt marshes, wet meadows and rough pastures. Drainage of inland wetlands poses problems for inland breeders.

The song, given in a hanging flight, on quivering wings, echoes beautifully over the marshes — but noisy alarm calls have an hysterical ring to them as redshanks dive at potential predators.

Length: 27-29cm
Weight: 100-160g
Where to look: winter — muddy and sandy coasts; summer — wet meadows, marshes. **Nest:** lined cup in tussock, well hidden. **Eggs:** 3-5, variable colour, spotted; April-May. **Food:** creatures from mud. **Voice:** loud *TEU-hu-hu*.

Spotted Redshank

❊

TRINGA ERYTHROPUS

Taller and more slender than the redshank; longer legs and a much longer, thinner tipped bill. Feeds with a jerkier action. Red legs darker than redshank's in summer; scarlet in winter.

In flight, shows a long white oval up the back; no wingbar, long thin shape.

This slim, active wader has many techniques for capturing its prey. At times it resembles a redshank, steadily walking and pecking at surface items; its gait is more jerky yet it seems to peck more delicately. At other times it forms lively parties, and group members seem to chase food items in almost exact unison. The bird usually wades in fairly deep water, but often swims, almost up-ending like a dabbling duck. Only about 1,000 can be found in Britain during the main migration period — July to September — and about 100 stay for the winter, nearly all in Wales and in the southern half of England. Despite its scarcity, migrants can be found on many estuaries and inland; they are usually first noted by the distinctive, clear chu-it call. Stunning in velvety black summer plumage, they are worth seeking in late June on the east coast.

Length: 29-32cm
Weight: 130-160g
Where to look: shallow water inland, estuarine creeks. **Food:** invertebrates, small fish, tadpoles. **Voice:** a clear, sharp, whistled *chu-it*, usually given in flight.

Winter birds are white below, mid-grey above, with pale stripe over eye.

Greenshank

TRINGA NEBULARIA

Length: 30-34cm; **Weight:** 170-200g
Where to look: peat bogs, lakes, estuaries.
Nest: hollow on ground. **Eggs:** 3-4, olive, spotted dark; May-June. **Food:** worms, fish.
Voice: a ringing *tu-tu-tu.*

The loud, clear trisyllabic call draws attention to the greenshank, for these notes penetrate through other wader calls. In flight it gives the impression of being rather thick-set compared with similar species. Perhaps as many as 1,500 pairs breed in Britain, but they are restricted to northern Scotland, and choose some of the most beautiful, yet wildest, countryside. In winter up to 400 remain here, almost all on western coasts, with at least as many again in Ireland. They are scattered in small muddy estuaries or on sea-lochs. For most of the time birds feed with a fairly steady, elegant walk, pecking at the surface, but at times they chase small fish in shallow water, running erratically with the bill held slightly open. The largest numbers are found in autumn, when Scandinavian migrants pass through to Africa. In winter, greenshank are mostly solitary although they may form loose and temporary associations with others of their kind.

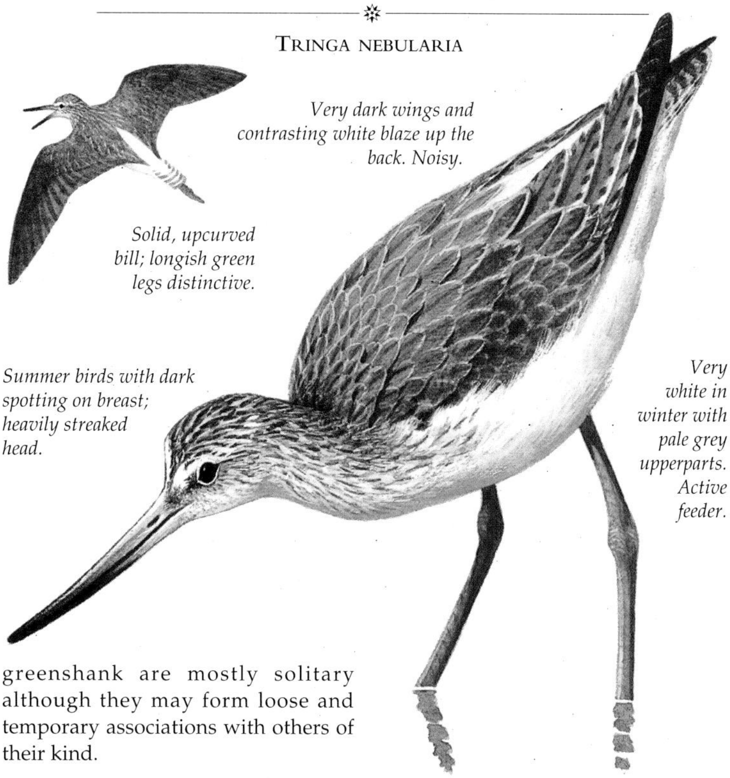

Very dark wings and contrasting white blaze up the back. Noisy.

Solid, upcurved bill; longish green legs distinctive.

Summer birds with dark spotting on breast; heavily streaked head.

Very white in winter with pale grey upperparts. Active feeder.

Ruff

PHILOMACHUS PUGNAX

Length: 26-32cm; **Weight:** 75-200g
Where to look: edges of lakes, shallow, flooded grassland; in summer wet meadows. **Nest:** in grass tussock. **Eggs:** 3-4, pale grey-green, boldly spotted; May-June. **Food:** small invertebrates.

An unusually shaped bird. Long legs but shortish, slightly down-curved bill. Head seems too small for the longish neck. Usually has pot-bellied, hump-backed shape.

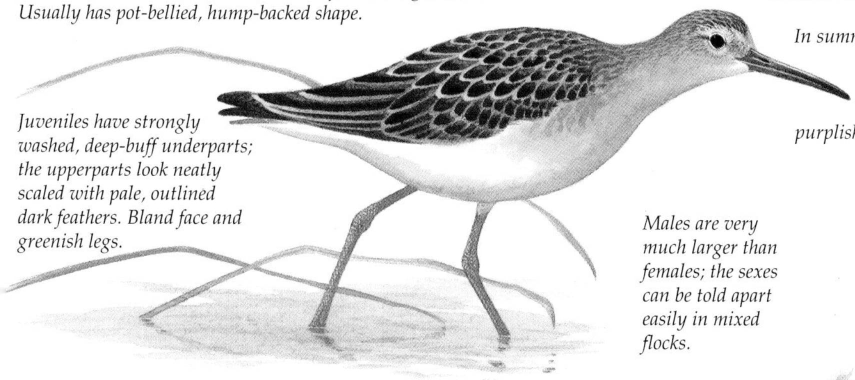

Juveniles have strongly washed, deep-buff underparts; the upperparts look neatly scaled with pale, outlined dark feathers. Bland face and greenish legs.

In summer, males are extraordinary, with huge variably coloured ruffs and head tufts. Main colours are white, chestnut-brown and purplish-black. Legs of adults are reddish. Ritualized display at lek.

Males are very much larger than females; the sexes can be told apart easily in mixed flocks.

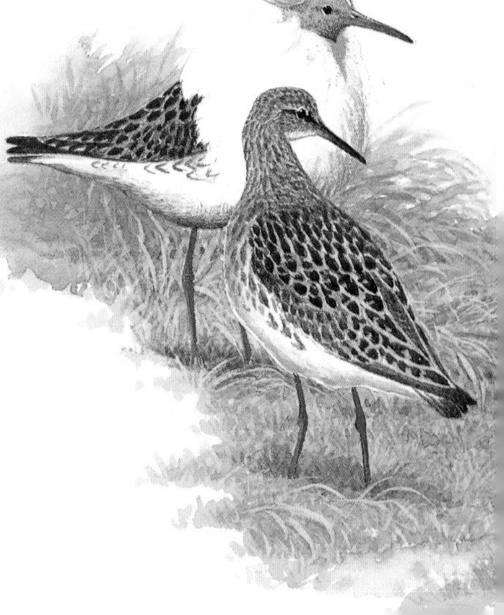

Britain is on the western edge of the breeding range of the ruff, and fewer than ten pairs breed here each year, mainly on wet meadows in East Anglia. The males' communal dancing display (called lekking) is a complex ritual carried out on traditional leks (display grounds). Females watch and then choose with which male to mate. They then depart and bring up the young alone. The ruff is unusual not only in its display, but also in appearance. In many ways (size, shape, feeding action) it resembles a redshank, but it is actually more closely related to the dunlin. In sthe autumn, migrants from Scandinavia and the USSR pass through Britain, some staying for the winter. About 1,500 remain, most on the Ouse Washes, and at Pagham Harbour, in Sussex. However, several million winter south of the Sahara in Africa. Interestingly, most wintering in Britain are males, but in Africa most are the smaller females.

Common Sandpiper

❊

ACTITIS HYPOLEUCOS

Dark with white wingbar; flies on strongly bowed, stiff wings

The rhythmical, bobbing walk makes the common sandpiper one of the most distinctive small waders. It feeds along the edge of lakes, rivers, even sea-lochs and rocky shores. Food is usually pecked from the surface of the mud, but sometimes the bird can be watched stalking insects with head held horizontally and slowly extended before a sudden snap to catch the prey. The bird is nearly always found singly or in very small groups. Many are seen on migration, especially in autumn, but only about 50 spend the winter here, mainly in south–western Britain; most migrate to sub–Saharan Africa. Breeding birds are found in upland areas of Wales, northern England and Scotland, and about 18,500 pairs breed in Britain. The flickering, down-curved wings, combined with the penetrating whistled call, given almost continuously in flight, are distinctive.

Length: 19-21cm; **Weight:** 40-60g
Where to look: summer — upland rivers, lake sides; passage — water edge anywhere. **Nest:** hidden in hollow near water. **Eggs:** 3-5, buff, dark spots; May-June. **Food:** invertebrates. **Voice:** noisy, a thin piping, penetrating *tse-we-wee*.

Slight stripe over eye, and glossy green-brown above in summer.

Dark; white point between breast patch and win; legs green-grey.

A horizontal wader with a long tail and short, straight bill. Walks with strong bobbing action.

Red-necked Phalarope

❊

PHALAROPUS LOBATUS

Breeding adult with red and grey neck, and white chin. Female is brighter.

Very thin, black bill; small size. Autumn young (left) show thin, golden edges on the dark back feathers.

Grey Phalarope

PHALAROPUS FULICARIUS

Grey phalaropes are very similar to red-necks in juvenile and winter plumages. Note the stocky appearance and thicker, shorter bill, often a little yellow at the base.

Sadly, the beautifully marked red-necked phalarope is now very rare in Britain, with only 30 pairs breeding, all in the far north of Scotland where they seek out well-vegetated lochans. A few appear at other times, mainly in eastern England after north-east winds in autumn. Huge flocks gather in winter in the Arabian Sea, and it is probably there that the British breeding birds go. It is an unusually late migrant in spring, with few arriving before June; most return south from late July, onwards. Most sex roles are reversed; it is the male who incubates the eggs and looks after the chicks, so he is less brightly marked and better camouflaged than the female. Juveniles and summer-plumaged birds have characteristic golden lines down the back, but in winter plumage they are very like grey phalaropes. Subtle points such as bill shape, body size, flight action and call need to be assessed. The bird is very approachable.

Length: 18-19cm; **Weight:** 30-40g
Where to look: a very few breed on pools in northern Scotland. Coastal pools in autumn. **Nest:** in grass by water. **Eggs:** 3-4, buff, blotched brown; June. **Food:** invertebrates. **Voice:** fairly low-pitched *twit*.

Green Sandpiper

❊

TRINGA OCHROPUS

A dark wader with white underparts seen walking steadily in shallow water inland is most likely to be a green sandpiper, for they are widely distributed across Britain during late summer and autumn. Nowhere do flocks of more than 30 appear, but in autumn the total number in Britain may be as high as 2,000. When feeding, they walk steadily, pecking at surface items, but with an occasional bob; if agitated they will bob vigorously before dashing away, calling very positively. In flight the black lining to the wings is an instant identification feature: the flight itself is very snipe-like with sharp flicks of the wings. They are often picked up by their calls when flying high overhead.

Between 200 and 300 remain for the winter, most having departed for Africa. In Britain, they seek fresh–water springs, chalk streams, or where rivers enter inner estuaries; all places where water rarely freezes. They have only bred twice in Britain. When breeding they seek old nests in trees, the young having to leap to the ground. They migrate back very early, and by late June many autumn passage birds are already in Britain; they seek the rich mud of sewage farms or reservoirs.

Looks very black in flight, with square white rump and white belly. Flickering flight, broad wings.

Relatively bulky for a smallish wader; always very dark above and white below; complete, but diffuse breastband. Small white stripe in front of the white eye-ring. Legs dull; often bobs.

Length: 21-24cm; **Weight:** 60-100g
Where to look: by edges of inland waters, in winter some on estuary creeks. Does not breed in Britain. **Food:** mostly insects, other invertebrates. **Voice:** a rapid high-whistled *Tuwit-wit-wit.*

Wood Sandpiper

❊

TRINGA GLAREOLA

This is one of the species to seek out in eastern counties of Britain, for it is very scarce on the west coast. Small numbers are seen in August and September, with most appearing on east winds which have blown them across from Scandinavian breeding grounds. Although resembling a green sandpiper, redshank or ruff, the yellowish legs, pale stripe over the eye and the slim, neat shape help to separate it.

Normally, wood sandpipers eat small invertebrates, but just occasionally are galvanised into action by tiny fish. Most of the time they wade in shallow water, especially where low vegetation is emerging, and walk steadily, pecking from the surface. They are quite wary and fly away rapidly, climbing quickly with peevish calls. Nearly all spend the winter in Africa, south of the Sahara. In spring a few are seen on passage and fewer than ten pairs remain to breed in Scotland. Here they give the melodic whistled song, delivered in a wing–quivering display flight, which is interspersed by glides on down–curved wings. Like many other waders nesting in wet, open woodland, they frequently perch in trees but are remarkably elusive.

Mid-brown above; square white rump. Feet extend past tail.

In summer, stripe over eye distinctly white. Bird rather greyish, with large white and brown speckles. Bars usually distinct on flanks.

Relatively slim and delicate for a medium-sized sandpiper; bill straight and rather short; legs longish, especially above knee. Bobs less than its relatives.

Juveniles are warm brown above with bright buff spots and buff wash to finely-streaked breast.

Length: 19-21cm; **Weight:** 55-80g
Where to look: edges of lakes and pools, floods. **Nest:** on ground among sparse trees, sometimes in old nests in trees. **Eggs:** 4, buffish, boldly spotted; May-June. **Food:** invertebrates. **Voice:** high, thin *chiff-iff-iff.*

Great Skua

❋

STERCORARIUS SKUA

Length: 53-58cm; **Weight:** 1,300-2,000g
Where to look: at sea and on coastal moors in far north. **Nest:** on ground. **Eggs:** 2, blotched dark brown. **Food:** mainly fish stolen from other birds; also birds and eggs. **Voice:** rather quiet calls in colony; silent at sea.

Often called 'bonxies', the traditional Shetlanders' name, great skuas are not easy to see in the south though they are relatively familiar in northern coastal waters and from eastern headlands in autumn. Shetland had 10 pairs in 1774, but that number had actually declined by the 1860s. However, with protection they survived, and birds spread to Orkney in 1915, the Outer Hebrides in 1945 and a few to mainland Scotland from 1949. There are now over 5,400 pairs in Shetland alone. Great skuas chase seabirds and terrify them into disgorging food, which they then eat. They also kill many birds in summer and are especially fond of immature kittiwakes which often breed close to the skuas themselves. They are bold enough to bring down a gannet, and aggressive enough to dive at humans (and sheep) with repeated headlong rushes that sometimes end with a severe clout from the bonxie's feet — so they are not popular with crofters! After breeding they leave for the mid-Atlantic and south American and West African coasts. Three-year-olds disperse most, spending summer far to the north; by five years old they are more attached to the colony and travel less widely in winter.

Raised wing pose used in display and aggressive encounters.

Chases many seabirds; can kill gulls and auks.

Stout, hooded, dark bill; triangular, capped head.

A heavy gull-like bird; broad wings with big flashes of white visible at a great distance; may look more or less tawny or paler around neck.

Arctic Skua

❋

STERCORARIUS PARASITICUS

Lazily drifting over the sea, well offshore, the dark shape of the arctic skua suddenly raises its tempo, accelerating in pursuit of a tern, which it then harries relentlessly, following each desperate twist, until the tern drops a fish. Few birds have the exciting aura about them that the skua has, and few have such elegance of form. Arctics are far more widespread in northern parts of the world than great skuas, but only about 2,500 pairs breed in Britain, 1,600 of these in Shetland. In winter they go as far as South Africa. Arctic skuas chase terns, kittiwakes and puffins, whereas great skuas chase mostly guillemots and gannets. Nearly half their attacks on terns end in success, whereas a far smaller proportion of chases after larger birds yield food, so most skuas prefer to follow the terns in autumn. This takes them into the North Sea rather than south along the Atlantic coasts where terns are fewer. They kill fewer birds than great skuas, but human intruders at the nest are equally likely to be attacked in fast, elegant, swooping dives at the head – though contact is rarely made.

Length: 41-46cm; **Weight:** 350-550g
Where to look: northern isles and coasts, headlands in autumn. **Nest:** on ground. **Eggs:** 2, brown. **Food:** fish. **Voice:** loud wail, short bark.

Pale adult has a dark cap, white belly and often a slight breastband; dark phase uniform brown. All show wing flashes and tail spike. Immature birds are warm brown with paler bars, buffish wing patches and short tail projection.

Chases and parasitizes other seabirds such as this kittiwake, forcing them to regurgitate food.

In calm weather has direct flight, easy and relaxed; in wind glides and tilts resembles shearwater; at colonies great heights are often reached.

Black-headed Gull

LARUS RIDIBUNDUS

Whether flying from a nest in a marsh to protest noisily at intrusion, following a plough to snap up worms, stealing bits of sandwich at the seaside or dipping into the fountain in Trafalgar Square, the black–headed gull is almost everywhere. A long drive in winter shows that it is one of the few birds so obvious in the landscape that it cannot be missed — gleaming white flocks in fields or thousands of them scrambling for food at rubbish tips catch the eye a mile away. Many breed inland, though the largest colonies are on coastal marshes and they are common on beaches all year round. Consequently, while many live on worms from the fields, others have a diet of fish scraps from harbours, all kinds of eligible refuse from tips, and whatever awful food they get from sewage outflows. Britain's breeding population is much higher than a century ago, perhaps up to 300,000 pairs, but in winter there may be three million of them — two thirds from the Continent (especially the Baltic countries) and well over a million of the overall number living inland.

Adults in winter have a dark spot behind the eye; bright-red bill tipped black and bright-red legs; unlike any other commonly seen gull.

Breeding adult has a dark brown hood and dark red legs and bill; white primaries tipped black.

Below the wings is a dark patch before a translucent stripe near the tip. Young birds have much more brown in the wing, with a dark trailing edge, but still have the blaze of white on the outer primaries and coverts that is so characteristic of black-headed gulls.

If you see a flock of gulls following a plough, the chances are they will be black-headed gulls. The species is an opportunistic and adaptable feeder.

Length: 34-37cm; **Weight:** 200-300g
Where to look: almost anywhere. **Nest:** on island or by pool from coast to upland moors. **Eggs:** 2-3, blotched, brown or blue. **Food:** worms, grubs, fish, scraps. **Voice:** long squealing calls; short, repeated yapping notes.

Little Gull

LARUS MINUTUS

Tiny gull; buoyant flight. Adult has jet-black head in summer, grey and white in winter. Upperwing grey with white border (some show small black marks at tip); underwing black with white rim.

Mediterranean Gull

LARUS MELANOCEPHALUS

Adult has pearly upperwing and eye-catching, white underwing; jet black hood, white eyelids, red bill in summer; ghostly pale, dusky mask, dark bill in winter.

Herring gull

❊

LARUS ARGENTATUS

The herring gull is so common and approachable that it is worth using as a standard against which to compare others. The plumage sequences can be worked out easily and, once the pearly–grey begins to appear on the back, it is not hard to identify. Because young gulls are brown and get progressively paler as they mature, it is possible to work out their

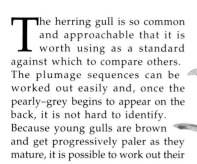

Second-year begins to get pale grey back, whiter head and body, paler bill; third-year more like adult.

First-year in flight; largely pale brows with dark tail and wing tips.

Adults are clean grey and white in summer with sharply defined black wingtips spotted white; pink legs, unlike lesser black-back's.

Bill of first-year has pale base; plumage fades with age.

In winter, adults streaked with grey-brown on head and breast; darker-backed birds frequent.

age much more easily than with most birds, the changing patterns being obvious at a glance. Larger, darker birds come here in winter from north Scandinavia — Britain's breeding birds are the smallest and palest in Europe — and on some southern coasts dark-backed, white-headed, yellow-legged birds from the Mediterranean can be found. These may even be of a different species, but the relationships of these large gulls are notoriously difficult to work out clearly. Winter flocks resting on fields or roosting on reservoirs are often wary and require care and patience for close views; quite unlike those that dive for scraps at your feet at any summer seaside resort, or wait in line on railings at fish quays, ready to pounce and fight for fish heads, guts or spilled herrings.

Length: 52-55cm; **Weight:** 750-1,200g
Where to look: cliffs, all kinds of coasts, reservoirs, tips, farmland in winter. **Nest:** on ground, cliff ledge or building. **Eggs:** 3, spotted brown. **Food:** fish, offal, refuse, eggs. **Voice:** loud squealing, wailing and laughing notes; deep *kyow–yow–yow*, short barks. Young birds have thin whine.

Glaucous Gull

Adult looks like a large herring gull with white patch at back. First-year neatly barred brown and cream, wingtips palest. Second-year (right) paler still and often fading to almost creamy white. Bill pale pink with sharp black tip in first year, not blended like Iceland gull's, later losing black and gaining yellow. Flight relatively ponderous.

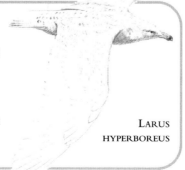

LARUS HYPERBOREUS

Iceland Gull

LARUS GLAUCOIDES

Adult very pale with wingtips all white. Young birds pale creamy fawn, with wingtips and tail palest.

Great Black-backed Gull

❋

LARUS MARINUS

Length: 62-65cm; **Weight:** 1,500-2,000g
Where to look: rocky coasts, beaches in winter, refuse tips and nearby fields, reservoirs, harbours. **Nest:** pad of greases, in hollow on clifftop. **Eggs:** 3, blotchy. **Food:** offal, fish, birds, eggs, dead animals and rubbish. **Voice:** deeper version of herring gull's wails and squeals and deep, barking *owk, uk–uk–uk.*

Characteristic of a windswept clifftop, under blue summer skies and surrounded by sea pink and campion, the great black-backed gull is one of Britain's most impressive birds, in a land of predominately small species. It does not, however, meet with universal approval, especially as it may eat a puffin or be seen feeding on a dead sheep. Even in winter a marauding great black-back will swoop at flocks of teal and coots, and it is quite capable of swallowing a big rat or a rabbit whole!

A flock of gulls resting in a field — which they do for hours at a stretch even in the shortest days of winter — may look a motley bunch, but when a great black-back flies down it simply dwarfs the rest, like a great bomber among lightweight fighters. On water, it is clearly the battleship of the fleet! About 25,000 pairs breed in Britain. In the north of Scotland, flocks of hundreds bathe in coastal fresh-water lochs and fly off to feed around passing trawlers. In

Larger size, leg colour and black (not dark grey) back and upperwing are the best distinguishing features from lesser black-backed gull.

Male gulls are larger (with bill and head bigger) than females, but their plumages are alike. This species is the biggest gull of all and the blackest on back; legs pale pink.

In winter adults stand out due to their size, white head and black back; young have a long black bill, a pale head and chequered upperparts.

This is the big, dominant gull of north and west coasts, but in winter it is also found in eastern estuaries and, increasingly, inland. It is a little longer than the lesser black-back but its bulk can make it look 'twice as big' (see weight); the breadth of the body is striking when standing or swimming head on.

winter it is very widespread, with over half of the European population on the shores of Britain, especially on the east coast.

Lesser Black-backed Gull

❋

LARUS FUSCUS

Slightly longer-winged than the herring gull. The best clue from beneath is darker primaries. Dark grey blends into blacker wingtips above, with small white spots.

As a breeding bird, the lesser black-backed gull is best known on Welsh islands, northern moors and thickly-vegetated areas above cliffs; it is less of a cliff-ledge breeder than the herring gull and is more likely to be surrounded by bluebells and campion as it sits on its eggs. Many leave Britain in winter,

though now thousands do stay to feed at Midland tips and to roost on large reservoirs. On most coasts it is simply a passage migrant. The summer adult, with soft slate-grey

back, and legs and beak of vivid yellow, is a most handsome bird and an elegant addition to the summer coastal scene. Juvenile birds are very dark and black-billed; in the winter they have all-dark flight feathers, unlike young herring gulls, and by the following autumn they are dark grey on the back like their parents, though still brown-winged and with black tail bands. In winter, adults have grey-brown heads and much duller yellow legs. A few birds from the southern Baltic may be seen in autumn, recognisable by their long wings, blacker backs and unstreaked white heads.

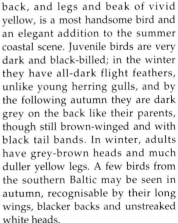

Longer-winged and shorter-legged than the herring gull. Slim and low-slung; legs yellow; red ring round eye; spot on bill. Shows white patches during autumn moult.

Length: 50-52cm; **Weight:** 600-1,000g
Where to look: islands, lakes and reservoirs, coasts, tips. **Nest:** on ground, on islands and moors, colonial. **Eggs:** 3, blotched brown. **Food:** fish, offal, worms, eggs, seabirds. **Voice:** deeper, more throaty calls than herring gull, abrupt *ow-ow-ow, kyoww;* longer wailing notes and squeals.

Kittiwake

※

LARUS TRIDACTYLA

At any great seabird colony, the most numerous species is likely to be the kittiwake. Vast ranks of gleaming white birds on ridiculously tiny, precarious nests, and hundreds more wheeling over the sea, create an eye-catching spectacle and a great volume of noise, all the birds calling their name (or perhaps it's sorry I'm late') in yodelling, nasal tones. It seems unlikely that a kittiwake will be misidentified, even when it goes to bathe or find nesting material at a nearby lake. But, from time to time, kittiwakes are seen inland, usually adults in early spring, or immature birds in autumn or winter after gales, and they frequently pass headlands a long way offshore. The bounding, banking flight (if there is a good wind), the mid-grey back fading out towards the wingtips, and protruding head and neck (looking brilliant white in summer) then make an adult identifiable a mile away — even if you cannot see the black legs and wingtips that would confirm it. Real birds of the sea, kittiwakes — unlike many gulls — do not scrounge at refuse tips or feed on beaches.

Black legs, yellow bill and 'dipped in ink' tips of wings identify adult; dark eyes, round shape, give head gentle expression.

Colonies found on sheer cliffs with nests on tiny ledges, often thousands of pairs; constant noise and activity make kittiwakes unmistakable.

Length: 38-40cm; **Weight:** 350-425g
Where to look: at sea; in summer on cliffs, beaches; in winter, harbours. **Nest:** on sheer cliff. **Eggs:** 2, spotted. **Food:** fish, offal from trawlers — not a tideline scavenger. **Voice:** quiet mew and ringing *kitti-way-ake.*

Common Gull

※

LARUS CANUS

Looking like a small, gentler version of the herring gull, the common gull is far less widespread as a nesting bird and only found over most of England and Wales outside the breeding season. It is not at all common in some inland areas, though often abundant on the coast and in some eastern counties, frequenting pastures and sports field where flocks spread out in search of worms. They are now seen more often in towns and on housing estates in winter. The greenish legs and bill, with no red spot, confirm that an adult is no herring gull, though in practice even at long range the slim shape, dark eye and darker back give it a quite distinctive look. Young birds have neat and attractive bands of brown, pale-edged wing coverts, and at first a scaly brown back, but this turns grey by the autumn; by the following spring the grey is often darker than the sun-bleached wings, which can be almost cream-coloured with pale, brown tips (on a young Mediterranean gull the back is always very pale). In winter, the head and upper breast of adults are heavily soiled with grey-brown streaks.

Wingtips have large black and white patches, more black than herring gull beneath; fluent flight.

Smaller than herring gull, back a shade darker with bolder white patches; greenish bill and long wings.

Length: 40-42cm; **Weight:** 350-450g
Where to look: lakes, coasts, farmland, tips. **Nest:** on ground near coast or on moor. **Eggs:** 3, blotched olive-brown. **Food:** insects, worms, fish, scraps. **Voice:** high, squealing calls shriller than larger gulls.

Sandwich Tern

❀

STERNA SANDVICENSIS

Length: 36-38cm
Weight: 210-250g
Where to look: all coasts; dunes, coastal lagoons. **Nest:** on ground, scrape in sand; in large colonies. **Eggs:** 1-2, mottled. **Food:** small fish, such as sand eels. **Voice:** rasping *kierr-ink* or *kirrick* is distinctive; short *kik*.

The Sandwich tern is the largest of the terns found regularly in Britain, and when flying over the sea or standing on a beach is noticeably the palest. Its whiteness is the best identification feature, along with the yellow-tipped black bill. The rhythm of the quick, double, or nearly triple call in late March or early April is also an instant pointer that the first Sandwich terns are back after their long winter in West Africa. Most birds reared the previous summer will spend their first year of life in the winter quarters, sometimes as far as South Africa (even on the east coast). In 1962 nearly 6,000 pairs bred in Britain and Ireland, then the highest 20th-century figure, but since then numbers have increased and are now stable at around 15,000 pairs. They are greatly helped by protection of their colonies on coastal dunes and lagoons, though they have a tendency to shift site for no very obvious reason after several years. Like all terns, they seem highly-strung, unpredictable birds, quick to take alarm and easily disturbed by insensitive intruders.

In direct flight, bill held level and wing-beats regular and strong: when fishing, looks down with bill pointing at water.

Tail deeply forked, but streamers short. Wingtips streaked with black, increasingly by autumn as paler grey gradually wears away.

Large, angular, long-winged and short-tailed; very pale; purer white beneath than common or Arctic terns; long head and bill.

Long, black bill with yellow tip unlike any other tern's; legs black; crested black cap.

Little Tern

❀

STERNA ALBIFRONS

Short yellow legs unique. Bill may show signs of black winter colour in autumn.

Often dives into breaking waves right at edge of beach; likes shelving shingle beach for fishing and nesting, but also breeds on sandier spots.

Yellow bill with very small black tip unlike any other tern's. Very pale except for strip of black along front of outer wing and black cap.

The little tern was once Britain's rarest breeding sea-bird, and its position is still near the foot of the table, but with recent special protection measures its numbers have increased again to over 2,000 pairs. Because they like to nest on stretches of fine beach and shingle ridges, they are always subject to human disturbance in summer — people tend to like exactly the same beaches on a hot weekend — and many of their colonies have only succeeded after being roped off and dotted with polite 'Keep Out' notices. In general, people have responded well, but the other problem — unusually high tides sweeping away eggs and chicks — is not so easy to guard against. Some colonies have even become the target of kestrels, and few chicks have been reared. Little terns arrive in Britain in April and leave by September, going south to spend the winter in the rich fishing grounds along the West African coasts. There they join others from most European coasts and also inland breeders from parts of France, Spain, Italy and eastern Europe. As with other terns, the one-year-olds remain all year in their southern quarters, enjoying the sun and surf.

Length: 25cm; **Weight:** 50-60g
Where to look: sandy and pebbly coasts, shallow coastal lagoons. **Nest:** on ground, sand or shingle. **Eggs:** 2-3, buff with dark spots. **Food:** small fish. **Voice:** fast, chattering *kirrikiki*, high, *quick kik-kik, kyik.*

Common Tern

❄

STERNA HIRUNDO

Arriving in April and leaving by October, the common tern is as much a harbinger of spring as the swallow. It is very widespread, but tends to be more southerly than the closely similar Arctic tern, and is much more often seen inland, but arctic terns do move through Britain on migration in April and May and large numbers sometimes appear briefly at reservoirs. It is always as well to check a tern's identify carefully, but good views are needed to see the details of bill colour and wing translucency; the pattern of the upper wing is more useful. Young birds are sometimes easier to separate than adults. Common terns often swoop for insects when inland, but usually they catch fish, hovering before a headlong dive. Their dives are more hesitant than the plunges of arctic and Sandwich terns. A tern colony has an air of belligerence and hectic activity about it; intruders are spotted from afar and greeted with noisy swoops from the brave, offended birds. They mix elegance with pugnacity. They are easily disturbed and colonies should be left well alone, though those on offshore islands can often be watched from the shore with no risk of harm being done.

Colonies along the north Norfolk coast are among the largest and strongest in Britain. Visitors to Blakeney Point, for example, can see hundreds of birds, some nesting alongside little terns and black-headed gulls.

Wingtips more streaked than on arctic tern, especially in autumn.

Inner primaries paler than outer ones, with central dark streak or wedge often obvious — useful as this is not seen on Arctic tern.

Slender, with a black cap and forked tail; more buoyant and slower flight than gulls; slim, pointed bill.

By late autumn adults show dark patch on front of wing, a white forehead and black bill.

Bill orange-red with black tip; rarely darker or without black.

Young bird much shorter-tailed and blunter-winged than adult; much browner in appearance.

Length: 32-33cm;
Weight: 100-140g
Where to look: coasts, lakes. **Nest:** on ground, often on island. **Eggs:** 3, mottled buffish or olive. **Food:** small fish and insects from water surface. **Voice:** short, sharp *kit, kikik;* high, grating, emphatic *KEEY-yah.*

Juvenile bird has ginger-brown tinge; bill pale orange with black tip; grey line near back of wing, so palest part is the centre.

Arctic Tern

❋

STERNA PARADISAEA

Summer adult has blood-red bill, a little shorter than common tern's and with no black tip; head smaller and more rounded on short, thick neck. Wings longer and tapering to more pointed tip.

Calls similar, but arctic has a more whistling, upward inflection to some notes at colony.

Shorter head and bill and longer tail give Arctic different flight shape from common, and wings are paler and cleaner at the tip.

All Arctic tern's flight feathers are pale and translucent from below (not just a central patch), and the dark trailing edge is thin and tapered.

Differences very subtle, but the heavier, broader-winged shape of common and rounder head of arctic become useful with experience.

dagger-like bill.

F ew birds exceed the elegance of the arctic tern — yet few exceed its vehemence in defence of its eggs and chicks. For many people a memorable experience is a visit to the Farne Islands, where the terns are almost tame enough to be touched; yet, should someone venture too close to the colony, they are quite ready to dive down and draw blood with that dagger-like bill. A few pairs are scattered among nesting common terns on southern coasts, but most are in the innumerable small colonies, and a few very large ones, around the Scottish and Irish coasts, especially in Orkney and Shetland. For several years in the 1980s the largest Shetland colony failed to rear chicks due to a lack of sand eels of a suitable size to feed to them. Orkney colonies suffered a similar fate, but eventually had a good year to make up the losses. Arctic terns nest as far north as any bird, but move so far south that a few get caught up in the strong westerlies of the South Atlantic and end up in Australia. They undertake one of the most enormous migrations of any bird.

Length: 32-35cm; **Weight:** 80-110g
Where to look: coasts, rocky islands. On migration in spring may visit inland lakes.
Nest: on ground, on rocks or shingly beach.
Eggs: 2, spotted and mottled brown and black. **Food:** small fish, especially sand eels. **Voice**: nasal, grating *pee-airr, kik, rising kee kee, keeyah.* Colonies very noisy.

Roseate Tern

❋

STERNA DOUGALLII

T he beautiful roseate tern is now very rare and the causes of its continued decline are not fully understood — which means that efforts to protect it are not always successful. Some — probably far too many — are killed in winter in Ghana, where small boys catch them in snares and with baited hooks on fishing lines. At the colonies in Britain they are killed by peregrines, foxes and rats. In Ireland some colonies have been deserted, for no clear reason. Yet there may be some other, unknown cause for a long-term decline in many parts of the wide range of this tern. It is a lovely bird, especially in spring, with extremely long tail streamers and a pink flush on the otherwise very white underparts. The very pale back and whiteness of its breast help to distinguish individuals in mixed tern flock. Bill colour (though with nearly as much bright red as a common tern's in late summer), flight action, wing pattern and other subtle differences also help to confirm the identify of an adult. Juveniles are coarsely marked and have dark foreheads, black bills and black legs.

Bill black in spring, dark red at base in summer, then half red.

Long bill, round head and long tail give recognisable profile.

Shorter, blunter wings than common or Arctic; flight action quicker and stiffer, with fast hover almost like little tern. Wingtip has blackish marks on top, but a white edge (no black) beneath – unlike common or Arctic terns.

Shape similar to Sandwich with long bill and black cap smoothed down over nape, rather chesty appearance — subtly different.

Length: 33-38cm; **Weight:** 95-130g
Where to look: rare away from colonies on rocky islets. **Nest:** in hollow, crevice, or under vegetation on ground. **Eggs:** 1 or 2, cream, blotched darker. **Food:** small fish.
Voice: distinct rasping *aakh* and whistled *chiv-y, chewit.*

Guillemot

✳

URIA AALGE

Birds with white
'spectacles' (detail below)
are known as 'bridled'
guillemots. Their
frenquency increases from
south to north, but the
reason is unclear.

Guillemots usually nest on narrow, densely packed ledges in colonies sometimes numbering tens of thousands of birds. The ledges are often so densely occupied that birds may be in physical contact with several neighbours, thereby defending the smallest-known nest area territory of any bird.

The guillemot's egg is perfectly designed for the bird's precarious nest site. It is pointed at one end, rounded at the other and rather flat-sided. If it rolls, it tends to do so in a circle, thereby avoiding the danger of rolling off the cliff.

On land the guillemot may appear rather awkward. In the water, however, it is streamlined and an excellent swimmer.

At colonies – sometimes numbering hundreds of noisy, squabbling and sparring birds – it breeds on tightly packed ledges.

In summer, adults in southern Britain have warm chocolate-brown upperparts, gradually becoming darker in colour further north, and almost black in Scotland.

Egg shape may have evolved to prevent it rolling off ledges, or perhaps as a consequence of the size and shape of the adult's body.

In winter, chin, throat and sides of neck are white. Note the dark line running back from the eye.

The colonies are all action, the birds noisy and aggressive, stabbing at neighbours with their dagger-like bills. This appears vicious, but they seldom seem to be injured. In contrast, paired birds commonly preen their partner's head and neck feathers most delicately (this is called allopreening). Like razorbills, guillemots are strong, but not agile, fliers and are superbly adapted for life in the sea. Underwater they are strong swimmers, propelled by feet and wings, and capable of diving to depths of over 50 metres (160ft). Like razorbills, the largest colonies are in northern Britain, particularly in Scotland. The numbers of birds have increased at many northern and eastern colonies, but the western colonies have shown little change. In the smaller colonies in the south, the declines recorded earlier this century appear to have halted. The breeding population of Britain and Ireland exceeds 700,000 birds, but guillemots are always vunerable to oil-spills.

Length: 38-41cm; **Weight:** 750-1,000g
Where to look: cliffs and sea at breeding colonies (March to July); otherwise out to sea. **Nest**: on cliff ledges, less often among boulders. **Egg**: 1, extremely variable colours. **Food:** mainly fish. **Voice:** prolonged whirring *aaargh*.

Black Guillemot

✳

CEPPHUS GRYLLE

The black guillemot, or tystie, as it is also known, is the most sedentary of Britain's auks, and the only one with white wing patches. It is widespread along the rocky shores of north and west Scotland and Ireland. In Wales it breeds only in Anglesey, and in England only at St Bees Head, Cumbria.

Tysties are usually seen singly or in small groups, but they do not nest together in large numbers like the other auks. They dive for food, usually submerging for up to a minute, and prefer the shallower inshore waters. The white patch on the wings makes it possible to follow diving birds underwater if watched from a clifftop using binoculars. Butterfish and sand eels are the most frequently taken foods. Only one fish at a time is brought to the chicks, and this is usually carried crosswise in the bill. Occasionally, a parent bringing food may be robbed by another parent from a neighbouring nest. Tysties are vulnerable to oil spillages near the shore and their eggs and young may be eaten by introduced mink, but are otherwise fairly free to enjoy their seaside existence.

Length: 30-32cm; **Weight**: 340-45 g
Where to look: on cliffs, boulder-strewn shores or on sea. **Nest**: in a crevice or among boulders, occasionally under driftwood. **Eggs**: 2, white. **Food**: mainly fish.
Voice: variety of high-pitched whistles.

In winter, appears pale grey, but retains the white wing patches.

The vermilion gape is only likely to be seen during threat or courtship display.

At close range, the adult's bright-red feet are even visible through the water when the bird is swimming or diving.

In summer plumage resembles a striking black, pigeon-sized auk, with white wing patches and red feet. Flies fast and low over water.

Razorbill

✳

ALCA TORDA

The square-ended, jet-black bill has two black and one white vertical ridges, and a white line joins the bill and eye.

Razorbills nest on cliffs and among bouldrs, usually in colonies with other seabirds, especially guillemots and kittiwakes. Although seldom as numerous as guillemots, some colonies number several thousand birds. The larger colonies are in northern England, Scotland and Ireland. Some colonies in Wales and southern England are now much smaller than earlier this century. At the colonies, birds are noisy and often quarrelsome, disputing territories with intruders or neighbours. They are rather ungainly on land, and though swift and strong fliers they lack manoeuvrability in the air. Landing usually requires several attempts, using tail and feet to aid control. They are at their most adept in the sea, where they dive for food, swimming underwater using feet and half-open wings. Outside the breeding season, birds disperse widely at sea, some travelling to the Bay of Biscay and even as far as the Mediterranean. Around 100,000 pairs of razorbills probably breed in Britain and Ireland – about 20 per cent of the world population. Overall, numbers appear to have changed little recently, although birds are often killed by oil pollution and by being trapped in fishing nets.

Length: 37-39cm; **Weight**: 590-730g
Where to look: cliffs and sea at breeding colonies (April to July); otherwise out to sea. **Nest**: in crevice, on ledge, or among boulders. **Egg**: 1, boldly blotched. **Food**: mainly fish. **Voice**: a deep growling *gurrrrrr* at colonies.

Between August and March the chin, throat and sides of the neck become white, and the markings along and across the bill fade into dull grey.

In summer, the razorbill's velvet black head, wings and back contrast with silky white below. Best distinguished from guillemot by the bill shape and pattern.

Puffin

❉

FRATERCULA ARCTICA

Standing on a grassy slope outside its burrow, the puffin is unmistakable. It is Britain's most colourful seabird, comical to watch and naturally inquisitive. The main colonies are in northern Scotland, the largest on St Kilda, west of the Outer Hebrides. Last century, St Kilda may have held over one million pairs, but now there are probably about one fifth that number. Numbers also declined earlier this century at other colonies, especially in southern England and Wales. The decline now appears to have halted, and some northern colonies may be increasing. The decline was probably caused by climatic change influencing sea temperature, which affected the distribution of fish rather than by pesticides or oil pollution. About 700,000 puffins now breed in Britain and Ireland. Most nest in burrows, many of which are regularly occupied from year to year. The birds may excavate the burrows themselves, or use those of Manx shearwaters or rabbits, with whom they sometimes share a common entrance. Early in the breeding season thousands of birds may be present on one day and almost none on the next. July is the best month to watch them. By mid-August they have left the colony, not to return to land until the following March.

Usually stands upright on land. Moves by shuffling or waddling, but may run, flapping wings.

The large, powerful bill is slightly hooked to help hold slippery prey. The feet are strong and used for swimming, for extra control when flying and for executing burrows. Puffins walk, and sometimes run, standing upright on their feet alone rather than using their legs and feet like other auks.

In flight, the large head and bill give a rounded profile to the front. The underside of the wing is darker than other auks'.

Adults may suddenly take flight, circling the colony in wheeling flocks of thousands of birds.

The triangular red, yellow and blue bill, white face, curious eye markings, black head, back and wings, white undersides and bright-red feet make puffins quite unmistakable. Amusing to watch, they walk with a waddle, display, fight each other, and cock their heads to one side to watch you watching them.

As evening approaches, puffins gather at their burrow entrances.

Length: 26-9 cm; **Weight:** 310-490g
Where to look: at colonies on grassy slopes or cliffs or on the sea from March to August. Attendance can be erratic, especially early in the season. Birds most numerous in early evenings in July. **Nest:** in a burrow 1-2 metres (36ft) long, less often in crevices on cliffs. **Eggs:** 1. Food: mainly fish, but also crustaceans. **Voice:** a low nasal *kaa–arr–arr* at the colonies, silent elsewhere.

Woodpigeon

❊

COLUMBA PALUMBUS

Shot in thousands, woodpigeons are reluctant to allow man too close. Yet when unmolested, in a town park or public grounds, they quickly become approachable. Only then does the full beauty and size of this pigeon become apparent. The dash and agility shown in a sudden, noisy escape flight through a shrubbery should hardly fail to impress — but pigeons are pigeons, and usually ignored!

Town woodpigeons start to nest in February with a peak in April and May. Rural birds start later, peaking from July to September. This is due to the different availability of food.

These pigeons have been thoroughly studied. They are very agile in trees, but feed mainly on the ground. Flocks have subordinate birds in front, with slower pecking rates than the birds in front, with slower pecking rates than the dominant pigeons. Their feeding rate increases to a peak just before they fly to roost, but most feed is taken in the afternoon. In the autumn stubble, only five to ten per cent of the daylight is spent feeding; but in winter ninety five per cent is spent feeding on pastures, and a little less in richer habitats.

When it takes to the wing in fright, the woodpigeon's wings may make a loud clattering sound.

Crescents of white on wing and the adult's neck patch are unique. The tail has a pale central band with a dark tip.

Underwing soft grey; head well forward on thin neck.

Large, heavy, deep-chested pigeon with long, broad tail. Bigger-bodied and smaller-headed than falcons and sparrowhawks.

Looks grey at a distance, but close views reveal browner back, pink breast, attractive eye and bill colour and a smooth appearance.

Length: 40-42cm;
Weight: 480-550g
Where to look: farmland with trees, woods, parks. **Nest:** thin platform of sticks in tree. **Eggs:** 1-2, white. Food: leaves, seeds, berries, buds, grain. **Voice:** *coo COOO coo, coo-coo*, in series, last with an extra *oo* at end.

Rock Dove/Feral Pigeon

❋
COLUMBA LIVIA

Feral pigeons occur in many colours.

Often has white rump and bars on wings; can be brown, white or pied.

The true rock dove is now restricted to northern coasts and islets. It has a blue body, greyer back, black wingbars and a white rump. The underwing is white, unlike the stock dove. Domestic birds gone wild (feral) often look very similar, reverting to this type on cliffs, but racers and town birds are all sorts of colours. All are swift, powerful fliers with the most pointed, swept-back wings of any large pigeon.

The rock dove is the ancestor of all tame and town pigeons. Escaped racing and dovecot pigeons long ago established themselves back in the wild, living off man's scraps in the cities or finding more natural places in quarries, or even on the sea cliffs where wild rock doves live. They provide colour and life in many a railway station or city street, but leave rather a mess, so they get no thanks in return. But the gleaming red eye of a pigeon is always worth a look! On the cliffs, they have inter-bred with the wild birds until many populations have become so tainted with domestic stock that few 'wild' birds remain. This is a pity, as rock doves are immaculate birds, more beautiful than many more highly-praised species and living a dramatic life in magnificent coastal cliff surroundings. Feral pigeons are treated as if they are not birds at all — no bird book does them justice — yet they are at least as much 'British birds' as pheasants and little owls. The wild rock dove is widespread, occurring in a variety of forms from Britain's seaboard to Alpine peaks and African desert cliffs.

Length: 31-34cm; **Weight:** 250-350g
Where to look: cliffs, fields, towns, quarries. **Nest:** on ledge in cave, on building. **Eggs:** 2, white. **Food:** cereals, seeds, buds, taken from ground. **Voice:** moaning *oorh* or *oh–oo–oor*, longer crooning in display.

Stock Dove

❋
COLUMBA OENAS

On the ground it looks a darker, bluer bird than the woodpigeon, with a shorter tail, rounder body and a neater shape.

Flight is fast; quicker action than woodpigeon.

Upperside shows pale centre and blackish edges to wings; no white, but two small bars near body.

Length: 32-34cm; **Weight:** 290-330g
Where to look: fields, woods, open spaces near gravel pits. **Nest:** hole in tree, ledge of cliff or building. **Eggs:** 2, white. **Food:** seeds, leaves, buds, flowers. **Voice:** deep series of *ooo–uh* or *orr–wump* calls, second note abrupt.

The stock dove is best-known as a bird of farmland and parkland with old trees, which give it nest sites in cavities and holes where branches have been wrenched away in gales. But it is also at home wherever a cliff ledge or cavity provides room to lay its glossy eggs, so long as this is within easy flying distance of suitable feeding grounds. Consequently, it can be seen, rather unexpectedly, high up on moorland crags or even on sea cliffs. The stock dove often visits open pools, such as new gravel pits, to drink at the water's edge. It is less likely to become tame or to live in a park than the woodpigeon.

Often overlooked, stock doves become easy to spot with practice — in flight they look like neat, rounded pigeons without the speed and dash of a racing pigeon, but far less ponderous, shorter-tailed and rounder-headed than the bigger, more numerous woodpigeon. On the ground, they are likely to be seen in pairs rather than huge flocks (though occasionally up to a hundred or two may gather together), and in good light, they look a lovely shade of slightly purplish blue. The call is also a give-away, especially from the depths of a big tree or from an overgrown quarry face. It has a loud, almost booming quality about it, with a rhythmic pattern quite unlike the lazy crooning of the woodpigeon.

The collared dove arrived in Britain in the 1950s. Its spread across Europe, from ancestral dry, hot habitats in India, to a cooler, damper environment closely connected with man and split grain, has been well documented. By 1964 about 3,000 pairs were breeding in Britain; by 1972 there were between 30,000 and 40,000 pairs, but the increase was beginning to ease off. The north-westward spread took the bird to the Faroes and Iceland, but the cause of the phenomenal expansion has not been fully explained. Collared doves are gregarious and good feeding sites attract flocks even in the breeding season. Town centres and open country where other pigeons are common are usually avoided, but gardens, shrubberies, allotments and farms are eagerly sought; these doves often come to birdtables. Unless persecuted, they become very approachable, but the monotonous *ku–koo–kuk* calls can be tiresome just after dawn in mid-summer, and are also the chief cause of over-optimistic reports of early cuckoos! The breeding season is very prolonged and there may be three, sometimes even six, broods of two young each reared by a single pair each year.

Pale grey-fawn with pink breast and thin black half-ring on neck.

Head paler and wingtips darker than basic colour; tail rather long, with white corners on top and black base with broad white tip below.

Small, slim dove with long broad wings and long tail held closed in normal flight. Flight active, with quick, rhythmic wing-beats, wings quite bowed or arched.

Collared Dove

❋

STREPTOPELIA DECAOCTO

Length: 31-33cm; **Weight:** 150-220g
Where to look: suburbs with conifers, parks, farms. **Nest:** in tree, near trunk.
Eggs: 2, white. **Food:** grain, seeds, fruits.
Voice: ku-KOO-kuk, abrupt at end; nasal *kwurr* or *ghee-gheee* in alarm and in gliding display.

Often seen in flocks in late spring, migrating along coasts; then in feeding parties in late summer on arable land.

Turtle Dove

❋

STREPTOPELIA TURTUR

As the pleasant cawing of rooks epitomises spring in wooded parkland and the bubbling of the curlew is the essence of early summer in the hills, so the long, rolling, deep song of the turtle dove means high summer in the country lanes of southern England. The main problem for the turtle dove, other than cool, wet summers that reduce the breeding success, is that the tall, ancient hedges which it loves so well are often grubbed out, so that there is less room for it than ever before. It needs big hawthorns, unkempt elders and small trees in farmland or on the edge of a broken, sunny wood if it is to survive in the face of agricultural change. Though happy to forage in the quiet lanes of a village, it is unlikely to nest close to human habitation and is far less of a garden bird than the collared dove. In the winter it makes for the Sahel, south of the Sahara, where the droughts of recent years, compounded by loss of forest and scrub may also affect its numbers. However, in some African areas large concentrations still occur. Sadly, huge numbers are illegally killed in southern Europe each spring.

Note blue on wing.

Upperside neatly patterned with light orange-brown and black; head pink.

Pattern recalls kestrel, but flight and shape quite different.

Agile dove, quick to fly off if disturbed, quieter than pigeon, but some clatter of wings; has no flight call, unlike the collared dove.

Length: 26-28cm; **Weight:** 130-180g
Where to look: woodland edge, lowland farmland, hedges. **Nest:** in hedge or tree.
Eggs: 1-2, white. **Food:** weed seeds, buds, leaves, cereals. **Voice:** purring song *coorrrr–coorrrr*, rather deep, lazy.

Cuckoo

❋

CUCULUS CANORUS

Cuckoos, wandering voices of the summer, are brood parasites, laying their eggs in the nest of other species, which raise their young for them. When the young cuckoos hatch they push out any other eggs or young they find in the nest, becoming the sole occupant. Cuckoos ususally choose the nests of the host species that brought them up, and their eggs will usually closely resemble the eggs of that species. Young cuckoos bear a close resemblence to sparrowhawks and even have the same white nape patch; this may be a disguise which helps to protect them from enemies. Cuckos are more often heard than seen and most views are of a slim grey bird flying away and directly into a tree or bush. Males and females are virtually alike, but the female can occur in a rare chestnut brown or 'hepatic' colour form. Cuckoos feed on hairy caterpillars that are poisonous to other birds. Their stomachs are protected from the irritating hairs of the caterpillars by a protective lining which can be shed and renewed.

Cuckoos start calling soon after their arrival in late April. They continue for another six weeks or so before becoming silent. By July, adult birds are beginning to contemplate the return trip to their wintering grounds.

The male keeps its bill closed, waves its tail from side to side and sways when calling.

The male's familiar call and the less well-known bubbling chuckle of the female are often all that indicates their presence.

Adult males are grey above and white with dark barring below. When perched, they tend to hold their tail above their wingtips.

Cuckoos are slender; with pointed wings, a long tail and a low, direct flight with shallow wing-beats. They are often confused with hawks.

Juveniles are dark grey-brown or rufous above, with dark barring and a white nape patch.

The young cuckoo will eject other eggs or young from the nest.

Length: 33cm; **Weight:** 105-13 g
Where to look: woods, dunes, farmland, moorland, reed beds. **Nest:** none of its own; parasitic on other birds. **Eggs:** 15-25 laid, one per foster-nest. Colour varies with host species. **Food:** mostly caterpillars and other insects. **Voice:** male has familiar *cu-coo*, female has a rich, liquid bubbling call.

Barn Owl

TYTO ALBA

The barn owl is one of the most widely distributed birds in the world. Those in Britain are at the extreme north-west edge of the range in Europe, and Scottish barn owls are probably the most northerly in the world. Sadly, in many areas the barn owl is now very scarce, or has gone altogether. This decline is known to have been going on for over 50 years, but it has clearly accelerated in the last 25 years or so. It is not known whether any long-term factor such as climate is involved, nor is it easy to be totally clear about other, more short-term causes. But it seems highly likely that the enormous changes in agriculture, especially in arable farming, during the last 20-30 years are at the root of the matter. The loss of prey-rich field edges and corners, rough pastures and similar areas has been critical; this habitat loss has been exacerbated by pesticides and also by the loss of nest sites as hedgerow trees disappear and farm buildings are pulled down, modernised or converted. Persecution has probably been minimal: barn owls have long been welcomed as neighbours on farmland. More research into barn owl habitat needs, and co-operative work with farmers, may provide some answers and some remedies.

Seen well, a barn owl is unmistakable. Note large, round-topped head with characteristic heart-shaped face and dark eyes, very long legs (looks 'knock-kneed' when seen from front). Always looks extremely pale and flashes ghostly white in car headlights — but beware deceptively pale look of all owls in headlights at night. Very rare snowy owl is much bigger and bulkier; male all white, female and young barred; yellow eyes.

Owls have relatively long, muscular legs; in most species (all those in Britain) these are feathered to the base of the toes — the reason for this is not fully understood.

The toes are powerful and equipped with long, sharp talons. The outer toe is reversible, giving a better grip on prey.

The barn owl's extraordinarily well-developed sense of hearing may be more important in hunting than vision: prey located by ear can be caught in total darkness.

The call of the barn owl is popularly described as a blood-curdling shriek, but is not familiar to many people. A variety of snores and hisses come from the nest site.

No nest as such: bird lays on floor, ledge, beam in building etc.

Nesting barn owls require freedom from disturbance: nest visits are illegal without licence.

Prey may be carried in bill as owl flies up, but is usually quickly transferred to one foot while carried to nest; then passed to bill again on arrival.

Length: 33-37cm; **Weight:** 250-350g
Where to look: mainly farmland, field edges, rough grassland. **Nest:** hole in tree, sometimes in quarries, or in ruins, barns or other outbuildings. **Eggs:** 4-7, white. **Food:** mainly rodents. **Voice:** snores, shrieks.

Eggs are laid at intervals of 2-3 days, but incubation begins with first egg laid: this results in a staggered hatch — first owlet in family eight days older than eighth.

Tawny Owl

✿

STRIX ALUCO

Adaptability can be the key to a species' success; this is certainly the case with the tawny owl. Originally purely a woodland bird, it has moved out into many man-modified habitats in the lowlands and, despite being absent from Ireland, is easily the commonest and most widespread of Britain's owls. It even lives in parks and large gardens in the hearts of cities. Woodland tawny owls feed mainly on wood mice and bank voles, but elsewhere they adapt readily to whatever small mammal species are available; in towns and cities they prey on small birds.

Tawny owls are thoroughly nocturnal and are thus seldom seen in daylight, unless found at a roost, where their presence may be revealed by the mobbing behaviour of small birds. After dark, they can often be found on the regular perches on their nightly 'beat', but are usually hard to see in treetops and other thick cover. They are more often heard than seen: the commonest call is a loud *kewick*. The tremulous, far-carrying song, so beloved of TV sound effects men, is almost too well-known to require description. The word 'hooting' scarcely does it justice, however. Occasionally an owl will hoot in the middle of the day, but the full performance is reserved until after dark.

Length: 37-39cm; **Weight:** 350-500g
Where to look: woods, parks, gardens, villages, towns — any area with trees.
Nest: in hole in tree, sometimes in ground or in building. Will use nestbox.**Eggs:** 2-5, white. Food: usually small mammals, but versatile enough to switch to birds in towns.
Voice: the commonest call is loud *kewick*. Song is loud, far-carrying musical *hoooo . . . hoo-hoo huhoooo..*

Plumage variable, but 'tawny' is a misnomer. May be more chestnut than shown, or much greyer. Note big rounded head, black eyes and stocky appearance.

Superb camouflage helps to hide tawny owl at (often regular) roosting place. Presence may be given away, however, by gathering of small birds mobbing owl and alarm-calling continuously.

Little Owl

✿

ATHENE NOCTUA

Small size, rather broad and flat-topped head readily distinguish the little owl. Usually looks squat and dumpy — yellow eyes very obvious. Habit of using conspicuous daytime perches a good identification point.

Over much of central and southern England, the little owl is much the most likely owl to be seen by the average birdwatcher. Although it does much of its hunting after dark, it is often abroad well before dusk, especially in summer. This is not a native British bird, but owes its presence here to a series of introductions during the latter half of the 19th century. Its spread has been limited by bouts of persecution, by occasional severe winters and by the use of agricultural pesticides. It may also have lost some ground in areas where intensive arable farming has caused widespread changes in habitat and, especially perhaps, the loss of old hedgerow trees. While it is a common and widespread bird in other parts of Europe, its distribution here is much more confined to the lowlands and — a direct reflection of the high proportion of insects and other invertebrates in its diet — is clearly also related to climatic conditions, especially winter temperatures. The loud, clear calls of this owl are not familiar to most people, yet give one of the best means of locating a pair in spring. They have a distinctive, clear quality and carry far, yet even experienced birdwatchers are often left puzzled by the sound.

Dumpy in flight, with its blunt head and rounded wings. Quick wing-beats, and characteristic heavy, bounding flight action.

Length: 21-23cm; **Weight:** 150-200g
Where to look: farmland, field edges, semi–open habitat with scattered trees, quarries, waste ground, etc. **Nest:** hole in tree, bank, cliff, or ground. May use nestbox.
Eggs: 2-5, white. **Food:** small mammals and birds, but also many insects and other invertebrates, including earthworms. **Voice:** song is repeated, plaintive *kiu*. Call is loud, ringing *werro*.

Long-eared Owl

❋

ASIO OTUS

Very often the first clue to the presence of this elusive bird is the 'squeaky gate' call of the young waiting to be fed. Breeding long-eared owls easily escape detection — the song period is short, and the low, cooing song quiet. Even the male's aerial display flying and wing-clapping can pass unnoticed. The birdwatcher's task is made no easier by the bird's strongly nocturnal habits and the fact that it chooses to nest in dense cover, generally preferring plantations and copses, but also using larger woods, shelterbelts and thick, tall scrub or bushes. Winter roosts, often in traditional sites, usually provide the best chance of seeing these owls, although birds feeding young may appear well before dark (and after dawn): hunting takes place over open areas, not in thick cover. The ear-tufts can be raised or lowered and the facial discs opened or closed, according to mood; alarmed birds often assume a characteristically slim, upright posture. In a tangled willow thicket

In flight, long-winged, but darker on underparts than short-eared owl.

Length: 35-37cm; **Weight:** 220-300g
Where to look: plantations, woods, copses, etc. **Nest:** old nest of magpie, crow; in some areas in cover on ground. **Eggs:** 3-5, white. **Food:** mainly voles, also other small mammals and birds. **Voice:** song is low, quiet cooing.

Facial discs are mobile, giving different expressions: open with ear-tufts erect when alarmed, shut and tufts down when relaxed. Orange eyes are often concealed by partly closed eyelids. Superb camouflage in tree foliage.

or hawthorn scrub they blend in amazingly well; even in a green pine they are surprisingly hard to spot.

Short-eared Owl

❋

ASIO FLAMMEUS

Unlike the long-eared owl, this bird is not too difficult to see. It is often abroad in full daylight and can be very conspicuous as it hunts over the open moors, heaths, rough grasslands and young plantations where it breeds, or the coastal marshes where it is often found in winter. The principal prey of the short-eared owl is, in most areas, the short-tailed vole. It is the abundance or otherwise of this small mammal which governs both the numbers and breeding of the owl: in years when voles are plentiful, short-eared owls will several numbers of eggs and rear large families. Similarly, the amount

Pale underwing very like long-eared owl, but upperwing looks more barred and underparts whiter.

Ear-tufts very small; seldom seen except on wary or alarmed bird.

In flight, typically looks pale and long-winged, moving buoyantly; perches on posts or level ground.

Always nests on ground in thick cover. Like other owls, male hunts for family and female remains at nest with young.

Yellow eyes surprisingly obvious, even on flying bird.

Length: 37-39cm; **Weight:** 280-350g
Where to look: open moorland, rough pastures, marshes, coasts. **Nest:** none made. **Eggs:** 4-8 (or more), white. **Food:** principally voles. **Voice:** least vocal of owls, but rasping and barking calls, deep *boo—boo—boo.*

of prey available in winter quarters dictates how many owls will be in an area, or whether, as often happens, they will be absent altogether. The classic relationship between the predator and its prey is strikingly illustrated by this species. It shows too how the effects can be very

marked with such a specialised predator: they are much less obvious with a more versatile bird like the tawny owl. In late winter and spring the short-eared owl may fly high up in display, calling with hollow, booming notes and clapping its wings rapidly beneath its body.

Nightjar

❋

CAPRIMULGUS EUROPAEUS

Secret and mysterious birds of bushy heaths and rough gorsy commons, nightjars are never easy to observe. Unless it is a clear, calm, warm evening there is no guarantee that they will be seen or heard, but late twilight on a midsummer evening is the best time to seek them. You may have to be content with hearing the sustained churring song, but with luck a pair will hunt for moths against the dim light of the sky, or come twisting and swirling around a birdwatcher's head as they would an isolated bush. During the day they sit along a log or on a patch of bare ground, almost impossible to find. They arrive here in May and leave for Africa in August and September, when several may migrate together. The British population is small and declining due to habitat loss and disturbance (sometimes by birdwatchers), pesticides and climatic change – a combination which is difficult to resist.

Nightjars rest on the ground. Their amazing plumage renders them almost invisible as they sit motionless, and with eyes shut, among fallen twigs and leaves. Not until they are almost trodden on will they actually fly.

Nightjars are best seen at dusk when they begin to call. They fly silently after insects with many sudden twists and glides.

The churring song is loud and vibrant at close range, far less high and metallic than song of grasshopper warbler.

Length: 7cm; **Weight:** 75-100g
Where to look: heathland, felled woodland, new plantations, moorland and dunes with bracken and scrub. **Nest:** on bare ground. **Eggs:** 2, mottled grey. **Food:** flying insects, mainly moths and beetles. **Voice:** song is a loud churring trill which rises and falls, given by perched male. Both sexes also have a deep *kooick* flight call.

Males have conspicuous white spots near the wingtips and on the outer tips of the tail. Females and young lack these.

Wings clapped loudly in display flight; also glide with wings raised and tail spread.

Superb camouflage when resting or nesting on ground.

Swift
❈
APUS APUS

The swift is a very remarkable bird: it is the only insectivorous bird whose young hatch at staggered intervals, thus ensuring that at least the oldest survives. Moreover, both eggs and young can survive long periods of chilling if the weather prevents the adults from feeding close by. Adults, too, are able to enter a state of torpor, and remarkable clusters of birds, clinging to walls like swarms of bees have, very occasionally, been recorded.

On leaving the nest for the first and only time, a young swift heads south to Africa immediately, without its parents, and may remain on the wing non-stop for two or three years! Swifts not only feed, bathe and 'sleep' aloft, but even on occasions mate on the wing. Only when nesting do they roost 'normally'. They may fly well over a million miles in their life of maybe ten years or more.

They probably eat more animals than any other British bird. Analysis of 12 food-balls intended for the young revealed more than 300 species of insects and spiders. One bird may catch 10,000 individual insects in a day. Although it does fly fast, a feeding swift takes insects in slow, steady glides.

Swifts prefer to nest in roofs of older houses where they have easy access to the rafters. They are semi-colonial, with often several pairs nesting in one roof and many more in nearby suitable houses. They are usually faithful to the same site year after year.

Adults are dark sooty brown, appearing black, with a pale chin. Young show more white on the throat and forehead, which is visible in flight.

Non-breeding swifts may undertake journeys of 200 miles or more to avoid heavy rain.

Although the bill is small, the gape is enormous to help catch its insect food.

Exceptionally long primary feathers and short inner wings create the familiar crescent shape, ideal for rapid sustained flight.

Parties of screaming swifts chase low over roofs on fine evenings.

The shallow-forked tail, usually closed, is used for greater control.

Every swift seems to carry more than its fair share of parasites, including the large, green, flightless louse-fly.

Length: 16-17cm; **Weight**: 35-50g
Where to look: in the summer sky, anywhere. **Nest:** hole in eaves, thatch, towers, rarely in cliffs; shallow cup of feathers and saliva. **Eggs**: 2-3, white. **Food:** insects, spiders. **Voice:** loud, shrill scream.

Kingfisher

❖

ALCEDO ATTHIS

On seeing their first kingfisher, most people are surprised how small it is. It is Britain's most exotic-looking bird and indeed is the widest ranging representative of a mainly tropical family of some 90 species. Often, all that is seen of this shy bird, first located by call, is a streak of brilliant electric blue flashing low and fast over the water surface. In Ancient Greece, a dead kingfisher was hung up as a protection against lightning!

Each young bird needs between 12 and 18 fish daily; youngsters are fed in rotation, the hungriest bird taking position at the front of the nest chamber. For such a beautiful bird, the nesting habits are distinctly insalubrious, the chamber becoming fouled with fish bones and scales — regurgitated as pellets and then trodden into the earth. The young excrete towards the light, so the tunnel also becomes filthy, and often shows a tell-tale white trickle below the entrance: on leaving the nest, the adults usually plunge-bathe to clean their plumage.

Kingfishers are highly territorial: they will even chase their own young away within three or four days of leaving the nest, starting a second brood almost immediately. Many young starve or drown in the first week, before they have learnt to fish.

Where small fish abound, adults are successful four dives out of five. They can handle fish up to 8cm (3in) long – half their own body length.

Perched motionless among vegetation, can be surprisingly difficult to see, the strong colour contrast breaking up the bird's outline. When fishing, often bobs head nervously.

Male and female share the same combination of iridescent blues, orange-red and white, with bright-red feet. The male's bill is all black, whereas the female has a red base to the lower mandible. Young are duller with dark feet.

Hving dived and caught a fish, the kingfisher struggles free of the water with strong wing-beats, returning to a same perch to beat its prey before swallowing it head-first. The dive is over in a trice.

Length: 16-17cm (of which bill 4cm)
Weight: 35-40g
Where to look: unpolluted, still or slow-flowing waters over much of Britain and Ireland, though rare in Scotland; sedentary, some moving to estuaries, sheltered coasts in winter. **Nest:** narrow tunnel 60-90cm (2-3ft) long, excavated in bank. usually over water. **Eggs:** 6-7, white, rather round, laid in shallow depression on bare earth, in chamber at end of tunnel. **Food:** small fish. **Voice:** loud, shrill *chee* often repeated; aggressive *shrit-it-it*; especially vocal in spring and autumn when establishing breeding and wintering territory.

Green Woodpecker

❀

PICUS VIRIDIS

The back is uniform yellow-green, with the primary feathers showing brown with white spotting. The undersides are an unmarked grey-green.

Dark cheeks and pale eye-ring are readily seen in the field.

In both the male and female the crown and central nape are deep crimson mottled with grey.

In flight, the pointed head and tail and brilliant yellow rump are striking.

Moustachial stripe of male has red a central streak which is difficult to see in poor light.

The main food throughout the year is ants and their pupae. Signs of green woodpecker attacks can often be seen on ant hills.

The green woodpecker is more often heard than seen; its loud almost laughing yaffle call carries a great distance, yet the bird itself is often shy and elusive. Britain's largest woodpecker, it is about the size of a jackdaw, and when seen is unmistakable, with green plumage, striking red crown and yellow rump. In flight the pointed shape of the head and tail and the short bursts of flapping interspersed with long swooping glides are characteristic. At rest it can be difficult to locate, often perching motionless for many minutes, occasionally giving an alarm call.

Old pasture and heaths are favoured feeding areas, for it is here that the bird finds the ants which are its staple diet. It uses its stout beak and long tongue to extract ants and pupae from galleries deep within the nest. The tongue can be extended up to 10cm (4in) and is used to explore the galleries, while the sticky tip is used to catch the prey. At most times of the year the birds are seen singly, but the young accompany their parents for a few weeks after fledging in July and such family parties can often be located by the loud begging calls of the young. Although they sometimes occur in well-wooded

Length: 30-33cm; **Weight:** 190g
Where to look: deciduous woods, parkland, heaths and commons. **Nest:** deep cavity excavated in trunk or large limb of mature tree. Unlined. **Eggs:** 4-7, glossy white, laid on wood chippings. **Food:** mainly ants and their pupae. **Voice:** loud, laughing yaffle.

gardens, green woodpeckers are extremely shy birds and at the slightest hint of disturbance they fly off, calling loudly in alarm with shouted, rapid notes, more screeching than the pleasant yaffle.

Length: 15-16cm; **Weight**: 32g
Where to look: a rare breeding bird in semi-natural pine forests in Scotland; in England and Wales only seen on passage in spring and autumn. **Nest:** any cavity, including nestbox' unlined. **Eggs:** 7-10, white. **Food:** ants and other insects. **Voice:** weak quee . . quee. . quee, similar to lesser spotted woodpecker.

On the ground it hops clumsily and collects food with a darting tongue. It often remains motionless for long periods, collecting ants that pass by.

Wryneck

❀

JYNX TORQUILLA

The wryneck is a close relative of the woodpeckers. Like the green woodpecker, it feeds almost exclusively on ants and uses its long mobile tongue to scoop them up. Unlike the woodpecker, it is seen mainly on the ground, does not often climb up vertical limbs and only rarely excavates dead wood. For a nest site it uses any available cavity, including artificial boxes. Another

The mottled brown back and barred tail are distinctive.

difference from Britain's true woodpeckers is that it is migratory, spending the winter in sub-Saharan Africa. At a distance it looks like a rather dull, long songbird, but close views reveal complex brown and lilac patterning on the back with two lilac and one blackish band running down from the nape. The undersides are barred and spotted and the tail has complex transverse patterning — all reminiscent of a small nightjar. In England the breeding population has declined to extinction in recent decades and now the only birds seen are occasional migrants in spring and autumn. These birds often appear in the most unlikely places, including suburban gardens, feeding on ants. A small number now breed in Scotland; these are though to be an offshoot of the large Scandinavian population.

The bill is used to peck at decaying wood to obtain food and to excavate the nest cavity

Great Spotted Woodpecker

❉

DENDROCOPUS MAJOR

A distinctive black, white and red bird, the great spotted is Britain's most widespread woodpecker. It is about the size of a blackbird and can be encountered almost anywhere where there are trees. In the breeding season it prefers mature broadleaved woodland, but at other times may wander widely and be found in isolated trees and copses. The first indication of its presence is often a loud repeated *tchik* call. After searching,

Adults and immature birds of both sexes have brigh-red under-tail coverts.

The male is readily distinguished from the female by the brilliant red patch on his nape.

In flight, the large white wing flashes, white-barred primaries and brilliant red undertail coverts are obvious.

the bird can usually be found high in a tree or glimpsed as it flies off. Its territorial drumming is the most evocative early morning woodland sound in spring, and is often punctuated by aerial chases through the canopy with two or three birds chattering loudly. Most of its food is obtained by pecking at dead and decaying wood to extract insects and larvae — crevices and decayed spots are attacked with rapid blows of the beak. In spring, the young are fed on caterpillars. A new nest cavity is usually excavated each year and this can take the birds one or two weeks, depending on the hardness of the chosen tree. Dead birch stumps and oaks are preferred.

Length: 22-23cm; **Weight:** 80g
Where to look: coniferous and deciduous woodland, hedgerow trees and gardens. **Nest:** cavity excavated in dead or decaying tree, unlined. **Eggs:** 3-7, white. **Food:** insects, seeds. **Voice:** loud *tchik* and rattling trill.

Lesser Spotted Woodpecker

❉

DENDROCOPUS MINOR

This small woodpecker is only the size of a house sparrow. It spends much of its time high in the tree canopy feeding among the smallest branches; with a rapid sewing-machine-like action of its beak it searches out its insect food. In winter it often joins mixed feeding flocks of tits. For a few weeks in early spring its *pee. .pee. .pee. .* calls, conspicuous butterfly-like display flights and weak drumming betray its breeding areas. The drumming is much softer than that of the great spotted woodpecker, and each burst lasts for well over a second. Both male and female drum, usually from high in the crown of a tree. The nest cavity is excavated by both birds and can be between

one and 25 metres (3-75ft) above the ground, often placed on the underside of a dead limb. The entrance hole is only 3cm (1in) in diameter, distinguishing the nest from those of other woodpecker species. The nest is usually very inconspicuous and difficult to find.

Usually high in woodland tree, but will also feed close to the ground in hedgerows and scrub.

When feeding, flutters more like a perching bird than a woodpecker.

Distinguished from great spotted woodpecker by its small size, barred black and white wing pattern without any large white flashes, and lack of red vent.

Male has distinct red crown which is absent in female.

Length: 13-14cm **Weight:** 20g
Where to look: deciduous woodland, parks, orchards and gardens. **Nest:** cavity excavated in decaying wood, unlined. **Eggs:** 3-8, white. **Food:** insects. **Voice:** slow, nasal *pee pee pee pee*; weak *chick*.

Skylark

❋

ALAUDA ARVENSIS

These familiar birds of the open countryside are often visible only as small specks in the sky as they hang in the air, singing non-stop. They are numerous throughout the country in the breeding season, but in winter many leave the bleaker upland areas for more hospitable lowland fields. Large numbers of skylarks from northern Europe arrive here in October and November to spend the winter. During very severe winters Britain's skylarks may move south to warmer parts of the Continent. Skylarks give their glorious song all year round, but tend to go quiet in August and September when they moult. They have probably benefited more than any other bird from the advent of arable farming and the deforestation of the countryside, which has provided the open cultivated areas that the species prefers. They rarely even feed close to a tall hedge.

In flight, the white trailing wing edge, white outer tail feathers and loud chirrupping call help to identify them.

The crest is not always easily seen, but can be raised when the bird is excited or alarmed.

The aerial song is a familiar sound, with the bird often too high to be seen. The song flight can last for anything up to five minutes. Skylarks also sing from perches.

Length: 18cm; **Weight:** 33-45 g
Where to look: open fields, moors, dunes and salt marshes. **Nest:** on ground in grass tussocks with fine grass/hair lining. **Eggs:** 3-5, white with heavy brown markings. **Food:** insects, seeds and worms. **Voice:** loud, clear, very rapid warbling in flight. Call a liquid *chirrup*.

Woodlark

❋

LULLULA ARBOREA

Woodlarks are very patchily distributed in southern and eastern England with, until recently, a few in Wales. They are often difficult to find, feeding inconspicuously on the ground, but they perch on the tops of trees and bushes. They sing beautifully through most of the year, especially from March to June, and often at night. The song flight is different from a skylark's, with the male circling at a constant height with a more fluttering action. In flight, the short tail, undulating flight and call — *tit-looeet* — help to distinguish them from skylarks. They are particularly fond of forestry plantations where trees have been felled or recently planted. Their numbers have been declining both in Britain and on the Continent. It is thought that habitat loss combined with climatic change may have caused this. It is very sad that their lovely song is now so rarely heard.

Small crest and clear buff-white stripes over the eyes which meet at the back of the head.

In flight shows very short tail with brown sides; broader, more rounded wings than skylark's.

Compared to skylark, flight is weak and fluttering. When flushed, the bird flies low over the ground.

Black and white mark at bend of wing is visible when perched

Length: 15cm; **Weight:** 24-36g
Where to look: heathland with scrub, plantations. **Nest:** fine grass lining in sheltered hollow. **Eggs:** 3-4, pale, brown-speckled. **Food:** insects and seeds. **Voice:** melodious descending song phrases; *tloo-ee, titlooeet* calls.

Swallow

❊

HIRUNDO RUSTICA

Britain's swallows winter in Africa, as far south as the Cape, returning between March and May to take up territories around buildings, but in less urban areas than house martins. The male sings from a wire or on the wing, and soon the pair will be dashing through an door, a broken window, even the observation slit in a bird-watching hide to build their mud-saucer nest. A chimney-stack or old mine-shaft may also be used: one nest in Cornwall was 17 metres (53ft) below ground. A nest may be occupied several years in succession by the same birds — a tribute to amazing navigation skills. Food-balls of small insects and individual larger ones are brought to the young. When they have fledged, the young sit in a prominent spot, often on a branch, and wait to be fed; they must soon learn to feed themselves and to drink and bathe on the wing. A classic autumn sight is that of swallows gathering on wires; at the same time reed-beds roosts may hold thousands of birds. Swallows melt away south in September and October, with stragglers hanging on till November. Soon after their arrival in spring and also in late summer, swallows and other hirundines often feed over water.

Swallows are glossy blue-black above; below they vary from nearly white to orange-pink, with a blue band across the breast. The throat and forehead are a rich, deep red. The dark tail has oval white spots.

Their long tails give them great manoeuvrability near ground or water, and around obstacles such as grazing animals.

Females have shorter tail streamers than males. The young are duller, with more orange foreheads and throats.

Length: 18-20cm
Weight: 18-19g
Where to look: open country. **Nest:** of mud and dry grass on a ledge in an outbuilding.
Eggs: 4-5, white, dark-speckled.
Food: insects taken on the wing. **Voice:** *tswit-tswit;* alarm *tswee;* prolonged song of calls and a rolling trill.

With tail feathers splayed, white dots are revealed.

Swallows will sometimes take food while perched, but they are predominantly aerial feeders.

Flies and sometimes butterflies are important sources of food.

House Martin

❋

DELICHON URBICA

Before men built houses, house martins nested on cliffs. A few still do so, but most now build under eaves (or other sites such as street-lamp shades) in villages, towns and city suburbs. Some have even nested on sea-ferries (including a cross-Channel vessel), the adults feeding the young between voyages and raising them successfully! Nesting may be delayed by drought, as mud is the main building material. The adults gather this in their bills and apply it with trembling movements of their chins. The bird is social and some sites have dozens of nests: why some houses are chosen and others not is still not clear. Old nests may be repaired and re-used and artificial nests may encourage birds to colonise. Fledglings of earlier broods often help feed the latest young. Unlike the swallow and sand martin, which make up the trio collectively called the hirundines, this bird rarely roosts in reed beds; it may use trees mainly, or sleep on the wing, but this, and precisely where it spends the winter in Africa, is still mysterious.

Parents feed fledged young both in the air and perched on wires.

In bright light, upperparts can look jet black without any bluish tinge.

House martins are among the first migrants to arrive in this country in spring. Pairs feed over gravel pits and lakes but soon move to likely nesting sites. Here they gather on wires and collect mud from puddle margins. Over a period of several days, the mud is used to construct their sound and solid cup-shaped nests. Their presence on a house is considered by most people as a sign of favour.

Length: 12.5cm; **Weight:** 18g
Where to look: around houses, over open areas and wetlands. **Nest:** of mud pellets and a little dry grass, under eaves, occasionally on bridges and cliffs; often colonial. **Eggs:** 4-5, white. **Food:** insects taken in flight. **Voice:** *chrrrp*; alarm a shrill *treep*.

Underparts look very clean and white, seeming much brighter than swallow or sand martin.

Adults are blue-black above with a white rump and underparts; and white feathering on their short legs. Young are browner above and below.

Gathering mud at edge of puddle for nest building.

Sand Martin

❉

RIPARIA RIPARIA

Swallows and martins have wide gapes for collecting food, water and nest material on the wing.

Young birds have brighter edges to the feathers of the upperparts.

Plain brown above, off-white below with a brown band across the breast. Tail only slightly forked.

The sand martin is often the first summer migrant to arrive in the spring, beating the swallow by several days. Flicking low over some reservoir or gravel pit in March, it was once perhaps taken a little for granted. No more: catastrophic declines in sand martin numbers have followed the long drought (aggravated by man) in the southern Sahara, the Sahel, where the birds spend winter. Some long-established colonies are empty, and those still active are at a low ebb; it remains to be seen whether the species can make a come-back.

Sand martins are the smallest of Britain's hirundines and rather delicate-looking, yet in excavating their burrows in sand or soil, they may dig in 2 metres (6ft) or more (usually half this) and move stones four times heavier than themselves. Living in colonies has several advantages, notably 'safety in numbers' and more eyes to spot predators. The bird has a special alarm call to warn of birds of prey; nevertheless many are taken.

Migrants roost in reed beds, often with swallows.

Like their relatives, swallows and house martins, sand martins feed primarily on insects which are caught mainly on the wing. During periods of prolonged bad weather, sand martins sometimes have great difficulty in feeding. During such weather, and also in late summer prior to migration, many hundreds will gather over suitable lakes and gravel pits to feed. They dip low over the water, feasting on midges and mosquitos in particular. Nesting in somewhat inaccessable cliffside colonies, sand martins are relatively immune to attacks from ground predators. They are, however, frequently subject to predation by hobbies whose speed and agility enable them to catch the martins on the wing

Perches freely on wires, branches and on the ground, where it may drink, and even bathe in, dew.

Length: 12cm;
Weight: 13-14g
Where to look: fresh-water wetlands, especially near mineral workings. **Nest:** in colonies, in a tunnel in a bank or cliff, occasionally in man-made holes, eg pipes. **Eggs:** 4-5, white. **Food:** insects taken in flight. **Voice:** a dry, hard *chrrp;* alarm sharper; song a series of call-notes.

Rock Pipit

❄

ANTHUS PETROSUS

Almost exclusively coastal, rock pipits search for food among rocks, seaweed and shore vegetation. They always make their nests close to the shore, in sheltered gullies and coves. Breeding usually begins in April and two broods are not uncommon; in some areas they are a host species for cuckoos. Lack of suitable rocky coastline from North Humberside to Kent means that they are absent from that whole stretch of coast.

They are difficult to spot among the rocks, and their presence is often first noticed as they fly up, calling as they go. In winter they may eat more than 15,000 small molluscs and larvae each day. They are usually solitary and territorial, but may form flocks in winter and can be quite approachable. Rock pipits are resident and most do not move from their home territories, although in winter birds are found on coasts where they do not breed and in March and October, especially, a few turn up by reservoirs inland. Birds of the Scandinavian race migrate south and appear regularly on the east and south coasts of England. In spring they can be distinguished from Britain's rock pipits by their browner upperparts and whiter belly.

Habitually perches on rocks. Often seen in small parties feeding on the shoreline.

Big, dark, dull dark-legged pipit — usually beside the sea.

A heavy-bodied pipit with dark olive upperparts and buff underparts with poorly defined breast streaks. Dark legs and grey outer tail feathers.

Length: 16cm; **Weight:** 21-30g
Where to look: rocky coasts and salt marshes. **Nest:** in rock crevice. Grass cup, lined with hair. **Eggs:** 4-5, white with grey/brown spots. **Food:** seeds, marine animals and insects. **Voice:** loud musical song. Call – strong *feest.*

Water Pipit

❄

ANTHUS SPINOLETTA

In spring, the water pipit is a very attractive bird, with a brown, almost unstreaked back, greyish head and unstreaked underparts which have a warm, pinkish flush. The white tail sides are not easy to see, but the bold, pale stripe over the eye and wingbars stand out. Water pipits breed in the mountainous regions of Europe; they leave the upland pastures between August and November, moving down to lowland regions, often dispersing some distance. The nearest breeding birds to Britain are probably in the Alps. No more than a hundred are recorded in Britain each winter, usually between October and April. They like watercress beds, coastal fresh water, inland marshes and rivers. Most are seen in southern and eastern England. They are often hard to see well, as they fly up at a distance and may move several hundred yards before settling again. After a while they will be found back at their preferred feeding place. Until recently, water pipits were regarded as a race of the rock pipit, but the two have been split into separate species along with the American water pipit, or buff-bellied pipit, a rare accidental visitor to Britain.

Length: 17cm; **Weight:** 21-36g
Where to look: lakes, watercress beds in winter and spring. Does not breed in Britain. **Food:** insects and seeds. **Voice:** song similar to meadow pipit. Calls are a sharp *dzit* and a short *drrt.*

Bold stripe over eye, white outer tail, dark legs, white throat all year.

In winter, browner and plainer above than rock pipit; white wingbars and belly.

In summer, breast is pinkish and unstreaked. Head is grey.

Bigger, browner and shyer than meadow pipit, with dark legs.

Meadow Pipit

❋

ANTHUS PRATENSIS

Meadow pipits are classic 'little brown birds'. Often only seen as they fly away from rough grass, the best clue to their identity is the thin, squeaky call, repeated persistently. They are often hard to see when on the ground, as they run between clumps of grass, occasionally pausing in the open. They are widely distributed throughout the country in the breeding season, but in winter leave the high ground for lowland areas, often feeding in urban parks and gardens and living secretively in weedy fields. Many of Britain's northern birds migrate south to southern and south-western England and Ireland and some will travel as far south as Spain. Migrants from northern Europe arrive here each autumn and may spend the winter. Meadow pipits are important hosts for the cuckoo, especially in Ireland. They make up a large part of the prey of species such as hen harrier, merlin and kestrel, too.

Length: 14cm; **Weight:** 16-25g
Where to look: moors, meadows and dunes. **Nest:** on ground in tussock of grass with fine lining. **Eggs:** 4-5, white with grey/brown spots. **Food:** insects and seeds. **Voice:** accelerating song with trill. Call high *tseep* repeated.

The squeaky call and white outer tail are distinctive in flight.

The upperparts can vary from grey to olive-buff. Underparts yellowish to pale grey; pale legs.

Display flight is like a tree pipit's, but starts from the ground; song is less musical.

Always prefers ground to trees.

Tree Pipit

❋

ANTHUS TRIVIALIS

The song is given after an upward flight from a tree during a 'parachute' drop.

As their name suggests, tree pipits make more use of trees than other pipits, especially in the lovely display flight. They feed on the ground, but when disturbed they will fly up into a tree or bush. They are summer visitors, arriving from April to June and leaving for tropical Africa from late July to October. Males usually arrive first and take up territory, announcing their presence with spectacular song flights.

They fly upwards from a tree perch and begin to sing as they reach the top of their ascent, descending with wings open and tail spread. The birds need song posts for display, as well as clear ground to feed on, and so choose heathland, commons and pasture with scattered trees or woodland edges. Newly-planted conifers are readily used, and recently felled areas with some trees still standing are favourite sites. Tree pipits have spread north in Scotland during the last 100 years, and now breed extensively in mature birch woods. They are still absent as breeding birds in Ireland and only occur there as rare migrants.

Breast lightly streaked and yellower than a meadow pipit's.

Solitary, perching on trees, but feeding on ground. Stronger bill, stouter build, bolder actions and different call from meadow pipit.

Weight: 15cm
Length: 20-25g
Where to look: plantations, heaths, scattered trees and scrub. **Nest:** grass cup with fine lining in tussock or bank. **Eggs:** 4-6, variable with dark spots. **Food:** insects and seeds. **Voice:** loud song with trills. Call a hoarse *teez*.

Yellow Wagtail

❋

MOTACILLA FLAVA

Yellow wagtails are among the most colourful summer visitors, the males shining out from grassy meadows like buttercups. They arrive from March to May and leave in August and September. There are occasional reports of over-wintering birds, but care must be taken not to confuse them with grey wagtails. Yellow wagtails are a race of the blue-headed wagtail and breed only in England and Wales, except for a few pairs in Scotland and even fewer in Ireland. Blue-headed wagtails breed from Scandinavia eastwards into Asia, and are seen as rare passage migrants in Britain in spring by their blue-grey crowns and ear-coverts with a white stripe over the eye and white chin. Odd ones turn up now and then in spring wagtail flocks.

Male mostly brightly yellow; long, spindly legs, fast walk, wingbars; unlike any other yellow bird.

Female is paler yellow with browner green upperparts.

Found in damp meadows and fields by water; often feeding on insects disturbed by cattle.

Length: 17cm; **Weight:** 16-22g
Where to look: water meadows, pasture, moors and lakesides. **Nest:** on ground in grass. Roots and grass lined with hair. **Eggs:** 5-6, buff with darker spots. **Food:** mainly insects. **Voice:** a loud *tswee-ip* warbling song.

Long white-edged black tail is a useful feature in flight.

Grey Wagtail

❋

MOTACILLA CINEREA

Grey wagtails live up to the family name more than the others as their longer tail accentuates the vertical wagging motion. They delight in the rush and tumble of upland streams and rivers, perching on boulders and flying out after passing insects. They also feed on the ground, running quickly and pumping their tail up and down each time they stop. In winter they leave the upland areas and move to lower ground, frequenting lakes, reservoirs, farmyards and sewage farms. Some birds travel south, even as far as France and Spain. Britain's residents are joined by northern European birds which arrive here for the winter. Grey wagtails suffer badly in severe winters, in common with other birds which feed by fresh water that becomes frozen. Watercress beds then become favourite haunts of these delightful and attractive birds.

Length: 18cm; **Weight:** 15-23g
Where to look: fast rivers and streams. **Nest:** ledges, holes in walls and banks near water. Moss, grass and leaves, hair lining. **Eggs:** 4-6, buff with grey/brown marks. **Food:** insects. **Voice:** infrequent warble, call a high *tzitzi* sharper than pied's.

In summer, male has a black throat.

In winter, male and female are similar with buff-white throat.

Often seen perched on rocks and overhanging trees near streams.

Often mistaken for yellow wagtail, but legs pink.

Grey crown, yellow underparts, yellow-green rump, long white-edged tail; very sharp call.

Pied Wagtail

❋

MOTACILLA ALBA

Length: 18cm
Weight: 19-20g
Where to look: farmland, open country. Often near water. **Nest:** holes in walls, sheds, banks, ivy; grass and moss lined with feathers and hair. **Eggs:** 5-6, pale grey with speckles. **Food:** insects and seeds. **Voice:** twittering warble; shrill *tchissick, tchuwee*.

Highly territorial in spring, they will even attack their reflections in the wing mirrors and hubcaps of parked cars.

Pied wagtails prefer short grass, also tarmac, where they can run along ground. They are agile and can dart rapidly or fly up to catch passing insect prey.

Black and white plumage and a long bobbing tail make this an easily recognisable bird as it chases across short grass for insects.

Pied has greyer back and a white throat in winter, but keeps crescent of black on the breast.

Females have a greyer back and a smaller bib than males.

The black and white plumage and constant tail-bobbing of the pied wagtail make it a distinctive bird, found commonly in open country, especially farmyards, parks and gardens. It can be seen in paddocks and fields, trotting along the ground and dashing after insects scared up by the horses or cattle.

In many parts of Britain the pied wagtail is a familiar bird of urban environments, favouring in particular school playing fields and even supermarket car parks. Small groups may be seen flying overhead towards dusk, making their way to a communal roost, where hundreds noisily gather on a tree before flying to a reed bed, bush or even a building ledge for the night.

Pied wagtails breed over the whole country with the exception of the Shetland Islands. In winter, northern birds move south to spend the winter in central and southern England, although many go to France, Spain and even Morocco. Pied wagtails are a race (ie sub-species) of the white wagtail and only breed regularly in Britain and Ireland. White wagtails breed from Iceland to the Mediterranean and are seen in Britain on passage in spring and autumn, especially on the west and north coasts. There have been records of white wagtails breeding in England and of hybridisation between the two races.

In flight, note the long tail and distinctive call.

Great Grey Shrike

LANIUS EXCUBITOR

Flight is deeply undulating, often low, with a sweep up to perch. Bold, white wing bars are obvious.

Red-backed Shrike

LANIUS COLLURIO

Colourful but increasingly rare. Coastal breeder, now most likely to be seen on migration. In flight: 'too big for a warbler; too small for a thrush'.

Starling

❊

STURNUS VULGARIS

Song is a long mixture of trills and rattles, unmusical but full of energy; wings waved vigorously during song: Many starlings mimic other birds and mechanical sounds.

Though familiar in gardens, parks and even town centres, the starling's life-style still holds secrets little known even to the keenest observer of birds. As with so many species, research reveals fascinating facts. A male in spring, having built his rough nest, sings with puffed-out throat and drooped wings to attract a mate. Should a female come close he will sing in a frenzy of wing-waving with his back hunched and tail fanned. If she stops near by, he will sing from the nest itself, to attract her in, and she will complete the lining. If there are several pairs of starlings in an area, by some unknown means they will synchronise their breeding and start laying eggs at the same time. Some females lay an egg in another's nest and bright blue eggs can often be found on a lawn, mysteriously intact — removed from a nest by a starling, but whether by an intruding female is not known. Some males are polygamous, leaving one mate on eggs, while going off with another, often younger, female. The male incubates eggs for a small part of the day, leaving the rest and all night to the female.

In spring, the male is very glossy and colourful with blue base to beak (female has a pink patch on bill).

Length: 22cm; **Weight:** 75-90g
Where to look: widespread. **Nest:** in hole in building or tree. **Eggs:** 4-6, blue. **Food:** seeds, fruit, caterpillars, leatherjackets, ants. **Voice:** trills, buzzy and screeching calls; a good mimic of birds and of other sounds.

From December onwards the bill turns yellow and in spring the legs change from dull brown to orange or reddish. Pale feather tips weaken and crumble away to reveal glossy colours beneath, most obvious in males. Females often keep more orange-brown on wings than males in summer.

Waxwing

❊

BOMBYCILLA GARRULUS

Females tend to show less intense black bibs and less bright yellow and red markings on the wings and tail, but sexing is not easy.

Every winter, British birdwatchers hope for an invasion of these gorgeous birds. Such 'irruptions', caused by overcrowding and food shortages on their normal wintering grounds in northern Europe, occur irregularly and may be becoming less frequent. Nevertheless, in most winters there are at least a few along the east coast of England and Scotland and, in some years, they are more numerous and get as far as the west, Wales and even Ireland. Waxwings are remarkable in many other ways: they turn up regularly in gardens and parks and allow a close approach. This will show their handsome plumage, including the secondary feathers with their extraordinary red blobs of 'sealing wax' at the tips, which give the bird its name. Very occasionally, the buttercup-yellow end of the tail will show these tips too. Waxwings feed acrobatically among the branches of berry-bearing shrubs and trees, sometimes gorging themselves to a state of total inactivity.

Gregarious and tame, waxwings may feed in one bush for some days.

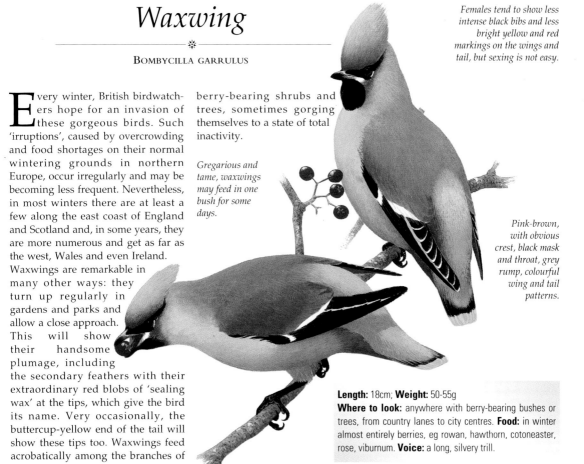

Pink-brown, with obvious crest, black mask and throat, grey rump, colourful wing and tail patterns.

Length: 18cm; **Weight:** 50-55g
Where to look: anywhere with berry-bearing bushes or trees, from country lanes to city centres. **Food:** in winter almost entirely berries, eg rowan, hawthorn, cotoneaster, rose, viburnum. **Voice:** a long, silvery trill.

Jay

❊

GARRULUS GLANDARIUS

Jays are widespread in wooded counties of England and Wales, absent from the southern and northern counties of Scotland, but occur in a band from Argyll to the east coast. They were badly persecuted in the last century, but this is lessening and the bird is now increasing, spreading into suburbs, and into upland areas where coniferous woodland has been created.

Jays eat a wide variety of foods, but acorns are the most important and persecution is quite unjustified on the grounds of their eating habits. They are responsible for the large-scale dispersal of acorns in the autumn, probably involving several thousand acorns per bird. This helps to sustain the birds, and is also vital for future survival of oak woods.

Jays do not normally move far in Britain, although large movements occur on the Continent in autumn, and in most years some birds reach southern and eastern Britain. Huge movements of jays were recorded in southern Britain in autumn 1983, caused by the widespread failure of the acorn crop both in Britain and on the Continent. In rural gardens, jays will sometimes come to bird feeders and take nuts and fat. Despite this apparently bold behaviour, they are, nevertheless, always wary of humans.

Crown is whitish, streaked black, and forming a small crest when erect. The 'moustache' is black.

The most colourful of the crows. The body is pinkish, browner above than below, with a white rump and black tail. The wing has a bright white panel and a patch of blue with black bars.

White rump, small red mark on inner black wing feather oddly repeated on bullfinch.

In autumn jays feed on acorns. Excess acorns are buried in soil and dug up when needed.

Length: 34cm
Weight: 140-190g
Where to look: deciduous and conifer woods, wooded farmland, parks, gardens.
Nest: well-hidden, of sticks. **Eggs:** 4-5, pale bluish, spotted. **Food:** almost anything, especially acorns. **Voice:** a harsh *skraaak*, quiet mewing.

Jays are easily disturbed and are most often seen flying away.

Magpie

❊

PICA PICA

Unmistakable as this bird is, it is often the call that gives away the magpie's presence. Except for large parts of Scotland, magpies are common in Britain. They are found in many habitats, though their preference is for grassland with thick hedges or scattered trees. Recent years have seen an increase in numbers, especially in towns and suburbs with thick shrubberies, though in eastern England, where many hedgerows have been removed, magpie numbers have declined.

The magpie, beautiful and intelligent, is much persecuted, especially in game-rearing areas, and is not appreciated in gardens where it is accused of eating too many eggs and chicks of small birds (though it is far less of a nuisance than the domestic cat and eats far fewer birds than protected hawks and falcons). Magpies eat mostly invertebrates in summer and seeds and berries in the winter. They do not move from their home territories, and no Continental birds arrive in winter. One of the commonest ways of seeing a magpie these days is feeding on animal road casualties. This rich source of food undoubtedly helps magpies thrive.

The magpie often hoards food. It makes a small hole in the ground with its bill, regurgitates food into it and covers it, reclaiming the cache one or two days later.

Even at a distance, the black and white plumage and long, graduated tail are unmistakable – as is the distinctive 'machine gun' call.

Bill, legs and feet are black and the eye is dark brown.

Sometimes comical on the ground. Walks with high-stepping gait and often hops or bounces sideways when excited or seeking food.

When observed closely, the wing feathers have a purplish-blue iridescent sheen, and the tail is iridescent green, with a band of reddish-purple near the tip.

On the ground the tail is usually held elevated, and rarely spread.

Juveniles have very short tails and lack the brightness and gloss of adults' plumage. Initially the flight is weak, and the birds hide in the foliage. The family party remains together until autumn.

Length: 40-45cm;
Weight: 200-250g
Where to look: farmland, open country with scattered trees or bushes, also increasingly in suburban and urban areas.
Nest: large, domed, of sticks lined with earth and fine roots. **Eggs:** up to 8, normally 5-6. **Food:** omniverous. **Voice:** a loud, rapid *chak-chak-chak*.

Chough

❊

PYRRHOCORAX PYRRHOCORAX

Adults have slim, down-curved red bills and red legs. Juveniles' bills are shorter and orange.

Choughs are slightly larger than jackdaws, and the scarcest of Britain's crows. Although once common, they are now confined to the cliff coasts of Wales, the Isle of Man, some of the Inner Hebridean islands, and Ireland. A few pairs breed on inland cliffs in Wales.

Choughs are gregarious, even in the breeding season, often flying along the cliffs in small flocks. Their flight is superbly graceful, agile and buoyant, often with aerobatic swoops and dives. The noisy calls are distinctive and far reaching; though usually pronounced 'chuff', the English name may originally have been 'chow' in imitation of the call. They feed on the maritime heath and pasture above cliff tops. The loss of these areas to arable farming has contributed to the chough's recent decline. About 1,000 pairs breed in the British Isles, the majority found in western Ireland.

Plumage glossy and entirely black. Walks, runs and hops.

May advertise its presence with noisy calls and wing flicking.

In flight wings are broad and the primary feathers on the wings well separated, giving a characteristic silhouette.

Length: 40cm;
Weight: 280-360g
Where to look: sea cliffs, very occasionally inland at rock faces and quarries. **Nest:** of sticks, lined with wool or fine grass, on a ledge or crevice, often high on rock face. **Food:** chiefly invertebrates. **Voice:** *kwee-ow; chee-a!*

Jackdaw

❊

CORVUS MONEDULA

Jackdaws are widespread throughout the British Isles, except for parts of Scotland (although numbers have increased and the breeding range has expanded there this century), yet oddly rare in places. They nest in loose colonies, often using the same nest sites year after year. Almost any suitably large crevice or hole, which the birds fill with a tangle of sticks, might be used as a nest site. Less material is used at cliff sites, where the nest often occupies a rabbit burrow. Jackdaws usually eat vegetable matter, especially grain and seeds, and surface-dwelling invertebrates, but will take almost any food. They readily exploit temporary abundances of food, such as the large numbers of leaf-eating caterpillars in woodlands in May or June, or animal foodstuffs. In winter they commonly scavenge at domestic refuse tips. Some migration occurs in winter when British birds move west, sometimes to Ireland, and birds from the Continent arrive on the east and south coasts.

Quicker and more active on the ground than other crows. Flight also quicker, and primary wing feathers only slightly separated. Has pale eye.

Gregarious at all seasons, often roosting and feeding communally with other crows, notably rooks.

Plumage is entirely black except for the ash-grey sides of the neck, nape and back of the head.

Noisy and sometimes aggressive. fluffs out feathers and spreads tail when defending nest site.

Length: 33cm;
Weight: 220-270g
Where to look: towns, cities, farmland, parkland, woodland and sea cliffs. **Nest:** pile of sticks in holes or crevice in trees, buildings or rocks. **Eggs:** 4-6, blue-green. **Food:** virtually anything. **Voice:** *kow, chuck-chuck, jak.*

Rook

❄

CORVUS FRUGILEGUS

What would the countryside be without its lively, noisy, busybody rooks! The very essence of lowland farmland, but less common in the uplands, they are gregarious, quarrelsome birds, nesting in tree-top rookeries which sway precariously in the wind, with anything from a handful to several thousand nests. Life at a rookery is fascinating and easily observed, since nesting begins well before the leaves appear. In winter a rookery may become a traditional roost.

Travelling flocks of rooks, using set routes, may amalgamate into spectacular gatherings of several thousand birds. The amiable 'caws' are among the essential countryside sounds. Accused of damaging crops, rooks eat mainly worms and leatherjackets, though grain undoubtedly forms a large part of the diet when they can reach it. On balance, rooks seem to be beneficial and it would be a sad loss if the village rookery or the roaming flocks of big, black birds were to disappear from the rural scene. British rooks are resident, but numbers are boosted by Continental birds in winter.

Length: 46cm;
Weight: 460-520g
Where to look: farmland, grasslands, parks and wooded suburbs. **Nest:** communally in rookeries in trees, re-using stick nest from previous year. **Eggs:** 2-7, usually 4-5. **Food:** omnivorous. **Voice:** a deep *caw* or *kaaah*.

Walks sedately, probing the soil and picking at invertebrates or seeds. Gregarious when feeding.

The communal roost, which may be at a rookery, attracts rooks from several other rookeries, as well as jackdaws and carrion crows.

The face and chin of adults lack feathers, and are pale grey. The base of the bill is also grey.

Activity and noise reach a peak at the rookery in early spring. Birds quarrel over territories, make pursuit flights around the rookery, and display by bowing, tail fanning and wing drooping.

The all-black plumage has a purplish gloss, and the long thigh feathers give the 'baggy trousers' appearance.

The iridescent sheen of the feathers gives a silvery effect when viewed against the sun.

Carrion and Hooded Crow

❈

CORVUS CORONE

The all-black carrion crow is found throughout England, Wales and most of Scotland. The grey and black hooded crow occurs in north-west Scotland, in Ireland and the Isle of Man. They are distinct forms, or sub-species, of the European crow. Although they have separate breeding ranges and different plumages, they are regarded as the same species because they inter-breed freely where their ranges overlap and they produce fertile offspring (often called hybrids). The zone where inter-breeding occurs is rather narrow, which indicates that the hybrids are less successful breeders than either of the pure forms. Both forms are usually resident, although there is some dispersal of young in autumn. Numbers of hooded crows are boosted in winter by the arrival in northern and eastern Britain of birds from Scandinavia. Crows will eat almost anything, and scavenge widely in winter, including at refuse tips and on the shore. They are widely considered to be pests, eating gamebird eggs, or causing damage to trapped sheep or young lambs. Although some damage is caused, it is rarely as serious as often suggested — hoodies eat a lot from tips and cattle troughs! People some-

The hooded crow has a grey back, breast and underside, and is grey underneath the front of the wing.

times confuse carrion crows with rooks. A rule-of-thumb way of distinguishing the two is to observe their social behaviour: rooks are invariably seen in large groups, while crows are usually solitary or seen in pairs.

The powerful dagger-like bill is capable of tearing flesh.

The carrion crow is entirely black, with a blue and green gloss.

Both hooded and carrion crows often mob birds of prey, such as this buzzard, and are usually successful in driving them away.

Length: 47cm
Weight: 540-600g
Where to look: farmland, open woodland, heaths, coasts, towns and parks. **Nest:** usually in trees, made of sticks and earth, lined with wool or hair. **Eggs:** usually 4, greenish, spotted. **Food:** omnivorous. **Voice:** *kaaaw.*

Where hooded and carrion crows inter-breed, the young may have mixed black and grey plumages.

Raven

✻

CORVUS CORAX

The spectacular raven is an inseparable part of the upland and coastal scene in western and northern Britain and much of Ireland. More widespread at the turn of the century, it has withdrawn westwards due to persecution. There has been a slight recovery since 1914 in places adjacent to ancient strongholds, partly due to a return to tree nesting by birds unable to find a suitable, unoccupied crag. More recently the range has contracted again, and large conifer plantations, which result in the removal of sheep, trigger a decline. In Ireland, where conifer planting is less concentrated and the food supply (largely dead sheep) consequently less affected, ravens may be on the increase. The British and Irish population is still less than 5,000 pairs. Most ravens are crag-nesters, ideally suited to the harsh and expansive upland environment or the windswept sea coast, but trees, quarry faces and old buildings are also used for nesting. Ravens with territories stay in them all year round, but young birds disperse and non-breeders form sizeable itinerant flocks. At a suitable windy crag they dive and roll in the upcurrents in an expression of sheer exuberance in their mastery of a difficult environment.

Length: 64cm;
Weight: 800-1,500g
Where to look: sea cliffs, woods and crags on valley sides, mountains and moors. **Nest:** usually on rocky crags and ledges, less often in trees; large and built of small branches and sticks, lined in layers, first with earth and roots, then plant material, mainly moss, then wool, hair and fine grass. **Eggs:** 3-7, (usually 5) laid in March. **Food:** omnivorous, but sheep carrion forms the majority of the diet. **Voice:** a deep croaking *prruk* often repeated. Also an almost bell-like *toc* and quiet, rattling 'song'.

The principal food is dead sheep, which may be abundant after hard winter weather. In the lambing season the placentae are eaten.

Ravens eat small mammals, frogs, lizards, insects and even refuse.

The larger, heavier and more powerful bill helps distinguish the raven from the carrion crow. The feathers on the throat are rather shaggy, giving the bird a distinctive profile.

In flight, note well-separated tips to primary wing feathers, large head, and long, wedge-shaped tail.

Flight is direct, with deep, heavy wing-beats; rather slower than carrion crow. May spread primary wing feathers, making wing-beats very noisy. Glides, and frequently soars on thermals.

The largest crow in Britain. Entirely black plumage with blue, purplish and greenish gloss, and black bare parts. Readily told from other crows by large size.

Perches on rocks and boulders, also on the ground. Has a stately walk. Hops clumsily when hurried.

Dipper

❄

CINCLUS CINCLUS

Living chiefly in the north and west of Britain, dippers love fast, shallow water. A bird will stand on a rock in mid-stream, 'curtseying' every few seconds as if on springs, then slip smoothly beneath the surface and walk along the stream-bed, or 'fly' underwater — tricks that no other songbird can achieve: the plumage is soft and dense for good insulation in the water.

Dippers sometimes perch on trees or wires, and they even search house gutters for food at times! Usually solitary or in pairs, several birds may roost together in winter, in a sheltered spot such as under a bridge. In winter, too, some birds move to lowland rivers or even to the coast, and some reach the south-east — although a winter dipper there may well be in the 'black-bellied' race from Europe, which lacks the chestnut of British birds. A hazard for upland dippers could prove to be acid rain, which may reduce populations of their animal food.

Brown head, slate-grey back, with dark 'scaly' markings only visible at close range.

Juveniles are greyer than adults, and more 'scaly' in appearance.

Dippers are unique among songbirds in feeding underwater. Despite unwebbed feet, they swim very well.

Brilliant white chin, throat and breast separated from dark belly and undertail by a chestnut band. White eyelid obvious when blinked.

Length: 18cm; **Weight:** 60-65g
Where to look: fast-flowing upland streams; less often lowland rivers, mill-races, weirs. **Nest:** under bridge, bank overhang, tree roots, behind a waterfall. Domed.
Eggs: 4-6, white. **Food:** aquatic invertebrates; some small fish, tadpoles. **Voice:** piercing, rasped *zit* or metallic *chink*; song a long warble of liquid and grating notes.

They fly low and fast on shore with whirring wings, following the course of the stream or river.

Wren

✻

TROGLODYTES TROGLODYTES

Most British and Irish wrens look the same as European ones, red-brown and buff, barred darker. However, there are four other subspecies on British islands — on St Kilda, on Fair Isle, in the Hebrides, and in the Shetlands. The first two races are greyer than mainland birds, the last two darker. One day they may form different species: at present, they all share the restless and excitable nature of the familiar woodland wren, and its explosive calls and song.

Few people would name the wren as the commonest British bird, and yet in many years it is exactly that, with perhaps ten million pairs. Its ability to survive and breed from southern heathlands to northern sea-stacks is the reason for its success in these years. But hard winters are murderous for the species: sometimes seven out of ten are killed. Some wrens combat severe weather by moving to better feeding places. Some roost communally in natural or artificial holes, and at dusk over 60 have been watched going into a standard-size nestbox! Special roosting nests are occasionally built, or old breeding nests may be used. How the birds all learn of such roosts is a mystery. Their live-food diet is one reason for wrens' winter vulnerability, but they can be helped by sprinkling grated cheese under hedges and in other likely places.

Tiny; red-brown above with darker bars; buffish below. Short, cocked tail. Both sexes, and young birds, look alike.

Wrens thread invisibly through the undergrowth, then pop up to sing or to scold the observer.

A wren's nest is an intricate structure. Usually spherical in shape, it has a neat opening on one side.

Normal flight is whirring, direct and low, the bird quickly diving back into cover again.

The male builds several nests and the female (or females when the male is polygamous) lines one with feathers. A second brood may be reared in the same nest.

Wrens often spend winter in odd places such as reedbeds.

Length: 9.5cm **Weight:** 10g
Where to look: low cover anywhere from gardens to remote sea cliffs, but especially in woodlands. **Nest:** domed, usually low in tree, ivy or crevice. **Eggs:** 5-6, white, spotted red. **Food:** insects, spiders. **Voice:** a hard *chiti;* dry rattle. Song is startlingly loud outburst.

Dunnock

❋
PRUNELLA MODULARIS

'Still waters run deep', the proverb says, and the dunnock is a perfect example. Sober in colouring and demeanour, it has a reputation among birdwatchers for being a bit boring, and yet it has an enormously interesting sex life! A male may have a single mate, two or even three; a female might have two or three males; and sometimes several males are associated with several females. The commonest arrangement is a simple pair or a female with two males.

Because of these complications, it is a biological advantage to a male to ensure that he is the one to fertilize the eggs: to do this, before mating he uses his bill to stimulate the female to eject sperm from any previous mating. In a two-male/one- female relationship, one male tends to be subordinate and may be prevented from mating: if so, he will not help to feed the young, which may not even be of their own species — dunnocks are frequent victims of the cuckoo, the speckled eggs of which they are unable to distinguish from their own unmarked ones.

Dunnocks are widespread in Britain. They occur in a wide variety of habitats, from upland areas of moderate elevation down to windswept headlands around the coast. The one thing all these different locations have in common is good ground cover, be it bramble or bracken.

Length: 14.5cm **Weight:** 20-22g
Where to look: gardens, woodland, hedges, open spaces with bushes. **Nest:** low in hedges, bushes, often in evergreens. **Eggs:** 4-5, turquoise. **Food:** insects; mainly seeds in winter. **Voice:** a piercing *peep*; song is a high, pleasant warble, like wren's, but weaker, more rambling.

Adult dunnocks are a rich brown above, streaked with black, slate grey on the head and underparts. They have a thin, buff wingbar.

Once commonly known as the hedge sparrow, the dunnock is sparrow-like in colouration, but with a quite different lifestyle.

Dunnocks have the fine bill of an insect-eater, though they mostly eat small seeds in the winter.

Not usually sociable, but in winter loose feeding flocks of a hundred or more birds may gather at food-rich sites.

They hunt for food under hedges, on lawns, along field borders and in root-crops and weed-patches.

Dunnocks have a distinctive gait, hopping slowly and deliberately, body close to the ground.

Sedge Warbler

❋

ACROCEPHALUS SCHOENOBAENUS

Old country names for the sedge warbler include mock nightingale and Scotch nightingale, for this lively summer visitor sings night and day when it first arrives back in Britain. A mass overnight arrival can be very exciting, with singing birds occupying every riverside bush where the previous day there were none. Often a bird will suddenly emerge from the depths of the vegetation where it has been feeding low down, and burst into its exuberant song, full of mimicry, seldom repeating itself, suddenly halting, then tearing off again, and always sounding vaguely irritated. It may also fly up vertically and spiral down, with fluttering wings and spread tail, singing excitedly.

Normally weighing only about 10g (⅓oz), the sedge warbler feeds avidly on plum-reed aphids before migration and puts on large fat deposits which may double its weight. This enables it to cross the Sahara in one hop from France or Spain, a distance of some 3,800km (2,400 miles). The Sahel drought in West Africa has caused a decline in numbers since 1968, as returning birds use this zone for feeding prior to spring migration.

The sedge warbler is primarily an insect feeder. The waterside vegetation which forms its ideal habitat is a rich hunting ground for flies of numerous species, as well as mayflies and caddis flies; moth caterpillars are also important in the sedge warbler's diet.

Inquisitive, often sidling up vertical stems to investigate an intruder or strange noise.

Often seen in jerky, low flight. Broad, creamy stripe over the eye, streaky back, and upstreaked tawny rump; tail spread and depressed. May perch horizontally, looking rather furtive.

At close range, the orange-red gape of the singing bird can be seen.

Length: 13cm; **Weight:** 10-13g
Where to look: waterside vegetation, cereal fields, plantations. **Nest:** deep cup of grass, sedge, low in brambles, etc.
Eggs: 5-6, pale olive, and well speckled.
Food: insects, larvae, aphids. **Voice:** impatient chatter of harsh and sweet notes.

Grasshopper Warbler

LOCUSTELLA NAEVIA

Perhaps Britain's most mouse-like bird in its movements. Will drop into low vegetation when disturbed, and run and creep in preference to flying. The song is insect-like, or perhaps recalls a freewheeling bicycle.

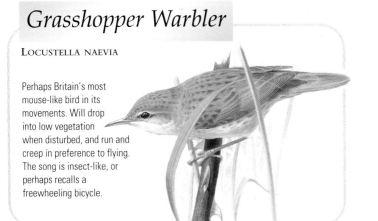

Cetti's Warbler

CETTIA CETTI

Dark, thick-set, whiter beneath; dark bars under rounded tail. The song is given in incredibly loud bursts.

Reed Warbler

❈

ACROCEPHALUS SCIRPACEUS

Seasonal and age variation in plumage colour, though always with warm red-brown hues, especially on the rump.

The neat, woven nest has living reed stems incorporated into its structure.

Though nesting in reed beds, they regularly forage in nearby bushes, especially willows. Often seen far from water on migration.

Very agile. Clings to vertical stems with both feet, or to adjacent stems, thereby doing the splits! Moves up and down in jerks, or hops and flits from plant to plant.

On the edge of its range in Britain, the reed warbler has spread west and north to occupy most suitable red beds in England and Wales. Large numbers may nest in one reed bed, though the birds themselves are not social, and are highly aggressive to others of their kind. Along with the meadow pipit and the dunnock, this bird is the main host of the cuckoo in Britain. Studies have shown that the proportion of reed warbler nests parasitised has more than doubled in recent years, and that 'reed warbler cuckoos' are significantly more successful in having their young reared to maturity than those using other hosts. Because of high cuckoo predation in reed bed colonies, nests outside reed beds are, paradoxically, more successful from the warblers' viewpoint.

For such small birds, reed warblers are long-lived. Ringing studies have revealed several 10- and 11-year-old birds.

The song may recall that of the sedge warbler at first, and like that species includes mimicry, but it is much more repetitive, with a steadier rhythm. Unlike the neurotic sedge warbler, the reed warblers' song sounds rather 'laid-back', perhaps in keeping with drowsy summer days by the waterside.

Like its relative the sedge warbler, the reed warbler feeds mainly on insects. Both adults and larvae are taken, and the diet includes moth larvae, grasshoppers, caddis flies and aphids. The bird is an agile climber and can move through reeds and tangled vegetation with ease, using its fine bill to pluck an unsuspecting insect from a leaf or stem.

Marsh Warbler

ACROCEPHALUS PALUSTRIS

Reed and marsh warblers both have long bills and legs, long undertail coverts and rounded tails. Voice only reliable distinction, that of the marsh warbler being rich and mimetic.

Length: 13cm; **Weight:** 10-15g
Where to look: reed beds across southern Britain. **Nest:** deep cup of grasses woven around reed stems, over shallow water. **Eggs:** 4, greenish-white, mottled darker. **Food:** variety of insects. **Voice:** like sedge warbler, but more relaxed, each phrase repeated.

Blackcap

❋

SYLVIA ATRICAPILLA

Often sings from high in an oak tree in spring. In jerky flight from tree to tree, the longish tail shows no white, ruling out whitethroats.

Although (like other warblers) they are primarily summer visitors, increasing numbers of blackcaps now spend the winter in Britain. At this time they most often live in gardens, where they feed on birdtable scraps, fat, bread and, not infrequently, even peck at hanging nut bags. British breeding birds migrate to the Mediterranean and North Africa; those seen in Britain during winter have come from eastern Europe. The habit of overwintering is not new, but it is growing, with perhaps 2,000 birds now, some regularly as far north as Aberdeen. Although smaller than many other garden birds, blackcaps are usually very aggressive, and may be the dominant bird present at the 'feeding station'. They often puff out their feathers to appear larger than they really are, and as an added protection against the cold.

The full song consists of short phrases, often with a terminal flourish of loud, clear notes, and is regarded by many as equal to the nightingale in quality. By contrast, the call is a *tac-tac*, harder than that of the garden warbler. However, the softer, more rambling subsong is very garden-warbler-like and many people are happier identifying them by sight, not sound.

Female unmistakable with bright, red-brown cap. Juvenile similar but more rusty-brown, less olive-brown above, yellower below, with orange-brown or dark brown cap.

In autumn, blackberries are regularly and greedily taken; in winter, ivy and holly berries. Rather clumsy feeder.

Length: 13-15cm; **Weight:** 14-20g
Where to look: woods, parks, gardens, birdtables in winter. **Nest:** compact grass cup. **Eggs:** 5, pale, spotted brownish. **Food:** insects, berries, also fat and scraps in winter. **Voice:** beautiful loud, rich, pure warbling.

Garden Warbler

❋

SYLVIA BORIN

No outstanding features, other than a beautiful voice.

The nondescript garden warbler more than makes up for its lack of looks with its beautiful song. It is always with a feeling of satisfaction that one catches sight of the songster to confirm the sound

When in full song, it has few rivals, and must rank in the British 'top ten' songsters. Note greyish-brown sides of nape and hind neck, and, in close view, narrow pale eye-ring.

identification, for it can be tricky to separate the songs of garden warbler and blackcap. The former sings longer phrases with shorter intervals, and the song is quieter and mellower, more rapid and even, without the almost abrupt outburst of the blackcap.

The garden warbler arrives later than the blackcap. Competition between the two species is largely avoided by the garden warbler's preferences for feeding in lower vegetation. The male builds several 'cock's nests' of dried grass before the actual nest site is chosen.

In autumn, late migrants hang on well into October, and then turn to fruit and berries to supplement the basic insectivorous diet. Like many birds, the garden warbler is rather inappropriately named, rarely occurring in the average garden, and unfamiliar to most garden birdwatchers. Only small numbers breed in Ireland, and it is scarce in the north of Scotland.

In flight, note shortish square-ended tail without 'white outers', longish wings and rather plump appearance.

Length: 13-15cm; **Weight:** 16-23g
Where to look: woods, scrub, overgrown hedgerows. **Nest:** loose cup of dry grass, usually low. **Eggs:** 4-5, white or buff, blotched darker. **Food:** insects, larvae, fruit. **Voice:** rich, sustained, even warbling. Call *check-check.*

On migration, may be seen in hedgerows, eating berries. Rather secretive. In worn plumage, upperparts greyer-brown, paler buff below, throat white, grey neck spot. Moults in winter quarters.

Whitethroat

❖

SYLVIA COMMUNIS

In spring, the male is a very smart bird with grey head, white throat and beautiful, pinkish wash across his breast.

In the spring of 1969 birdwatchers were asking 'where have all the whitethroats gone?'. Until then they had been among Britain's most abundant birds. Subsequent analysis showed that less than one bird in four had returned, and that the factor responsible was the disastrous drought in the arid thorn-scrub zone of the Sahel, south of the Sahara, which holds Britain's whitethroats in winter. The population has never recovered, though the rather tetchy song remains a characteristic summer sound. The old country name of 'nettlecreeper' reflects the bird's favourite nesting site.

The males return a fortnight before their mates to set up territory. They are restless birds, forever complaining, raising their crown feathers or fanning the rather long, prominently white-edged tail. The song may be given while on the move inside bushes, from an exposed perch or (especially where there are no trees or taller features in the territory) in a jerky, dancing, short song-flight, the bird bouncing as if on an invisible piece of elastic.

His mate is rather duller, with a browner head. Note also the white eye-ring and pale eye.

Easily told in all plumages from lesser whitethroat by the rusty fringes to the flight feathers, pale legs, longer tail and large-headed, often rather unkempt, appearance.

Length: 13-15cm; **Weight:** 12-18g
Where to look: low hedgerows, scrub, woodland edge. **Nest:** low cup of dry grass, roots. **Eggs:** 4-5, blue/green, spotted grey. **Food:** insects, berries. **Voice:** vigorous, scratchy warble. Calls include *whet-whet-whet*.

Lesser Whitethroat

❖

SYLVIA CURRUCA

Male and female similar. Not shy, but often stays well concealed.

Dark face and lower edge to ear-coverts.

In flight, shows less white on outer tail than whitethroat.

One of a small group of birds which migrates south-east to spend the winter in north-east Africa (mainly in the Sudan and Ethiopia), lesser whitethroats take different routes in spring and autumn. Ringing recoveries have shown that British birds pass through northern Italy *en route* to Egypt, where they follow the Nile, but when returning north they pass to the east of the Mediterranean, through Cyprus and Turkey.

Lesser whitethroats are rather retiring birds, but once their song has been learnt, it will reveal the species to be quite common over much of England. Care must be taken not to confuse the far-carrying, rattled song with that of the now rare cirl bunting. Birds often sing while on the move, almost always from within a thick hedge, or concealed in the canopy of a tree. At close range, a soft, inward whitethroat-like warble can be heard preceding the song proper, which is a simple, quick rattle sounding like *chakakakakaka*.

In autumn, young birds may be seen in gardens, diligently searching bushes for insects, or taking berries. Their presence may be announced by a hard *tac* or, occasionally, a high-pitched squeak.

The song makes up for its lack of musicality by its carrying power.

Length: 14cm; **Weight:** 10-16g
Where to look: tall, thick hedgerows, scrub. **Nest:** flimsier than whitethroat's. higher above ground. **Eggs:** 4-6, cream, speckled darker. **Food:** insects; fruit in autumn. **Voice:** unmusical, loud rattle. Call hard *tac-tac*.

Dartford Warbler

❄

SYLVIA UNDATA

Until recently Britain's only resident warbler, this entirely insectivorous bird is badly hit by hard winters, and by fragmentation of its specialised heathland habitat. It was first described in 1773 from Bexley Heath, near Dartford in Kent, but has not occurred in that county for many years other than as a vagrant. Nowadays it is confined mainly to Hampshire and Dorset, with outlying groups in Surrey and Devon. Birds which occasionally appear elsewhere probably come from the French population.

Often hard to find, because they skulk and (for a small bird) have large territories, the males may sing from the tops of gorse bushes, or ascend in a song flight. At other times the birds usually reveal their presence by a soft churring call, almost a buzz which, once learnt, is very characteristic. A bird may appear briefly on top of a gorse bush, tail cocked and flicked, and crown feathers raised, before diving abruptly out of sight, leaving the observer excited but anxious for more.

The male builds a series of flimsy 'cock's nests', but the actual nest, often decorated with spider cocoons, is built mainly by the female.

Identified by distinctive flight silhouette and jerky action, together with restricted habitat.

Both sexes appear all dark at any distance. Male is dark chocolate-brown with slate-grey head above, and dark wine colour below with white belly, the pale throat spots invisible except at close range. His mate is paler, greyer; young greyer still.

A restless, agitated bird, its long tail constantly cocked, fanned and flicked.

Note relatively large, angular head, and pale-based spiky bill.

Length: 13cm; **Weight:** 9-12g
Where to look: resident on southern heaths with gorse and heather. **Nest:** cup of dead grasses, moss. **Eggs:** 4, pale, speckled grey. **Food:** insects, in winter mainly spiders. **Voice:** scratchy warble. Call a soft *tchirr.*

Wood Warbler

❄

PHYLLOSCOPUS SIBILATRIX

Clear yellow stripe above eye; yellow throat and upper breast sharply divided from white lower down.

Largest of the green warblers, the wood warbler is peculiar in having two totally different songs. Only the willow tit shares this characteristic. A beautiful, silvery shivering trill, uttered with head thrown back and causing the whole bird to vibrate, is the regular song, but interspersed less frequently in these phrases is a powerful, rather melancholy repetition of the call note *pew.*

Though nesting on the ground, the wood warbler spends more time in trees than the willow warbler or chiffchaff. The beautiful spiralling courtship display flight of the male in and below the canopy attracts the attention of the female, in the open woods with little undergrowth which are its favoured habitat.

Wood warblers are seldom seen on spring passage, as they head straight for their breeding grounds. In autumn, like the lesser whitethroat, they move south-east through Italy to their equatorial wintering grounds in central and eastern Africa.

Unlike other leaf warblers, wood warblers do not give their nests a cosy feather lining. The parents are kept busy feeding their young for a month after fledging, and thus only have a single brood.

Adults become duller and browner above as season progresses.

Yellow fringes to tail and wing feathers, forming paler panel.

Bright colours harmonise with fresh greens in late spring sun.

Length: 12-13cm; **Weight:** 7-12g
Where to look: oak and beech woods with sparse ground cover, local. **Nest:** dome of dead leaves; grass on ground. **Eggs:** 5-7, white, speckled reddish. **Food:** insects. **Voice:** accelerated shivering trill, or repeated *pew-pew.*

Willow Warbler

❋

PHYLLOSCOPUS TROCHILUS

Call distinctly nearer two syllables than chiffchaff's 'hweet'.

Migrants from Scandinavia, and many Scottish breeders, are brown and white, rather than olive and yellow.

May hover briefly, or sally out after flying insects, like a flycatcher.

Gilbert White, of Selborne fame, was the first to distinguish the three species of 'willow wren' — willow warbler, chiffchaff and wood warbler — noticing that their songs were quite different.

For many bird-watchers the first real feeling of spring comes with the overnight arrival, in early April, of willow warblers — their effortless, beautiful cascade of sweet, liquid notes coming from still leafless trees and bushes. They are the commonest summer visitors, with some three million pairs in Britain and Ireland, their huge range stretching right across northern Eurasia. East Siberian breeding birds undertake a 10-11,000km (6-7,000 miles) journey twice a year to and from their winter quarters in East Africa — an astonishing journey for such tiny bundles of feathers. Their resilience is further evidenced by the record of a bird, alive and well, but completely transfixed by a thorn which must have pierced it some time previously, for dead skin surrounded the thorn.

Willow warblers are the only British birds to undergo two complete moults annually — once in summer, and again in West Africa in late winter: a remarkable fact considering the extra energy requirements needed to form a complete new set of feathers.

Legs usually pale in willow warbler, dark in chiffchaff, but not always! Much variation in both species, but willow warbler less drab, sleeker and usually with clearer and longer stripe above eye. Call different.

Length: 10.5-11.5cm; **Weight:** 6-10g
Where to look: woods of all types, scrub.
Nest: dome of grass, lined with feathers, on ground. **Eggs:** 6-7, white, speckled red-brown. **Food:** small insects, larvae.
Voice: falling cadence of pure notes. Call soft *hoo-eet*.

Freshly arrived adult – brown-olive above, whitish buff below, with yellowish breast and stripe over eye. 'Brighter' plumage than chiffchaff.

Chiffchaff

❋

PHYLLOSCOPUS COLLYBITA

Juvenile browner above and yellower below than adult, less bright than young willow warbler.

Like the cuckoo, the chiffchaff derives its name in many European languages from its rather monotonous, but unmistakable, song — *chiff chaff chaff chip chap chiff chep*. Many who recognise the song have little idea of the appearance of the singer, for this tiny bird, the first summer songbird to arrive back, in late March, usually sings from high in a tall tree. Most spend the winter around the Mediterranean, with small numbers braving the British winter, mainly in the south-west, and often at sewage farms. These residents may occasionally include the greyer Siberian-race birds, with their different, chick-like call. Bright autumn days may cause migrants to burst into unseasonal song.

The males play little part in the nesting cycle, leaving nest building, incubation and most of the feeding of the young to the female.

This short-haul migrant has shorter, more rounded wings than the long-winged, tropical-wintering willow warbler.

Though requiring more mature trees than willow warbler, it also feeds more regularly on the ground, especially on migration and in winter, hopping in an agile way, flicking its wings and tail frequently.

Brownish-olive upperparts, dirty white underparts with yellow tinge on breast. Rounder-headed, dumpier than willow warbler, with clearer eye-ring.

In worn plumage in midsummer, becomes browner and whiter.

Length: 11cm; **Weight:** 6-9g
Where to look: woods, scrub with trees. In winter, often by water. **Nest:** grass dome, just above ground. **Eggs:** 5-6, white, lightly marked darker. **Food:** small insects. **Voice:** repeated *chiff-chaff*. Call emphatic *hweet*.

Goldcrest

❋

REGULUS REGULUS

A long with the similar but much rarer firecrest, this is Britain's smallest bird, weighing only as much as a 10p coin. It is sobering to spot a minute dot heading over the waves towards land on the east coast in late autumn, at last pitching into a bramble where lively actions and a thin high call note reveal its identity. That such a tiny,

Pugnacious birds; the crown stripe flares in anger, even at its own reflection. Juveniles lack the black and yellow crown markings.

Large, beady black eye in bare face gives a rather 'surprised' expression. Yellowish feet.

Lively actions: hovering or flycatching like a leaf warbler; flicking wings while carefully searching the tiniest twigs and pine needles.

entirely insectivorous bird not only survives the British winter, but chooses to migrate here from Scandinavia, is one of nature's wonders. In Yorkshire, it was known as the 'woodcock pilot', arriving at the same time as that species, and in Norfolk it was even thought that they sometimes hitched a lift on the backs of short-eared owls!

Often joining tit flocks in winter, the restless and confiding goldcrest keeps in constant touch by means of its thin contact call. Along with the coal tit, it may be the dominant species in conifer plantations, both in summer and winter. Its ability to exploit these alien trees has resulted in a huge increase in numbers.

Length: 9cm; **Weight:** 5-7g
Where to look: woodland, parks, gardens with conifers. **Nest:** tiny suspended cup of moss, cobwebs. **Eggs:** 7-8, white with faint spots. **Food:** tiny insects. **Voice:** thin, high, rhythmical song, ending in flourish.

Firecrest

❋

REGULUS IGNICAPILLUS

I t is always a tremendous thrill to see this tiny gem, surely one of Britain's most beautiful birds. Formerly only a rare visitor on migration and in winter, mainly to the south and south-west coasts, breeding in Britain was not recorded until the early 1960s; since then, though breeding remains sporadic, numbers have slowly increased and small colonies are now scattered over a number of English and Welsh counties. These initial attempts at colonisation follow an increase in western Europe this century. The song has similarities with that of the goldcrest, and it is likely that the bird is often overlooked. Evidence of the close relationship of these species is shown by reports of cross-breeding.

In Britain, at least, Norway spruce is usually present where firecrests nest, with some deciduous trees and often holly, too. Firecrests often feed closer to the ground than goldcrests. On migration they frequent bracken, bramble and sea buckthorn. The thin

call is very similar to that of the goldcrest, but to the practised ear sounds harder and slightly lower-pitched, a repeated *zit*, the last note rising a little in pitch.

Bright orange sheen on shoulder patches, greener above and whiter below than goldcrest. Males have richer, fiery orange central crown stripe, best seen in display.

When displaying, males flash their brilliant crowns at a potential mate or intruder.

Length: 9cm; **Weight:** 5-7g
Where to look: less reliant on conifers than goldcrest; woods, coastal scrub. **Nest:** like goldcrest. **Eggs:** 7-11, white or pinkish, faintly marked. **Food:** tiny insects. **Voice:** song — simple, repeated crescendo of one note, without end flourish.

Juveniles lack the striking head pattern, though may be identified by suggestion of adult markings.

Pied Flycatcher

❊

FICEDULA HYPOLEUCA

This is a classic bird of wooded hillsides in the west and north of Britain. In spring, the male calls attention to himself with his repeated, musical song and his flashing plumage. The female is much more discreet, and she incubates the eggs alone.

The male is sometimes bigamous and may then hold territories up to 3.5km (2 miles) apart, perhaps in order to convince the second female that he is unattached! But if both the clutches hatch, he will only help feed the young of the first. Many broods are raised in nest boxes, and the provision of these has undoubtedly helped the bird to maintain or increase its numbers in some areas.

Feeding among leaves, on trunks and branches, and on the ground, pied flycatchers take a good deal of non-flying prey, particularly caterpillars, and occasionally even worms. Snails are also eaten, and the bird has been observed hammering a snail on a road to break open the shell, in the manner of a song thrush.

Once the young have fledged the family moves up into the canopy and becomes silent and difficult to find. In autumn they depart and, at the same time, the east coast of Britain may receive 'falls' of Continental pied flycatchers on migration.

Length: 12.5cm **Weight:** 13-14g
Where to look: mature deciduous woods.
Nest: in a hole, usually in a tree; nest-boxes.
Eggs: 5-9, unmarked pale blue. **Food:** mainly insects. **Voice:** a sharp *squick* or a soft *wheet*. The song is a short, sweet warble.

Although they do take prey in the air, pied flycatchers frequently pick food from leaves and branches, as well as the ground.

Some males in autumn retain the white forehead and black on the wings and tail. A spring moult restores the pied plumage.

Smaller and stouter than the spotted flycatcher; juveniles difficult to distinguish, but more white in tail of pied flycatcher.

Pied flycatchers do not sit bolt upright like spotted flycatchers: they appear more restless, flicking a wing, or wings, and waving their tails.

The male in spring is most striking. Females, young birds and males in autumn are grey-brown above and white below, with obvious white patches in the wings and on the sides of the tail.

Spotted Flycatcher

❊

MUSCICAPA STRIATA

The bird flies out in pusuit of passing insects, often returning to its original perch. Flight may twist and turn with the chase; frequently low over the ground.

Length: 14cm
Weight: 15-16g
Where to look: woodland edges, clearings, parks and gardens. **Nest:** in natural and man-made crevices and ledges, creepers, etc. **Eggs:** 4-5, white, blotched red. **Food:** chiefly insects. **Voice:** thin, high calls and song.

Preferred location on the edge of woodland or in open clearings; may also be seen in parks and spacious gardens, especially with mature trees and old walls to offer nesting sites.

Juvenile birds are truly 'spotted' on the breast and 'scaly' above, and may be confused with the juvenile pied warbler.

Characteristic broad-based, flattish beak, as other flycatchers; wings comparatively long, tail square at end; brownish spots over throat and breast.

Adults are grey-brown above, with blackish, pale-edged wings; off-white, streaked with grey, below; noticeably pale. Similar plumage for male and female.

The bird perches in a distinctive upright pose in a prominent place on a bare twig or fence post.

So great is its dependence on insects and because it needs to be quite sure of the supply of its food, the spotted flycatcher is among the last of the summer migrants to return to Britain from Africa.

One day in late May the spotted flycatcher will be back, sitting erect on a dead bough, or perhaps a post or a wire. It launches out in agile pursuit of some insect, catches it (sometimes with an audible snap of its bill) and perches again, often in the original place, with a flick of its wings. It pursues most flying insects, including butterflies, bees and wasps, and it strikes large and dangerous victims against its perch to subdue them. In colder, wet weather, it will hunt among branches for aphids and the like. The female will also eat snails and woodlice for the calcium she needs to form egg-shells. To avoid competing with each other, males and females may feed in different parts of their territory.

A favourite nest site is provided by a climbing plant against a wall or tree trunk, but spotted flycatchers will nest anywhere from an old nest to a corpse hanging on a game-keeper's gibbet! Open-fronted nest-boxes will often attract them.

Wheatear

❋

OENANTHE OENANTHE

Breeding throughout the British Isles, from the south coast of England to the Shetland Isles, the wheatear demonstrates how a population can vary in plumage and size. The males of the southern birds are smaller and paler, being almost pure white on the underparts compared with the rich buff of birds further north. The northern birds are also bigger and heavier.

When flying away, all wheatears show the distinctive white rump and black 'T' shape on the tail.

The long, black legs and upright stance are characteristic.

The song is frequently delivered from a hovering flight.

Spring males are clean, clear- cut, handsome birds.

Spring females are a uniform, rich buffish-brown.

Wheatears are typically birds of open country, from mountain tops to moorland, from heaths to sandy coastlands. They are ground-living birds with long legs and short tails. Highly active and very distinctive, when disturbed they fly away to display a gleaming white rump and base of the tail. A frequent perch is the top of a stone wall or exposed fence post, but as a substitute they will hover some distance above the ground, giving their harsh warning alarm note.

They have a wide distribution, from Greenland across Europe and Asia to Alaska. Throughout the range they are summer migrants, all individuals migrating south each winter to tropical Africa. Some of the migratory flights are particularly spectacular: a regular crossing being from Iceland to northern Spain, for example. They are among the earliest of the returning spring migrants, the first individuals reaching the south coast of England before mid-March. The sudden surprise of a flashing white rump announces the return of what, for the moment, seems the prettiest bird of spring.

The autumn male loses his striking markings.

Autumn females and juveniles are similar.

Length: 14.5cm; **Weight:** 17-30g
Where to look: open country, particularly upland areas. **Nest:** in hole, ground or wall; grass, lined with hair and feathers. **Eggs:** 5-6, blue. **Food:** chiefly insects. **Voice:** song scratchy, often in flight. Call a harsh *chack*.

Stonechat

❀

SAXICOLA TORQUATA

The number of stonechats in Britain is highly variable, a result of their susceptibility to cold winters, when local populations may be eliminated. Although some individuals are migrants (there are records of British ringed stonechats being found in the Mediterranean in winter), the majority remain here all year, although they spread more widely around the coast. Even in winter they are strongly territorial and remain in pairs, always thinly spread. Slightly shorter and rounder than the whinchat, the stonechat has a less streaked back and never shows the pale stripe over the eye of the whinchat. The distinctive male in breeding plumage has a black head with a contrasting white collar and very red breast. There is usually a clear area of white on the rump and white flash on the wing. Females and young birds are less well marked, but retain the round-headed appearance with a large dark eye and at least a trace of a dark chin.

The stonechat has a clear attachment to gorse, which the male will use as a song perch and from which he will launch into the characteristic song flight, when he appears to dance in the air.

The distintive pattern of the male is visible, in subdued coloration, on the female.

In flight, the male shows prominent white patches on wings and rump.

Rather robin-like in general appearance, with a large rounded head, long legs and upright stance. The brightness of the red breast in the male may enhance this illusion. Always perches in an open position on top of a bush or fence post and has a close affinity with gorse bushes.

Length: 12.5cm; **Weight:** 14-17g
Where to look: open country with gorse, and near coast. **Nest:** on ground; grass, lined with hair. **Eggs:** 5-6, greenish, speckled with rust colour. **Food:** chiefly insects. **Voice:** song series of double notes, call harsh tsak, *whee-tsak-tsak.*

Whinchat

❀

SAXICOLA RUBETRA

A summer visitor from wintering grounds in tropical Africa, the whinchat is rather patchy in its distribution through Britain. Most numerous in the open countryside of the north and west, it definitely favours the open hillsides and edges of moorland where isolated bushes or fence posts provide suitable look-out points and song posts. It is extremely easy to locate within its territory.

For differences from the closely related stonechat see above, but the whinchat always shows a pale stripe above the eye and pale patches on either side at the base of the tail. The streaked upperparts contrast with the warmish flush of pink or buff on the underparts, and the male presents a contrasting white flash in the wing.

Rather resembling a rather short-tailed robin in shape, the whinchat sits very upright on long black legs. When perched on the ground it can be mistaken for a wheatear, but it differs in that it regularly bobs its body and flicks both wings and tail.

Ever alert, the whinchat lives on its nerves, perhaps aware of its dangerously exposed position.

Slimmer than the similar stonechat, with upright stance on long black legs. Favours exposed perches such as fence posts.

Less well marked, the female still shows the streaked back and pale stripe above the eye.

In flight, the male shows striking white wing flashes and tail panels.

The striking and contrasting plumage of the male is distinctive, particularly the black face mask.

Length: 13cm; **Weight:** 16.5-23.5g
Where to look: open country with bushes. **Nest:** on ground, of grass, lined with hair. **Eggs:** 5-6, bluish, finely speckled brown. **Food:** mainly insects. **Voice:** a sweet warbling song; mimics other species. Call note a whistle and a *tap-hweet-tak.*

Redstart

❋

PHOENICURUS PHOENICURUS

Although widely distributed throughout Britain, redstarts are very much birds of the western and northern oak woods. The older trees provide the holes and cavities that make ideal nesting sites, and the open spaces and leaf-litter give good feeding.

Among the earlier returning summer migrants, many redstarts are back from their African wintering grounds by the middle of April, when their arrival is announced by the distinctive song issuing from high on an exposed woodland perch. They are very active birds, constantly flitting and hovering through the branches. When perched, they bear some resemblance to robins, which are of a similar size.

In all plumages, redstarts differ from all but black redstarts in having contrasting dark central tail feathers in a chestnut-red tail that is continually moved up and down in a characteristic quivering motion. The adult males, with their strikingly patterned plumage of black, white, red and blue-grey, must be among the most distinctive and most beautiful of all British birds.

Lacking the bright plumage pattern of the male, females retain the tail colouration.

Appearance is rounded or sleek. Male is brightly coloured and distinctive.

Length: 11.5cm; **Weight:** 12-19.5g
Where to look: old woods or parkland.
Nest: hole in tree, will use nestbox. Nest of grass lined with feathers. **Eggs:** 5-7, unmarked pale blue. **Food:** mainly insects.
Voice: brief warbling song and plaintive call note *hweet.*

Black Redstart

❋

PHOENICURUS OCHRUROS

Until the middle of the 20th century, the black redstart was considered a migrant species, occurring in both spring and autumn on the south and east coasts of England. It was rare in the north and west, and on the few occasions when a pair remained to nest it was usually at rocky coastal sites in Kent. Following World War II, a remarkable colonisation took place at the London bomb sites and the black redstart became an established British breeding species. Since that time the numbers have increased, and although still very much of south-east distribution the bird can now be encountered in towns and at such places as power stations far from central London. Railway yards and canal wharves are often appreciated!

The presence of breeding pairs is easily overlooked, for although the brief song is distinctive (the final phase has been likened to a handful of metal balls shaken together), the birds are inevitably in a noisy urban setting and only in the very early morning, before the town awakens, can the song be easily heard.

The greyness of the female is good camouflage when on the nest.

The song, delivered high above the city noise, is only clearly audible early in the day.

Length: 14cm; **Weight:** 14-19g
Where to look: towns and buildings.
Nest: hole in wall; grass, lined with feathers, **Eggs:** 4-6, white. **Food:** mainly insects. **Voice:** quick warbling and rattle.

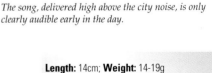

The black body plumage of the adult male contrasts with the white wing panel and red tail. Young males can closely resemble females — but they may sing, hold territories and breed.

Robin

❀

ERITHACUS RUBECULA

As Britain's 'national' bird, the robin must be familiar to everyone. Its association with Christmas dates from the 1860s, when greetings cards became fashionable and postmen wore red tunics and were known as 'robins'. Britain's robins are resident, and are joined by paler northern European immigrants in the winter. These European birds are less confiding and more skulking than Britain's birds — perhaps due to the continuing massacre of migrant birds in southern Europe.

Robins may live to be as much as ten years old, but only a quarter of all robins manage to live beyond their first birthday. The greatest enemies of robins are domestic cats and traffic, which both take a heavy toll. When nesting, the male robin defends the territory and responds to almost any small patch of red — a red flag to a robin would be a better saying than a red rag to a bull. Fights between males can be extremely vicious and may even be to the death. The perky little chap that waits on the spade handle for worms is really quite a nasty piece of work!

Although robins generally build their nests in hedges and shrubs, they will choose some unlikely spots too, including old kettles, and garden sheds are a favourite site.

Length: 14cm; **Weight:** 16-22g
Where to look: gardens, woods and hedges. **Nest:** in bank, ledge or nestbox. Leaves and moss, domed, with hair lining. **Eggs:** 5-7, white with red spots. **Food:** insects, worms and berries. **Voice:** fine song; call *tic-tic-tic*.

Male and female robins look the same and will sing in autumn to mark out winter territories. The autumn song is quieter and less forceful than in spring.

They stand very upright, bobbing their heads and flicking their wings and tail when excited.

Though mainly insectivorous, they will eat fruit and seeds. They are particularly fond of mealworms and can become hand tame if fed with them.

They are highly territorial and will display their red breasts vigorously to any intruders.

Robins pair up from late December to early March. The female chases the male until she is accepted and, once paired, the male feeds her as part of courtship.

Young robins are spotted and have no red breast. They moult into adult plumage in autumn.

During severe winters robins relax their territorial nature and several birds can be seen feeding at a birdtable together.

Nightingale

❋

LUSCINIA MEGARHYNCHOS

Nightingales have acquired a place in British folklore, not for their looks or familiarity, but for their voice alone. One of the earliest outdoor radio broadcasts included a nightingale from a Surrey wood. In fact, they can be extremely difficult to see as they are generally skulking birds whose brownish plumage hides them well in the dense vegetation that they prefer. Very much a species of south-east England, nightingales are scarce in the west and north even as migrants.

Returning as a summer migrant from wintering grounds south of the Sahara, the nightingale's far-carrying, rich and varied song fills some English woods from mid-April onwards, peaking during the first half of May. Contrary to popular belief, the nightingale does not only sing at night. Indeed, as a songster it is equally vocal in daylight, and can often appear to survive without sleep, as the singing will continue day and night during warm spring periods. By early June it is more sporadic and the brief song period comes to an end.

Although the plumage lacks distinctive features, when the bird is seen clearly the contrasting rusty-red tail, often held in a cocked position, is characteristic and gives the general impression of a rather outsized robin. The similar red tail of the redstart differs in having dark central feathers. Plainness in looks can be easily forgiven, though, when the bird has such a wonderful voice!

An extremely difficult bird to see, the uniform plumage blending with the shadows when well hidden in the foliage. Watch carefully for movement and look for the distinctive large black eye.

Principally a ground feeder, often sitting on a perch among the lower branches of scrubby bushes with head cocked on one side, carefully watching the ground below for movement. It will then drop onto any insect. Once on the ground, moves easily among the dead leaves and other foliage with a very agile hopping motion as it flicks tail and wings.

Length: 16cm; **Weight:** 18-26.5g
Where to look: scrub and dense thickets such as overgrown coppice woodland.
Nest: among vegetation close to ground, made of leaves, lined with grass and hair.
Eggs: 4-5, heavily speckled on bluish-green background. **Food:** insects, found on ground, plus some fruit and berries in autumn.
Voice: song rich, varied and vigorous, delivered day and night. Alarm a harsh, hard *tack, tack;* grating croak; loud *hweet.*

Ring Ouzel

❋

TURDUS TORQUATUS

Length: 24cm; **Weight:** 95-130g
Where to look: mountains and moorland.
Nest: of grasses and twigs among rocks and crevices. **Eggs:** 5-6, bluish-green blotched brown. **Food:** insects, berries and fruit. **Voice:** harsh rattle, piping song.

The ring ouzel spends the winter in the Mediterranean region, with some British breeding birds reaching North Africa. It is the only thrush that is a summer visitor to Britain. An early arrival, the first individuals reach southern England in early March and quickly return to the hills, where they occupy wild, open country.

Its upland breeding areas have earned the species the alternative name of 'mountain blackbird', and the differences between ring ouzel and blackbird are not always striking. The white breast crescent is only obvious in the adult males, but in all plumages the ring ouzel has a greyer look, caused by the pale fringes to the feathers. Paleness on the wing feathers results in a distinctive pale area visible on the upperwing as the bird flies.

Ring ouzel flight shows a somewhat similar quality to that of the blackbird, but it appears stronger on the wing and is rather erratic. The flight is accompanied by a deep, throaty, chattering call. The song is a simple, loud piping, audible over very long distances.

The largely black plumage gives the male a sooty appearance. The white breast crescent and yellow bill are obvious on the adult male, as are the pale grey fringes to the wing feathers.

The female is a brown, less strikingly plumaged bird.

Never as confiding as the blackbird, the ring ouzel is found in some of the wildest of mountain areas. Its behaviour is similar to the blackbird's.

Blackbird

❋

TURDUS MERULA

There can be few places in Britain where it is not possible to find the blackbird throughout the year. The British breeding individuals are resident, but each autumn large numbers of migrants from northern Europe arrive on their way south to milder wintering grounds. Spectacular arrivals on the east coast can be seen in late October and November when, at times, hundreds of blackbirds, accompanied by other thrushes, may drop from the sky.

Many of these migrants remain in Britain throughout the winter, joining the resident birds at communal feeding grounds (orchards with waste apples being a particular favourite), and at traditional roosting sites that may be used year after year.

Blackbirds are very susceptible to albinism and individuals often have substantial numbers of white feathers. On such dark birds these feathers are particularly obvious and at times may resemble the crescent shape on the ring ouzel. A few birds are occasionally seen that are pure white, especially in urban areas where they may not be receiving a proper diet. Such individuals are obvious not only to our eyes, but also to those of predators, and so seldom last for many seasons.

A blackbird searching the lawn for worms is a familiar sight. Mainly ground-feeders, they move about in a series of short hopping runs, pausing to cock their head as if listening (in fact looking) for food. The struggle between blackbird and worm as the prey is slowly but steadily drawn from the ground is a familiar garden sight.

The song, delivered from a very prominent song post, consists of loud clear notes combined to make phrases which last for some six seconds with a pause between of similar length.

They sing between March and June, whereas the mistle thrush starts in late December and has short phrases repeated over and over again.

Berries and fruit form a major portion of the winter diet. If the ground remains soft, worms predominate.

Length: 25cm; **Weight:** 80-110g
Where to look: dense woodland to open moorland, common in gardens. **Nest:** a little way up, in trees and hedges, sometimes in buildings. Constructed of mud and moss lined with grass. **Eggs:** 3-5, bluish-green, speckled brown. **Food:** insects summer, berries winter. **Voice:** rich fluty song, rattling alarm.

Males' wings look paler when flapped and catch the eye. Females are sooty brown, much darker than song thrush, but throat can be very pale, with dark streaks. Legs are dark, unlike thrushes'.

Song Thrush

❁

TURDUS PHILOMELOS

Although this is principally a resident species, found in towns and gardens throughout the year, some British song thrushes move south for the winter, to be temporarily replaced by arrivals from Scandinavia and northern Europe. Many of these birds, which are seeking the milder maritime winter climate, will pass on through Britain to spend much of the winter in western France or Spain. Most of the arrivals take place in October and are usually slightly in advance of the true 'winter thrushes' — the redwing and the fieldfare.

The presence of a song thrush in an area is often indicated by the discovery of a thrush's 'anvil', the site where snail shells are broken against a prominent stone or the concrete of a garden path to gain access to the soft, nutritious body inside. This behaviour is unique to the song thrush, although other species, notably the blackbird, have developed the habit of robbing the thrush as soon as the work of opening the snail has been completed, and flycatchers have occasionally been known to break a snail open.

Length: 23cm; **Weight:** 70-90g
Where to look: hedgerows, gardens and woodland. **Nest:** made of leaves and twigs, lined with mud. **Eggs:** 4-5, blue, spotted with black. **Food:** worms, snails, fruit and berries. **Voice:** alarm rattle, thin *sip* in flight.

The adult song thrush is a familiar garden bird; it was once more numerous than the blackbird, but this situation has now been reversed. The warm-brown upperparts of the adult, together with the buffish underparts covered in small, narrow black spots, distinguish it from the other thrushes. The stance is upright, but the body is more horizontal when running.

Song thrushes are regular visitors to birdtables and garden 'feeding stations', preferring to collect items dropped beneath the table rather than using the table itself. They can be attracted with fruit or grated cheese.

The long-legged, upright stance is typical of all ground-feeding thrushes. The birds are usually solitary, but will roost communally in cold weather.

The superb song is delivered from a lower perch than that of the mistle thrush, a low bush or building being typical.

Redwing

❁

TURDUS ILIACUS

The British breeding population of redwings is usually confined to northern Scotland, where nesting was first recorded in 1925. The population increased slowly, and now numbers some 100 pairs in most years. There is little evidence of a westward spread in range and it is speculated that Britain's breeding birds are migrants which have simply failed to return to Scandinavia, rather than being the vanguard of an extensive colonisation. Isolated breeding has been recorded as far south as Kent.

Two distinct populations reach Britain each winter, one from Scandinavia, the other from Iceland. The Icelandic birds spend winter in the west, around the Irish Sea, the Scandinavian birds in the east. Although at first glance the two populations are very similar, the Icelandic birds are in fact distinctly darker and larger. The greater size gives longer wings, necessary to carry them on the lengthy, oversea migration. The Icelandic birds have recently colonised the Faeroes and may also be responsible for some of the British breeding birds.

Length: 21cm; **Weight:** 55-75g
Where to look: open country and gardens. **Nest:** grasses and twigs in trees or bushes. **Eggs:** 5-6, greenish, with red-brown markings. **Food:** worms, insects, but also berries in winter. **Voice:** simply fluty song. Call distinctive *seeip*.

In flight, the smallness of this species can at times make it appear rather lark-like, particularly in a migrating flock. The tawny-red underwing can be very obvious and quite unlike the yellow-buff of the song thrush.

A standing bird will show distinctive lines or streaks on an almost white breast. Dull red flanks are usually visible. Note paler stripes on face.

Although a ground-feeder, flocks will gather on berry bushes such as hawthorn or ivy and feed until the supply is exhausted.

Slightly smaller and darker than the song thrush, the distinctive shade of olive on the upperparts is a good feature once noted.

Mistle Thrush

❖

TURDUS VISCIVORUS

The largest of the common thrushes, the mistle thrush is the earliest to start nesting. The song, often delivered from the top of a tall tree in very windy conditions (the bird's alternative name is 'storm cock'), can be heard from December onwards, and this is one of the few birds in full song at the beginning of the year.

Eggs may be laid as early as February, and young may have left the nest by the end of March.

When breeding, the mistle thrush can be very aggressive, showing a complete lack of fear in driving cats and dogs away from its nesting area. Some individuals will even attack man, to the extent of regularly striking at the head and preventing people from entering their own gardens!

Two identification features visible when the bird is in flight are the gleaming white underwing (obvious) and the whitish tips to the outermost tail feathers (less so).

This is the greyest of the speckled thrushes, most readily identified by the large size, large round spots on the underparts, very upright stance and pure white underwing that is easily visible in flight (when very distinct undulations are also apparent).

The song is always delivered from a very exposed position and consists of up to six blackbird-like phrases repeated again and again in regular sequence.

On the ground, the stance is very upright and birds move about with strong hopping, almost bounding, leaps. In winter the birds can often appear larger and rounder in contrast to the sleeker summer appearance.

Length: 27cm; **Weight:** 110-140g
Where to look: gardens and woodland. **Nest:** in fork of tree, built of roots and grass. **Eggs:** 3-5, variable in colour, but well spotted with brown. **Food:** fruit, berries and insects. **Voice:** loud, far-carrying blackbird-like song. Harsh, churring flight call.

Fieldfare

❖

TURDUS PILARIS

Fieldfares first nested in Britain in 1967, when a nest with fledged young was discovered in the Orkneys, but the subsequent colonisation has not been particularly dramatic. It is rare for more than ten pairs to have been recorded nesting in any one year, and these have almost always been in Scotland. The species has been steadily extending its breeding range westward through Europe, but this expansion may now have ceased.

Traditionally looked upon as a winter visitor to Britain, fieldfares may begin to arrive as early as August, but peak numbers are not reached on the east and south coast until late October or November. In suitable weather conditions, flocks of several hundred at a time will cross the southern North Sea, often arriving exhausted. Of all the winter visitors, the fieldfare is one of the latest to depart, with small parties regularly seen well into May.

Mixed thrush flocks in winter tend to be dominated by fieldfares and redwings, which behave in a noisy, nomadic fashion. Although fieldfares are usually found in the open countryside feeding on farmland and playing fields, cold weather will rapidly drive them into gardens where fruit and any remaining berries will be readily eaten and where they will join other birds at tables and feeding stations.

Length: 26cm; **Weight:** 80-130g
Where to look: parkland, open country.
Nest: in fork of tree, made of grasses and twigs. **Eggs:** 5-6, speckled greenish-blue. Rare and erratic nesting species in Britain. **Food:** mainly worms, insects, but fruit and berries in hard weather. **Voice:** nasal *ee-eep*; harsh *cha-cha-cha-chack* flight call. Song rather weak, blackbird-like.

Note red-brown back.

Flocks will suddenly arrive on berry bushes and remain until the supply is exhausted. Rotting fruit in orchards is eaten if weather is cold. Stubble and ploughed fields are also frequented.

The yellow base to the bill and contrasting plumage pattern, with smooth grey head and rump, makes the fieldfare the most elegant of all the thrushes.

Winter food will be largely insects if the weather remains mild and the ground unfrozen.

On the ground, behaviour is typical of all thrushes, with an upright stance and hopping run.

Comparing Finches

Finches comprise a varied group of seed eating species that have adapted to exploit the varied food supply that is available to them. All are characterised by deep, broad based bills, but some bills are more pointed – goldfinch – while others are blunt and conical – greenfinch – a reflection of the principal items in their diet. In all cases the males are more brightly coloured than the females, a reflection of the necessity for the females, which undertake the majority of the incubation and brooding activities, to remain hidden. The reed bunting often mixes with finches and may visit gardens.

Siskins

Goldfinch

Redpolls

Reed buntings (below) are associated with wetland habitats, the male strikingly marked with black head and broad white collar. The streaky brown female shown below.

Greenfinches (left and right below) exploit reeds and stubble, berry-bearing shrubs and bird tables, but are too heavy for slender stems.Greenfinch flocks swirl round fields, sweep into hedge if alarmed.

Less well marked than the male, female greenfinches (below) still retain a small yellow flash in the wing.

Chaffinches (male above female below) are the commonest of British finches.

The twite (female on right) is a moorland breeding species found in northern Britain.

Although they may nest in Scotland, bramblings (female above) are winter visitors, favouring beech woods.

Male brambling in winter.

Linnets often go un-noticed in such unlikely-seeming places as industrial estates and business areas. Above – female in winter and male above left.

Comparing Warblers

❋

Whitethroat: *(right) lively and excitable; horizontal posture. Key features: rusty-coloured wings, contrasting white throat, pale legs, long white-edged tail, peaked crown. Scratchy song.*

Willow warbler: *very active. Key features: small, slim, well-proportioned, longer-winged than chiffchaff, greenish and whitish, often with extensive yellow; fine bill, palish legs. Delightful song.*

Chiffchaff: *very active. Key features: very like willow warbler, but shorter-winged, duller, stripes above eyes less obvious, dark legs. Bright, repetitive song.*

Lesser whitethroat: *quieter, more unobtrusive than whitethroat, found in taller, thicker vegetation. Key features: white throat, dark ear-coverts, dark legs, no rust colour in wings, basically grey and white. Song hardly worthy of the name.*

Garden warbler: *secretive. Key features: compact build, gentle expression, soft browns, rather pale overall. Mellow song.*

Blackcap: *fairly active and lively, medium-sized. Key features: sharply defined black or brown skullcap, no white in tail. Beautiful, rich, fluty song.*

Marsh Tit

❋

PARUS PALUSTRIS

Marsh and willow tits are about as common as each other and, although not rare, are much less frequently seen than blue or great tits. They usually occur in ones and twos, and both marsh and willow tits join nomadic tit flocks in the winter. They pose one of the classic identification challenges and even experts cannot always tell them apart.

The two species live subtly different lives. Marsh tits prefer deciduous woodland, rarely occurring in conifer woods or scrub. They regularly drop to the ground, for instance to pick up beech-mast, and they hammer open this and other seeds, such as those of yew, honeysuckle and spindle. Marsh tits usually nest in ready-made holes in trees, walls and banks — perhaps doing a little enlarging work: for some reason they rarely use nestboxes. They come regularly to gardens and birdtables, and can often

In adults the cap is glossy black, the neck is 'slim', the bib neat, and there is little or no pale panel in the wing. The flanks and belly are a similar grey-white.

Marsh tits have strong bills and will hammer at tough seeds, such as beech-mast, while holding them under one foot.

Adult male and female marsh tits are alike in colour and pattern. The young bird has a browner cap and bib and is whiter below; it is very like the young willow tit.

be seen carrying food away to hide, usually in crevices under bark, but sometimes in the ground. Such food is regularly recovered, but whether by searching likely places or by precise memory is not yet known.

Length: 11.5cm; **Weight:** 11g
Where to look: deciduous woodland, gardens. **Nest:** in a hole, usually in a tree. **Eggs:** 6-10, white, spotted red. **Food:** insects, seeds and fruits. **Voice:** an explosive *pitchu*; *chika-dee-dee-dee*, etc. Song a repeated *chip-chip-chip*.

The female excavates a new hole each year, low in a rotten stump.

Willow tits do not prefer willows, nor marsh tits marshes! The willow tit is less confined to deciduous woods than the marsh.

Length: 11.5cm; **Weight:** 10g
Where to look: woods, scrub, gardens.
Nest: self-excavated, low in a stump. **Eggs:** 6-10, white, spotted red. **Food:** insects, seeds and fruits. **Voice:** a nasal *air-air-air*, high, thin calls, etc. Song is a clear *piu, piu*.

Both species sometimes occur in the same wood, and both join roving tit flocks, but it is rare to see them together.

Willow Tit

❋

PARUS MONTANUS

The willow tit has the distinction of being the most recent British breeding species to be recognised. It was only separated from the marsh tit at the end of the last century, and the differences between the two species can still be very difficult to spot in practice. Plumage differences are slight, especially in summer when adults have worn feathers: juveniles can be inseparable even in the hand. However, the calls and song are fortunately very distinctive.

There are other differences, too. Although they occur more patchily across the country, willow tits live in a wider variety of woods than marsh tits, including conifer plantations. This may explain their slightly finer bills, which could be useful for feeding among bunches of conifer needles. They feed low down, but only very rarely on the ground, nor do they appear to 'hammer' food. Yet they excavate a new nest hole each year, typically in soft, rotten wood, and ignoring older apparently suitable holes, even in the same stump. This may be to avoid a build-up of parasites, which live in old nests. Willow tits will use nestboxes, especially if these are filled with wood chips or polystyrene for the bird to excavate.

Compared with the marsh tit, adults have a duller black cap, a bull neck and a more diffuse bib; in fresh plumage, pale wing panel and bright buff flanks.

The marsh tit's distinctive sharp, sneezing 'pitchu' sounds annoyed. The willow tit's deliberate, very nasal, 'air-air-air' is unique. Both calls are frequent.

Blue Tit

❉

PARUS CAERULEUS

Blue tits literally put all their eggs in one basket, producing a single brood of chicks each year to coincide with the greatest abundance of juicy, nutritious caterpillars. If that brood fails, there is no second chance. This contrasts with the strategy of the blackbird, whose dependable supply of worms allows three broods of four at a time, spread through the summer.

The blue tit is one of the most popular and familiar garden birds in Britain. Despite its eagerness to profit from man — quickly discovering a bag of peanuts or sunflower seeds, searching the window frames of houses for spiders, using an artificial box for nesting — the blue tit is essentially a woodland bird, especially where there is oak or birch.

In winter the blue tit population spreads out, even feeding in reed beds and much more open places — almost anywhere, in fact, where food might be available. In a mixed feeding flock in a wood it is interesting to watch the great tits going to the ground using the bigger branches, while the blue tits tend to feed out on the slimmer twigs, using their extra agility to the full.

Pale yellow underside, with a thin dark streak. Young birds have greener wing coverts.

Extremely acrobatic and active, blue tits are so light that they can seek food at the tips of the thinnest twigs, unlike great tits.

Fledglings have greener caps and yellower faces than their parents, but the basic pattern still helps to identify them.

Blue tits may not easily be forgiven for stealing cream from milk bottles, pecking putty or even tearing wallpaper if they get the chance.

A fresh-plumaged, bright blue tit has a vivid blue cap, blue wings and tail and clean yellow breast. In dull light it tends to look rather drab, paler beneath, and the white face with black lines is then the best feature.

The great tit is bigger, with a blacker head; the coal tit has no blue, green or yellow. Blue tits feeding in tree tops with thin, high calls may easily be confused with other tits and goldcrests.

Length: 11.5cm; **Weight:** 9-10g
Where to look: broadleaved woods, especially oak and birch, less in conifers; gardens, widespread in winter. **Nest:** hole in tree, nestbox, almost any kind of cavity. Nest of moss with grass and bark strips, lined with feathers. **Eggs:** 7-13 (smaller clutches in gardens), tiny, white with red-brown spots. **Food:** insects in summer, insects and seeds in winter. **Voice:** high, thin notes, churrs and trills — *tsee, tsee-see-chuchuchuch.*

Great Tit

❄

PARUS MAJOR

Great tits are the 'tough guys' of the tit family, as anyone who has watched them at a birdtable can testify. They usually stop short of serious violence, but that stout beak, which can hack open a hazel-nut, is a formidable weapon, and there is evidence that they occasionally kill other birds and may eat portions of them. There is even a remarkable record of one killing a goldcrest and carrying it away in its feet, like a miniature hawk.

Despite these unendearing habits, the great tit is a fascinating species. It has been well studied, partly because it nests very readily in boxes, and also because it is reasonably easy to distinguish the male from the female — the black band on his belly is thick and unbroken, especially as it passes between the legs.

Males take little or no part in building the nest, but feed the hen when she is laying and incubating the eggs. If disturbed at the nest, she will hiss like a snake and this may frighten predators away, or startle them enough for her to escape.

Scores of different calls have been described for this species.

Most of these calls have a distinctive metallic or ringing quality which helps to identify them; in a wood, 'if you don't know the call, it's probably a great tit!'

The tail is blue-grey with obvious white outer feathers.

Females have less glossy caps, and less black on the belly.

Great tits are adaptable, taking advantage of unusual nest sites, such as pipes, letter-boxes, etc. Like blue tits, they have learned to open milk bottles and, in experiments, to perform very complex tasks to obtain food.

Their large size, plus the striking combination of white cheeks, yellow breast, black crown and bib, make great tits unmistakable

The young are fed, as in other tit species, mainly on caterpillars, and the birds time their families to coincide with peak numbers of these. This peak varies in timing from year to year. But how do the birds know — some weeks in advance — when the peak will be?

In Autumn and winter, great tits roam the woods in flocks, often with other species. They regularly drop to the ground, where they toss leaves aside and tear up moss and fungi in search of food.

Juvenile birds have washed-out, duller colours and their cheeks are yellowish, not white.

Length: 14cm; **Weight:** 19g
Where to look: woods, hedges, gardens. **Nest:** in a natural or artificial hole.
Eggs: 5-12, white with red spots. **Food:** mainly insects, seeds, fruits. **Voice:** very varied; calls are mostly metallic and ringing, such as *chink*. Song, a loud *teacheteacher-teacher*, very strident.

Coal Tit

❋

PARUS ATER

The large, white patch on the nape is unique and distinctive.

The coal tit occurs regularly in deciduous woodland, but it is with conifers that most bird-watchers associate it. In a mixed woodland, it will often be found flitting around in the top of a pine. It is even common in conifer plantations, where few other birds may be present. It overcomes the shortage of natural cavities in plantation trees by nesting in a hollow among the roots, or even in a mouse-hole. It often uses nestboxes and, given the choice, prefers one on a conifer to one on a deciduous tree.

In the winter, the coal tit often visits gardens, where it tends to be dominated by the larger blue and great tits. It manages quite well, however, by taking small pieces of food discarded by the other birds, and also by carrying food away and storing it.

The distinctive double wing bar is often easier to see than the nape-patch: at close range the bars show as separate white spots.

Another distinguishing feature is the obvious olive-grey hue of the back.

The black bib is more extensive than on other small tits.

Length: 11cm; **Weight:** 9g
Where to look: woods, especially coniferous; gardens. **Nest:** in a hole low in a tree, or in the ground. **Eggs:** 7-11, white, spotted red. **Food:** chiefly insects and seeds. **Voice:** bright, *peet;* song, great tit-like, but faster, softer.

The smallest of the tits, it often looks dumpy and short-tailed.

Males and females look alike, while juveniles have yellower cheeks, nape and wingbars. Fresh plumage, clean and bright.

Crested Tit

❋

PARUS CRISTATUS

Although a very few crested tits have occurred in England (probably all vagrants from the Continent), the only place in Britain where there is a realistic chance of seeing them is in the old pine woods of Highland Scotland, particularly in the valley of the River Spey. Even here, there are only a few hundred pairs, and the bird can be very difficult to find. The best approach is to choose a stretch of this ancient Caledonian forest (with plenty of dead wood, which the birds and their insect food love) and to listen for the soft, purring call. The first view may well be of an apparently drab, grey-brown and buff little bird, neck-achingly high in a pine.

However, with patience, the 'bridled' face pattern and the upstanding black and white crest may be seen, especially if the bird drops low to inspect some cracked or rotten stumps as a possible nest site. If, as our modern pine plantations age, more sites become available, or if crested tits learn to use nestboxes more regularly, they may well be able to expand their range.

This is the only small British bird with a crest, but this feature can be surprisingly difficult to see, especially on a bird overhead. Nor is the distinctive face pattern always obvious in brief views.

Males and females look alike; juveniles are a little duller with shorter crests.

Crested tits often feed by clinging to the trunk of a tree. They will join roving tit flocks, but are usually seen in ones and twos.

The favourite nest site is a rotten stump, but a fence post or a hole in the ground may be used.

Length: 11.5cm; **Weight:** 11g
Where to look: old pine forests. **Nest:** self-excavated in a stump, etc. **Eggs:** 5-7, white, blotched red. **Food:** insects, seeds and fruit. **Voice:** thin calls like other tits and a distinctive, purring *choorr,* repeated as song.

Bearded Tit

❉

PANURUS BIARMICUS

Adult males have 'moustaches', grey heads and black undertail coverts. Females plainer; shape and behaviour distinctive.

Young birds are more golden, with black backs and tail sides; males have yellow bills, females grey; males show black on face.

The fascinating 'beardie' is not a tit at all, but belongs to an Asian family, the parrotbills. It lives in reed beds, climbing with agility among the stems and often perching with each foot on a different reed. In windy weather it keeps low, but a chorus of unmistakable ringing calls will give away a flock, or the birds may fly, like tiny pheasants, just above the reed tops. Sometimes, with tails cocked up, they will feed on the ground, but always near reeds.

The bearded tit suffers badly in severe winters, but breeds prodigiously (a pair may raise four broods in a season!) and soon builds up its numbers again. After particularly good seasons, flocks 'erupt' from their breeding grounds, and appear in reed beds where they have not been seen for years, if ever.

Regular migrations also take place between summer and winter sites, often hundreds of miles apart. Birds may be very faithful to two such sites or ring the changes: it seems likely that they are influenced by others that they encounter — or perhaps by a new mate.

Length: 16.5cm; **Weight:** 15-16g
Where to look: reed beds. **Nest:** low in reeds. **Eggs:** 5-7, white speckled with black. **Food:** mainly insects in summer and small seeds in winter. **Voice:** unique and memorable: a metallic *ching* and a hard *tik*, repeated.

Long-tailed Tit

❉

AEGITHALOS CAUDATUS

Despite appearances, this bird is not really a tit, and may be related to the exotic babbler family: like them it has fluffy plumage and sociable habits. A flock in winter will defend its territory against other flocks and roost communally, the birds huddling together for warmth. In fact this bird seems to like tight places — both adults will roost in the nest with the brood of up to a dozen young! The nest is a wonderful, elastic construction of moss and spiders' webs, disguised with lichen (or even pieces of polystyrene!) and lined with hundreds, perhaps thousands, of feathers. It may be low in a thorn bush or high in a tree, and the adults sometimes take 20 days to build it. After the breeding season, family parties and larger flocks wander through woods and along hedges, often joined by tits and other small birds. Long-tailed tits take mostly insects, but they also peck lichen and green algae from trunks and branches. They are wonderfully acrobatic and will hang upsidedown by one foot, holding large food items in the other to eat them. They visit birdtables only rarely, but when they do decide to do so, they may come regularly, sometimes for more than one winter.

An unmistakable 'ball and stick' shape, both perched and in flight.

Adults are black, white and pale pink. Juveniles have dark cheeks, no pink and shorter tails.

Unique nest is an oval purse of moss, webs and lichen, feather-lined.

Roving bands of these birds move with agility through trees and bushes, crossing gaps in single file and calling ceaselessly as they go.

Length: 14cm; **Weight:** 8g
Where to look: hedges, bushes, woods in winter. **Nest:** in a bush or in a tree fork. **Eggs:** 8-12, white, spotted with red. **Food:** mainly insects. **Voice:** a thin *zi-zi-zi; tup;* a rolling *trrr:* all distinctive. Song rare.

Nuthatch

❋

SITTA EUROPÆA

Length: 14cm; **Weight:** 20-22g
Where to look: woods, parks. **Nest:** in a tree-hole. **Eggs:** 6-11, white, spotted with red. **Food:** insects, nuts, seeds. **Voice:** a variety of clear, ringing whistles.

A big-headed, short-tailed and perky little bird, rather like a miniature woodpecker in shape and actions, always on the move.

Nuthatches behave like sparrow-sized woodpeckers, but have the unique ability to climb down trunks and branches as well as up. They do this by moving obliquely, hanging from the upper foot and propped by the lower one. Unlike woodpeckers, they are no carpenters (they nest in ready-made holes), but they are plasterers, and exclude starlings and predators such as weasels with a hard, mud rim to the nest-hole. They even do this to a nestbox hole — and fill in any cracks in the top and sides as well! The young are fed mainly on insects, taken from both bark and leaves. In autumn, nuthatches pick up beech-mast, acorns and hazel-nuts, carrying them to a favoured branch, wedging them in the bark and hacking them open with energetic and noisy whacks of the bill. They sometimes visit birdtables, and access to this easy food supply may now be helping the bird to extend its range further north and west in England and Wales, though not as yet into Scotland or Ireland.

Blue-grey above, with white cheeks and corners to the tail; buff below. Chestnut flanks are brighter in the male.

The most striking feature is the broad, black eye-stripe.

The birds often plaster the nest-hole entrance with hard-drying mud, to keep out predators and larger competitors.

In a tree, the bird climbs just as readily down a trunk as up it, not using its tail as a prop. Flight silhouette is distinctive.

Treecreeper

❋

CERTHIA FAMILIARIS

The treecreeper is usually seen flitting across a clearing, landing low on a tree trunk and then jerkily working its way up, propped on the stiff and pointed feathers of its tail. The down-curved, fine-tipped bill is ideal for probing in crevices in the bark. The bird spirals as it goes (quite why is not clear) appearing and disappearing from view, and it climbs along under branches as readily as on top. At any point it may abandon the tree and fly down to the base of another: unlike the nuthatch, it rarely climbs downwards. In winter, treecreepers often join tit flocks; they do not visit bird-tables, but they will sometimes feed on fat if it is smeared into tree bark.

Some birds hollow out winter nests in the soft wood of certain tree trunks. (Wellingtonias are a favourite). The birds make several hollows and choose one on the lee side of a tree, according to the weather. Just occasionally treecreepers can be persuaded to breed in a wedge-shaped nestbox with a hole in the side. But beware if you are standing nearby when the young emerge — there is a record of a fledgling mistaking a man for a tree . . . and climbing him!

Treecreepers usually climb upwards; spiral round trunk and branches, then drop to the foot of another tree and start again.

Adults are warm brown above, streaked with buff; juveniles are greyer and more spotted.

A delicate looking bird, brown above and silvery-white below, with a fine down-curved bill.

Length: 12.5 cm; **Weight:** 9g
Where to look: woodland and parks. **Nest:** in a crack in a tree, or behind loose bark. **Eggs:** 4-8, white, spotted red. **Food:** insects. **Voice:** a thin, high *tsit* or *tsu*. Song is a penetrating *tsip-tsee-tsee-tsee*, ending in a flourish.

Treecreepers usually fly between one tree and the next. Longer flights are unusual.

Treecreepers, nuthatches and woodpeckers all cling to trees. The lesser spotted woodpecker is small enough to confuse, but is obviously black and white. The nuthatch is blue-grey with black eye-stripe. The treecreeper is brown, and thin-billed.

House Sparrow

❁

PASSER DOMESTICUS

Male has rather striking and distinctive plumage which is duller in winter than spring.

The rather drab female and young show distinctive broad pale band over eye; plain underparts (see greenfinch).

There is no species more closely associated with mankind than the house sparrow. From the centre of large cities to farm buildings in the most rural settings, this cheerful exploiter of human rubbish and wastefulness is found in abundance. They are inventive opportunists and have managed to colonise much of the world — especially those areas explored by Europeans. They followed the army camps across the North African desert in World War II, and they take rides on the London Underground and on cross-Channel ferries where discarded food is available. They appear in all kinds of isolated places where people settle — but how do they find them?

The normal breeding cycle is from May to July, often with three broods, but there has been an increasing trend towards year-round nesting, a sign of a very successful species. Any month with a spell of fine weather may trigger breeding activity and nest building, and although many of these out of season attempts are doomed to failure, an unusually long mild spell can result in fledged young being seen in mid-winter.

Length: 14.5cm; **Weight:** 22-31g
Where to look: associated with human habitation, rural and urban. **Nest:** untidy grass and straw, in buildings or hedges. **Eggs:** 3-7, greyish, finely speckled. **Food:** varied, mainly seeds and buds. Voice: noisy, twittering and cheeping notes.

In flight, the males exhibit a striking contrast between the clear grey rump, brown back and wings with white wing-bar and chestnut side of neck.

Food provided in gardens will always attract large numbers of house sparrows, which have learnt to feed from peanut feeders.

On the ground progress is by a series of hops or shuffles.

Tree Sparrow

❋

PASSER MONTANUS

Less widespread than the more familiar house sparrow, the tree sparrow differs in several distinctive ways. It is a smaller, plumper bird than the house sparrow, lively and bold, but less inclined to exploit gardens and human waste, and more characteristic of open woods, parks and farmland with scattered trees. To look at, there is no difference between the sexes and even the recently fledged young resemble the adults.

A hole-nesting species that will frequently take over tit nestboxes in a woodland, it is dominant over any tits using the chosen box. Tree sparrows have even built on top of a brood of young blue tits, which the parents continued to struggle to feed until they were eventually stifled by the accumulating nest material gathered by the sparrows. Another favoured nesting site is within the base material of a larger nest, such as that of a crow, magpie or heron. The owner of the main nest apparently tolerates the squatters quite happily.

Smaller than the house sparrow, but more active and jerky with tail almost permanently cocked and hopping movements on the ground.

Ground-feeding birds can appear to have a dark head and white collar, as in reed buntings.

Plumage lacks variation between sexes, age and season; these only distinguished by behaviour.

Male and female tree sparrows share incubation, unlike house sparrows, where the job is the female's. The female is always at the nest during the night, brooding the young until seven days old.

A regular migrant, there is an annual late-autumn immigration into Britain from continental Europe often associated with other finches.

White cheeks with contrasting black spot is very distinctive. Chocolate-covered crown and double white wingbars are good features.

In flight the shorter tail and rather more bouncy action separates tree from house sparrow.

The distinctive double flight call is somewhat reminiscent of the redpoll.

Length: 14cm; **Weight:** 19-25g
Where to look: areas of open woodland, farms and buildings in winter.
Nest: in holes of straw and grass. **Eggs:** 4-6, stippled brown. **Food:** Mainly seeds, but some insects. **Voice:** *cheep* call higher pitched and more metallic than house sparrow, flight note a double *tchur tchur* or *tek tek.*

Chaffinch

※

FRINGILLA COELEBS

The chaffinch, among the most popular spring songsters, is one of Britain's commonest and most widespread breeding species, with seven million pairs distributed throughout Britain and Ireland. Largely resident, British chaffinches rarely move more than 5km (3 miles) from home. The numbers are swollen each winter by a marked immigration from northern and eastern Europe. In these cases movements in excess of 2,000km (1,200 miles) are not unusual. Spectacular migrations can be watched on the east and south coasts during October and November and it is calculated that ten to 20 million chaffinches arrive each autumn.

Producing only one brood per year, chaffinches build a beautifully camouflaged nest in the fork of a tree or dense bush. The outside of the nest is covered with lichen stripped from the surrounding bark. They are extremely long lived for small birds, ringing recoveries indicating that individuals may survive for up to 12 years. Where cause of death is known, the majority have been killed by traffic or by cats.

In flight, the distinctive white outer tail feathers and wingbars are equally apparent.

Females show white in the wing; unstreaked; ground feeders.

The male's contrasting plumage is highlighted by the pink breast.

Winter flocks use a distinctive 'choop' flight call; no twittering.

Length: 15cm; **Weight:** 19-23g
Where to look: hedgerows, gardens and farmland. **Nest:** in bush or low tree, of grasses decorated with lichen. **Eggs:** 4-5, dark spotted, greenish. **Food:** varied. **Voice:** *spink* call; rattling song ends with flourish; *choop* in flight.

Brambling

※

FRINGILLA MONTIFRINGILLA

In shape and behaviour the brambling is very similar to the chaffinch, and the two frequently mix in winter flocks. The conspicuous white rump is the most striking field characteristic of bramblings when the birds are in flight and is the best way of spotting them in a finch flock. A more prolonged view will show the orange breastband of both male and female and the pale orange shoulder patch and, in spring, the black head of the male. The black is obscured by pale grey in winter.

In recent years small numbers have been recorded nesting in Scotland and northern England, but there has been little evidence of major colonisation. The species is still principally a winter visitor from northern Europe, arriving each autumn in October and early November in variable numbers. In peak seasons as many as two million may be involved, but this is quite exceptional. A roost site one winter in northern England was estimated to hold over 150,000 individuals. The wintering flocks, however, are very nomadic, wandering erratically, but remaining in each site long enough to exhaust the available food supply. They can be elusive, but a good flock is worth seeking out.

Length: 14.5cm; **Weight:** 22-30g
Where to look: beech woods or farmland. **Nest:** odd pairs may breed in Scotland. **Food:** insects in summer, beech-mast and other seeds in winter. **Voice:** twanging *sweek;* nasal greenfinch-like *dweeee;* hard *chup* in flight.

Mainly a ground feeder, the preferred food is beech-mast, but many small seeds are eaten.

Winter flocks may be found in woods or open farmland.

In flight, the prominent white rump is a key feature.

Both sexes show orange breast and white belly which distinguish them from the chaffinch.

The male is highly distinctive, with a striking black head.

Hawfinch

❋

COCCOTHRAUSTES COCCOTHRAUSTES

The massive bill and rather short tail give the hawfinch a most distinctive silhouette, both in flight and when perched. At times it will appear to be so 'top heavy' that it seems in danger of tipping forwards. The thick neck and large head add to a most striking flight appearance which is quite unlike any other British finch, but clear views are unusual.

Generally considered a shy and secretive species, often difficult to locate, it will frequently perch on the very top-most branches, but obtaining good views is not an easy task for the birdwatcher. The broad white patch on the wing coverts and border to the tail contrasts with the warm-brown back and provides a striking pattern as the bird flies away, but other details demand closer study, which in turn requires patience and care.

The exceptional structure of the bill, together with massive jaw muscles, enables the hawfinch to tackle food ignored by other finches. Cherry stones are a regular feature of the diet, but softer seeds are taken and dealt with in a delicate manner.

Mixed woods and orchards are preferred, but beech, hornbeam and wild cherry are most favoured.

Length: 18cm; **Weight:** 48-62g
Where to look: mixed woods and orchards.
Nest: roosts on foundation of twigs, usually in fruit trees. **Eggs:** 4-6, bluish green, spotted. **Food:** large seeds and fruit stones.
Voice: quiet whistling song, robin-like *tick* call.

A bird of tree tops, but will feed on ground when soft fruit is available in orchards.

Secretive when breeding, a little more obvious in winter when flocks form to roost communally.

Scattered populations throughout England, but mainly a south-eastern species.

Bullfinch

❋

PYRRHULA PYRRHULA

Length: 15cm; **Weight:** 21-27g
Where to look: undergrowth near woods and gardens. **Nest:** fine twigs, built in thick cover. **Eggs:** 4-5, clear green-blue. **Food:** buds, berries and seeds. **Voice:** a distinctive low, piping *teu*, which carries well.

Throughout orchards and gardens in south-east England bullfinches have a justified reputation for damage to buds on fruit trees, often seriously affecting far more than they eat and reducing the crop. Many birds are trapped and destroyed. Two factors may affect the amount of damage. The number of suitable nest sites near the orchard will determine the population level in the area, and the available 'natural' food supply in late winter controls the change of diet to buds. When the ash-key crop is good, bullfinches remain in the woodland and fruit farmers sleep more easily.

Although males have a re-markably bright plumage, bullfinches can be very secretive. Their presence in an area — and they are far more numerous in south-east England than the rest of the country — is revealed by the distinctive, far-carrying piping call and the prominent white rump which stands out as they fly away.

Never far from dense cover, keeping to bushes and trees, they rarely settle on the ground. When they do, movement is by a series of ungainly hops. Pairs remain together throughout the year, with family parties in autumn and occasionally small flocks in winter.

Colourful, but easily overlooked.

White rump striking in flight.

Males with contrasting plumage of grey back, jet-black cap and striking pink-red underparts. Inner flight feathers with red.

Unlike the male, the female has pinkish-grey underparts, but retains black cap and white rump. Young birds resemble female, but have no black cap.

In spring, rarely welcomed by gardeners concerned for the buds.

Greenfinch

※

CARDUELIS CHLORIS

Winter numbers are boosted by migrants from continental Europe.

Juvenile (left) streaked brown above, with faint yellow underneath; pale yellow flashes on wing and tail.

Although solitary when breeding, flocks form in winter, often mixed with other species in woods and open farmland. In competition will become aggressive.

The duller female is browner with subtle streaking on the underparts. The yellow flashes in wing and tail are more subdued.

The olive-green plumage of the male is off-set by varying degrees of yellow, brighter on older birds.

Note the very stout bill and short, well forked tail.

Length: 14.5cm;
Weight: 25-31g
Where to look: open woodland, gardens and farmland. **Nest:** of twigs and moss in hedges and bushes. **Eggs:** 4-6, spotted, off-white. **Food:** mainly seeds and berries. **Voice:** twittering song; drawn out nasal *tsweee*.

The yellow in wings and tail is clearly visible on flying birds.

Increasingly familiar garden birds, greenfinches have been attracted more and more to birdtables with sunflower seeds and other goodies. Together with house sparrows these confident, distinctive birds have quickly learnt how to feed from peanut feeders in winter and, being rather aggressive when competing for food, will drive away other more timid birds, including tits.

The stout bill on this rather heavily built finch enables it to deal with some of the larger seeds that become available, such as sea-buckthorn in the winter. In gardens they like mezereon, yew and cotoneaster berries. In spring they like tall hedges and are happy in big shrubberies and parks, their tinkling trills and wheezy notes livening up a sunny morning.

Flight, in common with all finches, is distinctly undulating, but in the breeding season the very characteristic song-flight of the male consists of a circling pattern on strangely erratic, slow, bat-like wing-beats, during which the bell-like calls are given non-stop. In winter, flocks burst up from the ground with a loud rush, swirling over a field or into the nearest hedge.

Siskin

❉

CARDUELIS SPINUS

As a breeding species the siskin is closely associated with conifers, and recent expansion of the population within Britain has almost certainly been the result of increased afforestation and the development of mixed ornamental woodland. At one time confined to Scotland, the species now nests in small numbers in scattered places throughout the British Isles, including several locations on the south coast.

On the breeding grounds the very musical twittering song, delivered in flight as the males circle the tree tops, is a sure sign of the presence of nesting birds. Indeed the song-flight will continue well after the female has settled to incubate the eggs, and consists of very exaggerated wing-beats, the wings appearing to meet above the back. At the same time, the tail is usually spread, flashing vivid yellow patches.

Like the greenfinch, this is predominantly a yellow-green bird, but it is smaller and slimmer, and the male has a black chin and throat and yellow rump. The female is very much greyer, lacks yellow and has paler, striped underparts. The neat, complex wing pattern can usually be seen on this tiny bird.

The bill shape is ideal for extracting seeds of birch, alder and larch.

Often mixed with redpolls.

In early spring, siskins will discover the red string bags containing peanuts.

Feeds on twigs like a party of tits.

Very active. Shows a distinct notch in tail in bounding flight.

Length: 12cm; **Weight:** 12-18g
Where to look: mainly conifers when nesting, alders by streams in winter. **Nest:** twigs and moss, high in conifers. **Eggs:** 4-5, deep blue, with pale spots. **Voice:** varied twittering song and shrill *tsewi* flight call.

Redpoll

❉

CARDUELIS FLAMMEA

Females lack the pinkish flush; some males vivid in spring. Juvenile (right) lacks red.

Feeding in tree tops, their behaviour is very tit-like and agile.

Variable in size and colour, larger and paler individuals from northern localities are occasional winter visitors.

The bouncy, undulating flight is accompanied by the distinctive three- or four-note flight call.

Breeding birds fly over a large area during display.

fallen birch seeds, bursting up into the trees if disturbed.

The presence of redpolls is frequently first indicated by the distinctive metallic twittering flight call; a close view will reveal the crimson on the forehead and small black chin patch. Some males have a noticeable pink flush to the underparts, but this may be absent from other individuals. Some are very colourful in spring.

Still rather sparsely distributed in south-west England, redpolls have increased and spread quite dramatically since the 1950s and are now widespread throughout the rest of Britain, although numbers fluctuate greatly from year to year.

In winter, redpolls often join siskins in mixed flocks. They feed together in the tops of alder and birch trees, extracting the tiny seeds. Their behaviour is very tit-like, birds often hanging upside down at the very end of the branches. Such flocks are often associated with areas of running water, cress beds or riverside banks. Migrant flocks can be found in open areas of scrub or waste ground, feeding on low clumps of vegetation such as seeding willow-herb. In spring they feed on the ground on

Length: 13-14cm; **Weight:** 10-13g
Where to look: birch and alder woodland. **Nest:** grasses on a twig foundation, usually high in tree. **Eggs:** 4-5, blue, spotted and streaked. **Food:** mainly seeds. **Voice:** trilling unmusical song in flight; call fast *chuchuchuh-uh*.

Goldfinch

❈

CARDUELIS CARDUELIS

One of the most colourful and distinctive of all the British finches, the goldfinch is the 'thistle-finch', with a decided preference for eating the seeds of thistles. It is particularly appropriate that the collective noun for such an attractive bird is 'charm'. A slim, delicate-looking finch, it is usually seen fluttering in a rather butterfly-like manner among the seed heads of low-growing vegetation. Although flight action retains the usual undulations of all finches, the goldfinch has a peculiar bouncing quality in its movements.

Where some finches are ground-feeders and others tree-top feeders, the goldfinch is very much a bird of the lower vegetation, favouring plants of open waste ground such as teasels and hawkweeds. It can hop on the ground but is more likely to be seen hanging from the seed-heads in a tit-like manner; flocks also feed in trees.

The striking plumage consists of a mixture of black, white, brown, yellow and red – goldfinches have white rumps, but this is often overlooked among the wealth of other bright colours. Sexes are similar in appearance, although the red extends behind the eye only in the male. Young birds are 'grey pates' without the colourful head pattern, and slightly streaked beneath.

At one time this was a very popular cage bird, and one form of trap for small birds is known as a 'chardonneret' — the French name for the goldfinch.

In all plumages the black feathering of the wings is contrasted with the bright yellow flash that gives the bird its name.

On leaving the nest, young birds lack the face patterns, but acquire these within two months.

The striking pattern on the head of all adults is unique. In spring there are patches of brown each side of the breast.

Outside the breeding season flocks rarely mix with others, but may be with siskins in alders.

In addition to the band of brilliant yellow, the black wing feathers each have a prominent pale tip. Black tail feathers have pale tips and oval patches.

Length: 12cm **Weight:** 14-17g
Where to look: gardens and orchards, rough and open ground. **Nest:** built of wool and moss at end of branch. **Eggs:** 5-6, spotted and streaked, bluish. **Food:** seeds, mainly thistles, and insects, **Voice:** liquid twittering calls and song.

Unforgettable and unmistakable. Identification is easy.

Linnet

❊

CARDUELIS CANNABINA

Feeds on bushes in summer, but a ground-feeder in winter.

Widespread throughout Britain, the linnet is often thought of as a bird associated with heaths, commons and gorse bushes. In fact it is also found in open country and farmland far from gorse. A semi-colonial species, small groups of ten or more pairs can often be located, and then the bird will appear absent for some distance until the next group is found. Large numbers form lively flocks in winter, but can be difficult to locate. Quite extensive areas can seem empty of linnets, but rather than there being a genuine reduction in numbers, it is just that all the birds tend to assemble in one place where there is plentiful food.

Although quite large numbers and concentrations may be encountered on southern and eastern coasts in late autumn, the amount of migration undertaken by linnets is still something of a mystery. It appears that a small number of British birds move south for the winter, travelling as far as Iberia; a somewhat larger number from Scandinavia probably arrives to spend the winter in Britain, spreading southwards from eastern Scotland.

Open farmland or coastal salt marshes are very much favoured during the winter months. Small seeds are taken all year round.

Length: 13.5cm; **Weight:** 15-21g
Where to look: areas of gorse in summer, farmland and shore in winter. **Nest:** grasses near ground. **Eggs:** 4-6, spotted, bluish. **Food:** small seeds and insects. **Voice:** varied, musical twittering song. Rapid flight call.

The male's strongly contrasting plumage of grey head and crimson breast and crown is lost in winter and absent in females.

In flight shows pink rump and very little white in wing.

Overall appearance of dark tawny brown with bright orange-buff colouring around face and breast; neat tawny wingbar.

Twite

❊

CARDUELIS FLAVIROSTRIS

The bill is rather greyish in summer, pale yellow in winter.

Colonial as a breeding species; small numbers grouping together. Flocks form in winter months.

plants, often in company with linnets and skylarks.

Flight, behaviour and shape are all reminiscent of the linnet, but this is a slightly smaller bird with a relatively longer tail. Generally much darker, it lacks the chestnut back and red crown of the male linnet. In mixed flocks twites can be distinguished by having pinkish rumps (males) and yellow bills in winter.

Lacking clear-cut identification features, the twite is probably frequently overlooked, but it is estimated that the British breeding population numbers some 20,000 pairs, with perhaps 100,000 individuals present in winter.

Very linnet-like in appearance, the twite is often known as the 'mountain linnet'. Although very much a bird of the higher ground, mountains and moorland, in summer it is also found nesting at sea level in northern and western Scotland and parts of Ireland. The breeding areas are largely deserted in winter and there is a general movement to coastal localities where it feeds on the seeds of salt marsh

Favours open country all year; breeds in Pennines, northern Scotland and western Ireland. Winters on coast.

Length: 13.5cm; **Weight:** 13-17g
Where to look: moors and mountains in summer, coasts in winter. **Nest:** built of grass near ground. **Eggs:** 5-6, blue with bold markings. **Food:** seeds. **Voice:** song a linnet-like twittering, call a very nasal *tsooee, dweye.*

Crossbill and Scottish Crossbill

❋

LOXIA CURVIROSTRA AND LOXIA SCOTICA

In flight the short deeply-forked tail, together with the heavy neck and bill and distinctive call, readily identify the crossbills.

Young birds resemble females, but with a greyish tinge.

Female

The increase in conifer plantations has produced a wider spread of the common species.

Crossbills are the most specialised of all the finches. Most obvious are the crossed mandibles, which enable the birds to extract seeds from pine cones. Other adaptations include particularly strong asymmetrical jaw muscles which assist the twisting movement necessary to extract the seed. In normal circumstances the feeding activity follows a regular routine. The cone is broken from the tree, usually requiring a considerable effort, with the bird apparently making use of every muscle. It is then carried to a convenient branch where it is held firmly by the feet while each seed is extracted in a systematic manner.

The numbers and distribution of crossbills in Britain vary greatly from year to year, for this is an 'invasion species'. Factors as varied as food supply and prevailing weather conditions will control the number of migrants reaching Britain in the autumn, and in many cases the subsequent size of the breeding population early the following year.

The Scottish crossbill is a different but very similar species, found only in Scottish pine woods.

Scottish crossbill (right) is a separate species with a larger, blunter bill and larger body; it is Britain's only unique species.

The Scottish crossbill (left) is confined to the Highlands.

The variation in colour of the red-plumaged males is partly a reflection of age, but many breeding males will not have attained the full red colouration.

The crossing of the mandibles can be in either direction, right or left-handed cross! This determines which is the stronger leg!

Crossbills are often detected by the pine cones, with seeds extracted, lying on the woodland floor.

Length: 16-17 cm; **Weight:** 34-48 g
Where to look: conifer woods and plantations. **Nest:** grasses on twig foundation, breeding between January and July. **Eggs:** 4, off-white with bold spots. **Food:** almost exclusively seeds from cones of pine, larch and spruce. **Voice:** loud, persistent *chip chip* flight call. Song of trilling notes followed by greenfinch-like calls.

Early nesting species, some pairs have eggs in January or February.

Yellowhammer

❋

EMBERIZA CITRINELLA

Long, notched tail shows white on sides when spread, less obvious than on reed bunting.

Juveniles are darker, well-streaked, and may show very little yellow, but plumage extremely variable.

Feeds almost exclusively on the ground. When disturbed, flocks fly up into bushes, coming back down in ones ands twos when the danger has passed.

The derivation of the curious English name becomes clear upon learning that the German word for bunting is 'Ammer'. The two languages have a distant common origin. The dark, irregular lines on the eggs have given rise to the yellowhammer's country name of 'scribbling lark'.

The phrase 'bread-and-cheese' recalls the song of this familiar bunting only in rhythm: in fact the song is rather variable and sometimes lacks the final (higher or lower) 'cheese'. On drowsy high-summer days it is often the only bird sound accompanying the hum of insects.

Aggressive when setting up territory, the male pursues his prospective mate in a rapid, twisting courtship flight. Once paired, both birds often feed together, and indeed gather food for the young, away from their nesting territory. The young are fed almost entirely on green caterpillars and insects.

In winter yellowhammers are social. They may roost in large numbers in rank vegetation, sometimes in reed beds with reed and corn buntings, and even on occasion in snow burrows. Ringing reveals that up to 70 per cent of adults spend the winter within 5km (3 miles) of the nest site.

Often makes long, circular flight, returning to a point close to where it took off.

Sociable in winter, often mixed with other buntings and finches.

When flying away, the unstreaked rusty rump is very striking in all plumages.

Length: 16.5cm; **Weight:** 27g
Where to look: farmland, heaths, scrub, hillsides. **Nest:** bulky, of grass or straw, with characteristic platform, low down or on ground in grass clump or bush. **Eggs:** 3-5, pale with dark 'scribbling' and spots. **Food:** cereals, grass seeds; insects in summer. **Voice:** familiar *'little-bit-of-bread-and-no-cheese'*. **Flight call** *twick* or *twitick*.

Corn Bunting

❊

MILIARIA CALANDRA

A bulky, clumsy-looking, sparrow-like bird; rather neckless appearance. Large, dark eye in rather pale face. No white in shortish tail.

Sexes alike in plumage.

May fly short distances with legs dangling, on fluttering wings.

Pursues rivals or prospective mates low over cornfields.

Paler, less buff in summer. Streaking most dense in centre of breast, forming diffuse dark spot.

Britain's largest bunting, this nondescript bird makes up for its drab appearance with a fascinating sex life! It is one of a very few truly promiscuous passerines, both male and female mating with several partners. The males return to the breeding sites in midwinter, the largest birds securing the best territories. The females do not leave the winter flock until April, and they alone deal with all the domestic duties, leaving males free to court other hens. Males sing, head thrown back, from a prominent low perch, or from overhead wires, in almost every month of the year, and at any time of day.

Although one of the few species at home in modern agricultural 'prairies', the corn bunting has, for reasons unknown, decreased this century to the point of extinction in much of the west and north. The British population is sedentary, flocking outside the breeding season to feed on stubble and in farmyards. Winter roosts in reed beds or scrub may contain a hundred or more birds. The distinctive flight call is a low-pitched dry but loud *kwit* or *quilp kwit-it*.

Length: 18cm; **Weight:** 44-54g
Where to look: open farming country.
Nest: large, loose, of coarse grasses, often in scrape on ground. **Eggs:** 3-5, usually pale with bold, dark scribbles and blotches.
Food: seeds, insects. **Voice:** unique, discordant jangling.

Cirl Bunting

❊

EMBERIZA CIRLUS

Length: 16.5cm; **Weight:** 22g
Where to look: farmland with hedges and tall trees, bushy slopes, cliffs. **Nest:** neat, well-concealed, of moss and grass. **Eggs:** 3-4, bluish-white, boldly marked. **Food:** seeds, insects. **Voice:** metallic rattle on one note.

Not discovered as a British bird until 1800, in Devon, the cirl bunting expanded its range during the 19th century to become widespread, if local, north to the Midlands and Wales. A decline was first noticed in the 1930s, accelerating since the late 1950s to the present precarious position of perhaps 150 pairs, almost all in Devon. The recent colder, wetter springs and summers are probably responsible, for the cirl bunting is essentially a Mediterranean species at the edge of its range in Britain.

The bird is easily overlooked until the song is learnt. Like the other farmland buntings, the song period is long: it may be heard regularly from late February to early September, and occasionally at other times, though bursts may be irregular, even during the main song period. It may recall a distant lesser white-throat, but with an unmistakable, sharper, bunting quality.

The breeding territory is unusually large, and given the bird's relative secrecy, and tendency to fly quite long distances, it can be very elusive. Nevertheless, a recent survey revealed that three out of five territories contained a house or farm building.

Call a soft, penetrating ssi.

Black and yellow head markings make male unmistakable.

Female distinguished by olive-grey rump, buffy rather than yellowish breast, with neat, dark streaks.

In winter, gathers into small flocks, or remains in pairs.

Breeding right around the Arctic Circle in Eurasia and North America, the snow bunting reaches further north than any other small bird, right up to the summer limit of ice in Greenland. The first British nest was found in 1886. These lovely buntings remain a prize summer find on the barren, hostile tops of the highest mountains, the sweet musical song being uttered in a short display flight. The nest often has a warm lining of ptarmigan feathers.

In winter, they are often delightfully confiding. Sometimes called 'snowflakes', a flock in flight does indeed fancifully recall a flurry of snow as each bird flies in deep undulations, seeming to dance along, then swooping low and fast before landing, flashing white in wings

Winter birds usually show lovely warm rusty-buff wash over crown and breast, reddest on females.

Snow Bunting
❀
PLECTROPHENAX NIVALIS

and tail. A feeding flock moves in rolling fashion, each bird running rapidly, pecking, leap-frogging over its companion in short flights, frequently calling.

Yellow bill with dark tip in winter. Some white always visible in the wing in flight.

Breeding male black and white, female cold grey-brown and white.

Inland lowland sightings are unusual, and reports in gardens can usually be related to partially albino sparrows.

Numbers wintering in Britain vary greatly. Highly sociable, flocks of a thousand or more on record, usually under 50.

Very long-winged, well-built bird. Flight strong and bouncing.

Length: 16cm; **Weight:** 30-40g
Where to look: rare breeder, high, mountain tops. Commoner in winter in northern hills, east coast. **Nest:** in crevice. **Eggs:** 4-6, off-white, blotched brown. **Food:** seeds, insects. **Voice:** rippling trill; *tew*.

The male's handsome black and white head and breast in breeding plumage are unmistakable. Note the long, deeply notched tail, typical of British buntings.

Usually perches rather upright on plant stem, with tail at rakish angle or twisted to one side.

Reed Bunting
❀
EMBERIZA SCHOENICLUS

The brief, unmusical song is delivered *ad nauseam* from a prominent song-post such as a tall reed or dock. A widespread bird, with breeding recorded from every county in Britain and Ireland, it is mainly sedentary, though deserting upland areas in winter when it moves into all types of open country. Most reed buntings move only a little way, yet, curiously, studies at roosts in central and southern England have revealed two males for every female: perhaps the females simply do not all come to the communal roost. Prolonged heavy snow cover may make it difficult for this ground feeder to find enough seeds to eat, and heavy mortality may result. They are increasingly visiting gardens for free handouts in winter.

Although primarily birds of wet and damp areas, there has been a trend this century for breeding to spread into the drier habitats normally occupied by yellowhammers or corn buntings, with little evidence of competition between these species where they coexist. More recently this spread seems to have halted. Farmland reed buntings do not require the taller trees favoured by yellowhammers, being content with low song-posts, more like their usual marshy homes.

Length: 15.5cm; **Weight:** 19g
Where to look: all types of wet areas, farmland, scrub, plantations, also gardens in winter. **Nest:** substantial, of grasses, on ground or low in tussocks, hedgerow bushes. **Eggs:** 4-5, buff, or olive-brown, boldly marked with dark streaks, smudges. **Food:** seeds, insects and invertebrates in summer. **Voice:** monotonous short song. Call shrill *tseeu*; high *see*.

INDEX

Accipter gentilis 47
Accipter nisus 47
Acrocephalus palustris 122
Acrocephalus schoenobaenus 121
Acrocephalus scirpaceus 122
Actitis hypoleucos 78
Aegithalos caudatus 144
Alauda arvensis 103
Alca torda 89
Alcedo atthis 100
Alectoris rufa 56
Anas acuta 35
Anas clypeata 35
Anas crecca 30
Anas penelope 30
Anas querquedula 34
Anas strepera 34
Anser albifrons 27
Anser anser 28
Anser brachyrhynchus 28
Anser fabalis 27
Anthus petrosus 107
Anthus pratensis 108
Anthus spinoletta 107
Anthus trivialis 108
Apus apus 99
Aquila chrysaetos 42
Arctic skua 80
Arctic tern 87
Ardea cinerea 22
Arenaria interpres 77
Asio flammeus 97
Asio otus 97
Athene noctua 96
Athya ferina 36
auks 13, 89, 90
avocet 61
Aythya fuligula 37
Aythya marila 37

Bahama pintail 41
bar-tailed godwit 62, 74
barn owl 95
barnacle goose 25
bean goose 27
bearded tit 144
Bewick's swan 24
birds of prey 42–52, 95–7
bittern 22
black grouse 54
black guillemot 89
black redstart 132
black-headed gull 81
black-necked grebe 17
black-tailed godwit 62, 74
black-throated diver 15, 31
blackbird 135
blackcap 123, 139
blue tit 141

Bombycilla garrulus 111
Botaurus stellaris 22
brambling 138, 148
Branta bernicla 25
Branta canadensis 26
Branta leucopsis 25
brent goose 25
bullfinch 149
buntings 156–7
Burhinus oedicnemus 66
Buteo bueo 43
Buteo lagopus 43
buzzard 43, 50

Calidris alba 68
Calidris alpina 69
Calidris canutus 68
Calidris ferruginea 70
Calidris maritima 71
Calidris minuta 70
Canada goose 26
capercaillie 54
Caprimulgus europaeus 98
Carduelis cannabina 153
Carduelis carduelis 152
Carduelis chloris 150
Carduelis flammea 151
Carduelis flavirostris 153
Carduelis spinus 151
carrion crow 116
cayuga mallard 41
Cepphus grylle 89
Certhia familiaris 145
Cetti's warbler 121
Cettia cetti 121
chaffinch 138, 148
Charadrius dubius 64
Charadrius hiaticula 64
Charadrius morinellus 65
chiffchaff 126, 139
chough 114
Cinclus cinclus 118
Circus aeruginosus 44
Circus cyaneus 45
Circus pygargus 45
cirl bunting 156
Clangula hyemalis 39
coal tit 143
Coccothraustes coccothraustes 149
collared dove 93
Columba livia 92
Columba oenas 92
Columba palumbus 91
common gull 84
common sandpiper 78
common scoter 39
common tern 86
coot 59
cormorant 21

corn bunting 156
corncrake 57
Corvus corax 117
Corvus corone 116
Corvus frugilegus 115
Corvus monedula 114
Coturnix coturnix 55
crested tit 143
Crex crex 57
crossbill 154
crows 116
cuckoo 94
Cuculus canorus 94
curlew 63, 75
curlew sandpiper 70
Cygnus columbianus 24
Cygnus cygnus 24
Cygnus olor 23

Dartford warbler 125
Delichon urbica 105
Dendrocopus major 102
Dendrocopus minor 102
dipper 118
divers 15, 31
dotterel 63, 65
doves 92–3
ducks 29–41
dunlin 62, 69
dunnock 120

eagles 42, 50
eider 38
Emberiza cirlus 156
Emberiza citrinella 155
Emberiza schoeniclus 157
Erithacus rubecula 133

Falco columbarius 49
Falco peregrinus 52
Falco subbuteo 49
Falco tinnunculus 48
falcons 49, 51, 52
feral pigeon 92
Ficedula hypoleuca 128
fieldfare 9, 137
finches
firecrest 127
flycatchers 128–9
Fratercula arctica 90
Fringilla coelebs 148
Fringilla montifringilla 148
Fulica atra 59
fulmar 19
Fulmarus glacialis 19

gadwall 33, 34
Gallinago gallinago 72
Gallinula chloropus 58

gannet 20
garden warbler 123, 139
garganey 34
Garrulus glandarius 112
Gavia arctica 15
Gavia stellata 15
geese 25–8
glaucous gull 82
godwits 62, 74
goldcrest 127
golden eagle 42, 50
golden plover 63, 65
goldeneye 31, 33
goldfinch 138, 152
goosander 32, 40
goshawk 47
grasshopper warbler 121
great black-backed gull 83
great crested grebe 16
great grey shrike 110
great skua 80
great spotted woodpecker 102
great tit 142
grebes 16–17
green sandpiper 79
green woodpecker 11, 101
greenfinch 138, 150
greenshank 62, 77
grey heron 22
grey partridge 56
grey phalarope 78
grey plover 63, 66
grey wagtail 109
greylag goose 28
grouse 53–4
guillemot 88
gulls 81–4

Haematopus ostralegus 60
Haliaeetus albicilla 42
harriers 44–5, 50
hawfinch 149
hen harrier 45, 50
heron 22
herring gull 82
Hirundo rustica 104
hobby 49, 51
honey buzzard 43
hooded crow 116
house martin 105
house sparrow 146
Hydrobates pelagicus 18

Iceland gull 82
jack snipe 73
jackdaw 114
jay 112
Jynx torquilla 101

kestrel 48, 51
khaki Campbell 41
kingfisher 6–7, 100
kittiwake 84
knot 62, 68

Lagopus lagopus scoticus 53
Lagopus mutus 53
Lanius collurio 110

Lanius excubitor 110
lapwing 63, 67
Larus argentatus 82
Larus canus 84
Larus fuscus 83
Larus glaucoides 82
Larus hyperboreus 82
Larus marinus 83
Larus melanocephalus 81
Larus minutus 81
Larus ridibundus 81
Larus tridactyla 84
lesser black-backed gull 83
lesser spotted woodpecker 102
lesser whitethroat 124, 139
Limosa lapponica 74
Limosa limosa 74
linnet 138, 153
little grebe 17
little gull 81
little owl 96
little ringed plover 64
little stint 62, 70
little tern 85
Locustella naevia 121
long-eared owl 97
long-tailed duck 39
long-tailed tit 144
Loxia curvirostra 154
Loxia Scotica 154
Lullula arborea 103
Luscinia megarhynchos 134
Lymnocryptes minimus 73

magpie 113
mallard 31, 32
mallards 31, 32, 41
Manx shearwater 18
marsh harrier 44, 50
marsh tit 140
marsh warbler 122
martins 105–6
meadow pipit 108
Mediterranean gull 81
Melanitta fusca 38
Melanitta nigra 39
Mergus merganser 40
Mergus serrator 40
merlin 49, 51
Miliaria calandra 156
Milvus milvus 44
mistle thrush 137
Montagu's harrier 45
moorhen 58
Motacilla alba 110
Motacilla cinerea 109
Motacilla flava 109
Muscicapa striata 129
Muscovy duck 41
mute swan 23

nightingale 134
nightjar 98
Numenius arquata 75
Numenius phaeopus 75
nuthatch 145

Oenanthe oenanthe 130

osprey 46, 51
owls 95–7
Oxyura jamaicensis 36
oystercatcher 60, 63

Pandion halaetus 46
Panurus biarmicus 144
partridges 56
Parus ater 143
Parus caeruleus 141
Parus cristatus 143
Parus major 142
Parus montanus 140
Parus palustris 140
Passer domesticus 146
Passer montanus 147
peewit 63, 67
Perdix perdix 56
peregrine 51, 52
Pernis apivorus 43
Phalacrocorax aristotelis 21
Phalacrocorax carbo 21
phalaropes 78
Phalaropus lobatus 78
Phasianus colchicus 55
pheasant 55
Philomachus pugnax 77
Phoenicurus ochruros 132
Phoenicurus phoenicurus 132
Phylloscopus collybita 126
Phylloscopus sibilatrix 125
Phylloscopus trochilus 126
Pica pica 113
Picus viridis 101
pied flycatcher 128
pied wagtail 110
pigeons 91–3
pink-footed goose 28
pintail 32, 35, 41
pipits 107–8
Plectrophenax nivalis 157
plovers 63–7
Pluvialis apricaria 65
Pluvialis squatarola 66
pochard 33, 36
Podiceps auritus 17
Podiceps cristatus 16
Podiceps grisegena 16
Podiceps nigricollis 17
Prunella modularis 120
ptarmigan 53
puffin 13, 90
Puffinus puffinus 18
purple sandpiper 71
Pyrrhocorax pyrrhocorax 114
Pyrrhula pyrrhula 149

quail 55

Rallus aquaticus 57
raven 117
razorbill 89
Recurvirostra avosetta 61
red grouse 53
red kite 44, 50
red-backed shrike 110
red-billed whistling duck 41
red-breasted merganser 40

red-crested pochard 10
red-legged partridge 56
red-necked grebe 16
red-necked phalarope 78
red-throated diver 15, 31
redpoll 138, 151
redshank 62, 76
redstart 132
redwing 136
reed bunting 138, 157
reed warbler 122
Regulus ignicapillus 127
Regulus regulus 127
ring ouzel 134
ringed plover 63, 64
Riparia riparia 106
robin 10, 133
rock dove 92
rock pipit 107
rook 115
roseate tern 87
rough-legged buzzard 43
ruddy duck 36
ruddy shelduck 41
ruff 77

sand martin 106
sanderling 62, 68
sandpipers 70–1, 78–9
Sandwich tern 85
Saxicola rubetra 131
Saxicola torquata 131
scaup 37
Scolopax rusticola 73
scoters 38–9
Scottish crossbill 154
sedge warbler 121
shag 21
shelduck 12, 29
short-eared owl 97
shoveler 33, 35
shrikes 110
siskin 138, 151
Sitta europaea 145
skuas 80
skylark 103
Slavonian grebe 17
smew 4
snipe 72

snow bunting 157
Somateria mollissima 38
song thrush 136
sparrowhawk 47, 51
sparrows 146–7
spotted flycatcher 129
spotted redshank 76
starling 111
Stercorarius parasiticus 80
Stercorarius skua 80
Sterna albifrons 85
Sterna dougallii 87
Sterna hirundo 86
Sterna paradisaea 87
Sterna sandvicensis 85
stock dove 92
stone-curlew 66
stonechat 131
storm petrel 18
Streptopelia decaocto 93
Streptopelia turtur 93
Strix aluco 96
Sturnus vulgaris 111
Sula bassana 20
swallow 104
swans 23–4
swift 99
Sylvia atricapilla 123
Sylvia borin 123
Sylvia communis 124
Sylvia curruca 124
Sylvia undata 125

Tachybaptus ruficollis 17
Tadorna tadorna 29
tawny owl 96
teal 30, 33
terns 85–7
Tetrao tetrix 54
Tetrao urogallus 54
thrushes 136–7
tits 8–9, 140–4
tree pipit 108
tree sparrow 147
treecreeper 145
Tringa erythropus 76
Tringa glareola 79
Tringa nebularia 77
Tringa ochropus 79

Tringa totanus 76
Troglodytes troglodytes 119
tufted duck 33, 37
Turdus iliacus 136
Turdus merula 135
Turdus philomelos 136
Turdus pilaris 137
Turdus torquatus 134
Turdus viscivorus 137
turnstone 63, 71
turtle dove 93
twite 138, 153
Tyto alba 95

Uria aalge 88

Vanellus vanellus 67
velvet scoter 38

wagtails 109–10
warblers 121–6, 139
water pipit 107
water rail 57
waxwing 111
wheatear 130
whimbrel 75
whinchat 131
white mallard 41
white-fronted goose 27
white-tailed eagle 42
whitethroat 124, 139
whooper swan 24
wigeon 30, 32
willow tit 140
willow warbler 126, 139
wood duck 41
wood sandpiper 79
wood warbler 125
woodcock 73
woodlark 103
woodpeckers 101–2
woodpigeon 91
wren 119
wryneck 101

yellow wagtail 109
yellowhammer 155

The following organisations can help you further your interest in birdwatching:

The Royal Society for the Protection of Birds (RSPB)
The Lodge, Sandy, Bedfordshire SG19 2DL
Tel:01767 680551

Wildfowl & Wetlands Trust
Slimbridge, Gloucestershire GL2 7BT
Tel: 01453 890333

British Trust for Ornithology (BTO)
The Nunnery, Nunnery Place, Thetford, Norfolk IP24 2PU
Tel: 01842 750050